Praise for *Busy*:

"This book has the power to change your life. In this thought provoking guidebook to today's world of 'too much', Tony Crabbe destroys the myth of 'busyness' and provides practical, thoughtful advice to help individuals (and their organisations) unleash their true potential."
—Dave Coplin, Chief Envisioning Officer, Microsoft UK, and author of *Business Reimagined*

"A life-changing book which reassesses what you are doing, why you are doing it and in what way."
—Carole Ann Rice, *Daily Express*

"Business psychologist Crabbe draws an amicably accessible blueprint for escaping a state of extreme activity . . . for anyone juggling an ever-expanding schedule in or outside the corporate world, this book might be worth fitting in."
—*Publishers Weekly*

"You'll want to ban 'busy' from your vocabulary after reading Crabbe's delightful takedown of busyness as an excuse . . . *Busy* is a very smart, fun and enlightening read."
—Margaret Jaworski, *Success Magazine*

BUSY

*How to Thrive in a World
of Too Much*

TONY CRABBE

piatkus

PIATKUS

First published in Great Britain in 2014 by Piatkus

Copyright © Tony Crabbe

This edition published in 2015

1 3 5 7 9 10 8 6 4 2

The moral right of the author has been asserted.

All rights reserved.
No part of this publication may be reproduced, stored in a
retrieval system, or transmitted in any form or by any means, without
the prior permission in writing of the publisher, nor be otherwise circulated in
any form of binding or cover other than that in which it is published
and without a similar condition including this condition
being imposed on the subsequent purchaser.

A CIP catalogue record for this book
is available from the British Library.

ISBN 978-0-3494-0120-1

Printed and bound in Great Britain by
Clays Ltd, St Ives plc

Papers used by Piatkus are from well-managed forests
and other responsible sources.

MIX
Paper from
responsible sources
FSC® C104740

Piatkus
An imprint of
Little, Brown Book Group
Carmelite House
50 Victoria Embankment
London EC4Y 0DZ

An Hachette UK Company
www.hachette.co.uk

www.improvementzone.co.uk

Acknowledgments

A big thanks go to everyone at Little, Brown and Grand Central; it has been a true partnership working with you. Thanks to Tim Whiting for his faith in me, and for shaping my initial ramblings into something much more valuable. To Zoe Bohm and Sara Weiss, my editors in the UK and the US; patient to the last, I have loved working with both of you. To Kate Hibbert and Andy Hine, who have sold this book all over the world; and to Rick Wolff, who brought this book to North America. Thanks to Megan Gerrity, the production editor, and Angelina Krahn, the copy editor, you have localized the English and improved my writing. Finally, thanks to Julie Paulauski, for all your imagination and energy in publicizing the book.

Dad, thanks for that "walk around the sheepfold" that saved me from a gray life of numbers. And thanks to Mum for being my foundation, my safe place (and my source of the world's best macaroni cheese). I couldn't imagine better parents or a better childhood. Paddy, thanks for always being the first to ask, and for endlessly encouraging me. Barry, you're an inspiration, a catalyst for me and so many others. Thanks for the endless support of Dulcie and me.

Martin, Pete, Fiona, Doug and Gerry: you're all my favorites! (Pete, by the way, this is the only bit of the book you need to read.) I love you all and I'm hoping this book might create an alternative nickname for me other than Spud! Dame, thanks for the invite to that conference, which triggered all of this, but mostly thanks for being a good friend and co-conspirator. Shiv, thanks for being such a brilliant pain in the neck to keep me writing. Dom and Kate, thanks for allowing me to drink all your tea and write the first half of this book in your garden shed.

To my children: Jack, the brilliant questioner and engineer; you have the courage to walk your own path—you're very special and I can learn a lot from you. Ben, my cheeky chappie who still skips down the street; your endless sense of fun always makes me smile. Seren, you're such a princess, punching above your weight in this family—full of fire, full of ideas and full of cuddles. Together, the three of you make me more happy than any daddy could hope to be, and you fill my life with shafts of pure joy. Thanks for being patient with me and this book. I am hugely proud of all of you: no wonder my favorite number is three!

To Dulcie: You have carried, cajoled and motivated me through this project. Like all our schemes, this was a team effort; a yin and yang pairing of opposites bound by a common purpose. This book could not have happened without you—you have given up such a lot to allow me to do this, and you have taken on such a lot too. Not only that, your smart business guidance over the years has brought me to this place; it helped me to find my own career path. In thanks, I dedicate this book to you, my wife and best friend, my soul mate, my love and my life.

Contents

Preface: Busting Busy   xiii

Getting
Started: Too Busy to Read This Book?   xxvii

Section One
Mastery

Chapter 1:   Stop Managing Your Time! (...and Go
Surfing)   3

Chapter 2:   Make Choices (Fighting Fish and
Terminal Consumption)   22

Chapter 3:   Manage Attention (How to Use Our
Blobby Tissue Better)   42

Chapter 4:   Negotiate for Your Life (To Keep Those
Missiles at Bay)   64

Section Two
Differentiation

Chapter 5:   Stop Being So Productive! (Become
More Strategic)   81

Chapter 6:   Impact Through Innovation (Don't Be
                the Invisible Man)   103

Chapter 7:   Busy Is a Terrible Brand (Develop
                a Better Brand)   116

Chapter 8:   Walk Your Own Path (Fixing Radios
                by Thinking)   129

Section Three
Engagement

Chapter 9:   Stop Striving for "More"! (Put Your
                Values First)   159

Chapter 10: Reconnect (Why We're Better Off with
                Fewer Friends)   179

Chapter 11: From Buzz to Joy (An Ode to Depth)   202

Chapter 12: Beyond Busy (Making Good
                Intentions Stick)   227

What I Have Learned   244

Other Books to Read   251

Notes   255

Index   269

BUSY

As the Buddha said two-and-a-half thousand years ago... we're all out of our fucking minds.[1]

—Albert Ellis (considered the second most
influential psychotherapist in history,
1913–2007)

How long does it take you to reach for your first shot of email each day? This is followed shortly afterward by a coffee, and the day starts in a rush. On the way to work you utilize your time wisely, crunching through more email and messages, making the odd call. You hit work at a run, bounce from meeting to meeting, task to task, juggling, responding and executing. It feels like demand after demand; you're drowning but you mustn't show it. So you plow on, faster, head down, doing, doing, doing.

At some point you leave the office; still working, you enter your home. Your family is wonderful, but a burden and a distraction as well. You spend an evening of split attention, email on tap; you get irritated easily. You know, of course, that in principle you should switch off and enjoy your time with your loved ones, but you are so busy at the moment. Anyway, you're doing it for them.

You try to relax with wine and the TV and go to bed exhausted (with a final check of the phone for email). Your sleep is shallow; your brain is still working and worrying. Tomorrow you'll wake up unrefreshed.

You can't escape the feeling that you're failing as a partner, a parent and a friend; failing to keep up and perform as you'd like; failing to lead the life you'd hoped for. You've become a little hollow, a little brittle and a little helpless.

The alarm sounds and you reach for your first shot of email . . .

BUSTING BUSY

We're Wrong

In 1996, eight climbers set off to climb Everest. They had all the right equipment, they were well trained and they were fit. They made good progress. Then things changed. It appears there was something of a traffic jam toward the summit, and there may have been some weather changes and so progress slowed. There is a rule on Everest that if you don't reach the summit by a certain time, you have to abandon your attempt. On that day, these really experienced but frustrated climbers should have turned back, but instead they kept going. They reached the summit too late in the day, had to climb down in darkness, and died.

Christopher Cave, a former stockbroker, heard about this and it bothered him.[1] It reminded him of what he'd seen happen in a lot of companies. Those companies would commit to a strategy. Then, as the business context changed, evidence would start appearing that the strategy was a bad idea. Instead of looking dispassionately at the new information and stopping to reflect on a better course of action, these businesses responded to their frustrated efforts with more activity. In effect, to avoid having to face the possibility that they were heading in the wrong direction, they increased their efforts in the wrong direction.

I see the same thing with individuals. The world has changed; you don't need me to tell you that. The problem is, we haven't. Despite all our technology and training, our strategies for coping and succeeding come from the Industrial Age. They haven't changed, despite the evidence piling up that they're not working. Despite everything we try, we remain overloaded at work and overcommitted at home, and it seems to be getting worse. Instead of facing the reality that our current approach doesn't seem to be helping reduce our sense of overwhelm, we redouble our efforts—smartphones never leaving our sweaty palms—in the wrong direction, killing ourselves with endless busyness. This book is an attempt to persuade you to stop, to rethink the way you respond to all the information, demands and expectations hitting you on a daily basis. This book suggests an alternative approach.

"Busy"

Let me start by explaining what I mean by "busy" (because this book is no manifesto for laziness). "Busy" is that frenetic, always alert multitasking that propels us through overburdened lives. It involves being always "on," glancing regularly at our phones and jumping from task to task. It is the juggling, cramming and rushing that makes up so much of our daily existence. It is urgency, distraction and exhaustion.

Why We Think We're Busy

We think we are busy because we have so much to do, at work and at home. Our organizations are more demanding than they've ever been, our inbox and to-do list are bulging and our calendars are crammed full of meetings. The pressure doesn't stop when we get home; we feel buried beneath the avalanche of chores and expectations, harried by nonstop errands and the constant shuttling of children from one activity to the next. We're trying our best, but it seems a hopeless task. We're just busy; that's life today.

Why We're Really Busy

Busyness isn't essential. Yes, there is a lot to do, but believing you're always busy because you have so much to do is both false and unhelpful. This is why you're busy:

Busy Is Easier

Busy is the easy option. We are busy because we don't make the tough choices. We allow the world and our inbox to set our agenda, rather than think for ourselves. It's easier to simply react; to choose to try to do everything, rather than make the difficult decisions and unchoose things—it takes more courage to do less. In fact, as Ben Hunnicutt explains, busy is actually one of the seven deadly sins; it is slothfulness. In the Middle Ages, slothfulness had two forms: one was lazy, the other—called acedia—was running about frantically. "There is no real place I'm going, but by God, I'm making great time getting there."

Busy Is Avoidance

All those things you keep meaning to do—those things that will make a real difference in your life and career—are hard to do. In the heat of the moment, when we have to choose between easy work and hard work, between skimming through email and grappling with that complex project, we more often than not choose the easy, busy activity. We throw ourselves into frenetic activity and give ourselves the perfect excuse for not doing the big-thinking stuff. In being busy we get to feel productive while procrastinating!

Busy Is a Brand

When we demonstrate our busyness to the world, and shout about it whenever we can, we proclaim our value. Somewhere deep down we think that if people realize quite how busy we are at work it will help us get promoted; outside of work it proves our importance. Busy is aspirational. So even if we try to make it sound like a moan, we are building our brand.

Busy Is an Addiction

There is a small squirt of the cocaine-like dopamine released each time you look at your email; and Google searches release opiate-like substances.[2] Which of us hasn't fought with the temptation to whip our phones out for a quick fix of social media or text, even when we know we shouldn't (on average every 6.5 minutes)?[3]

Busy Is What Everyone Else Is Doing

Our behavior is powerfully shaped by the social norm, what everyone else does. How many unbusy people do you know? Even if you have persuaded yourself you have a rational explanation for your busyness, a lot of it will be driven by unconscious biases. A lot of your busy behavior isn't yours; it's the behavior of the herd.

Is Busy That Bad?

I mentioned that busy is aspirational; in fact, as researcher Ann Burnett found, we even compete with our busyness.[4] How annoying is it when someone out-busys us? You know the scene: You have just explained, in some depth, your exhaustion and overwhelm, detailing the scale and the breadth of the demands you have faced this week. Only to have the other person *completely* outdo you! You feel somehow diminished. It seems we want to be busy (or at least appear so).

If we seem to be aspiring to be busy, and to brag about it, it can't be that bad, right? In fact, it is.

The Allostatic Load

Stress isn't bad for us, in itself. However, for many of us, our sense of being overwhelmed causes us to push ourselves to superhuman feats of persistence and production. To get through all we have to do, we fuel ourselves with stress (and caffeine). We push, push, push ourselves to stay busy. Terrified of dropping the ball, we seldom pause; we seldom recharge. We just keep on driving ourselves. Ever since 1972, the National Science

Foundation has found a steady rise in the percentage of people, both men and women, who "always" feel rushed.[5]

It isn't any specific intensity of stress or exertion that is bad for us; it is the persistence. The body and the brain aren't designed to be always on. The body is designed for switching between active and passive states: to fire up into an adrenaline-fueled, alert state, and then cool down to a calmer one.

The rush of busy isn't occasional; busy is constant. We are flatlining at full speed ahead. When we don't allow this pulsing between on and off, we fail to allow ourselves to recover. This causes an *allostatic load*[6]—best described as accelerated wear and tear on the body and brain. In Japan there is a word for the consequences of this: *karoshi*, which means "death from over-work." *Karoshi* happens when chronic fatigue, stemming from long hours and persistent stress, lead otherwise healthy young adults to drop down dead from a stroke or heart attack. Increasing your allostatic load through constant busyness reduces your thinking power, your performance and your memory, and increases all kinds of health risks: cardiovascular disease, reduced immune system performance and early death. Even beyond death and disaster, busy just isn't much fun.

Too Much

It's all too much. We have too much to do, too much information and too much pressure. Today you will consume the equivalent of 174 newspapers' worth of content (five times as much as you would have in 1986).[7] In the time it will take you to read this page, 300 million emails will be sent.[8] In the last minute, three days' worth of content has been uploaded to YouTube.[9] In the last ten seconds, one hundred people have discovered the Internet and email for the first time, joining nearly three billion others,[10] and are now adding to the noise.

In 2010, it was estimated that information overload is costing the US economy one trillion dollars a year.[11] We live in an age where computing power and Internet connection speeds are increasing exponentially along with sheer quantity of information and entertainment. We are constantly bombarded with the "seething static"[12] of limitless information, communication and choice. In this world of too much, we are simultaneously overstimulated and bored, enriched and empty, connected yet isolated and alone.

For information workers, the last twenty years have felt like drinking from a water fountain that has become a fire hose. As our tools for productivity improve, we produce more. As it becomes easier to communicate, we communicate more. For example, in 1986 the average worker produced the equivalent of two and a half newspaper pages of content each day. In 2011 it was estimated that this amount had risen to six complete newspapers each and every day.[13] That's a two hundredfold increase in output! Every action we take, every email we send, has a consequence for someone else. So as we are all able to do more we create more work for others, who in turn are doing more, which means we all have more and more demands on us.

The simple fact is that "too much" is here to stay, and will worsen each year. There is an inevitability to this. Year after year you will receive more electronic communication, be exposed to more information and be expected to be on top of more stuff. You *will* receive even more emails next year. None of us is going to turn the technological clock back thirty years, and our organizations are unlikely to start saying "Relax! Don't do as much work!"

The Three Faces of Busy

There are "three faces of busy." Each of these "faces" refers to a different way in which we relate to busyness. The first face sees "busy as an experience": the hopscotching, multitasking, racing and cramming that leave us feeling overloaded and overwhelmed. The second face is "busy as a success strategy": we think that by being busier and getting more done we will succeed in our careers. The third face is "busy as an approach to happiness": we become busy in an attempt to become happier in our lives. Each of these faces have strategies that underpin them. I will challenge each of these strategies throughout the book.

Busy As an Experience

Busy is an experience. We feel harried and overwhelmed for much of our waking moments. So what strategy do we employ to address this? For most of us, it is time management. We believe that if we could manage our time more effectively, we'd be more in control of our life and more effective. However, in a world of infinite demand, the more we manage our time, the more we can cram into our days. The focus on managing our time has three effects: We get more efficient, and so we do more things, and so we get busier. Our attention narrows and so we lose the perspective needed to make good choices, and as we get better at juggling more, our attention gets scattered and diffuse, meaning we don't appreciate anything. If we want to achieve calmer, more effective and happier lives, time management is not the solution. In fact, it's making things worse.

Busy As a Success Strategy

For the whole of human history we've been living in a world of scarcity. When there is too little, we constantly strive for more. Whether food, stuff or information, we try to get as much as we can. This applies in the workplace too. The basic principle of agriculture, manufacturing and even office life has been *the more the better.* So we play the "More" game. We assume that personal productivity is what will deliver success. However, in a world of too much, the last thing we need is more of anything. When everyone is so overwhelmed, the biggest scarcity is attention. In order to succeed, in your career or in a business, you have to cut through the noise and be noticed. In focusing on doing more things and being more productive, the big stuff—which requires thinking and creativity—gets squeezed out. We have become drudges, too busy to lift our heads and do the things we know will make an impact and differentiate ourselves. We don't need to be more productive; we need to do less, better.

Busy As an Approach to Happiness

We lead our lives with some taken-for-granted assumptions: that more money, more status and more popularity are good things. So we prioritize accordingly, putting our values, our relationships and our health on hold while we strive to make our lives better through acquisition. But this is a really dumb idea. First, research has shown that achieving these goals will have very little impact on our well-being.[14] Second, the things we sacrifice—relationships, meaning and health—are the only things that can make us feel truly happy. Third, people who focus on external values—money, stuff and status—are less happy and less healthy than people who focus on the things that busyness kills: relationships, personal growth or contribution to your community.[15]

Going the Wrong Way

As the strategies of time management, productivity and acquisition start letting us down, the most common response I see is that people redouble their efforts. They start relying ever more heavily on time management and all the efficiencies they can wring out of their technology. They start driving themselves even harder to work faster, to do more, for longer. They start reaching, ever more desperately, for the barren comforts of material possessions. Frustrated we may be, but unlike the climbers on Everest, we can't let that cloud our judgment. The world has changed; we need a different response.

Moving Beyond Busy

I guess it is clear by now that I want to reframe the way we talk about busy. I want to marginalize it; I want people to be slightly embarrassed to say they are busy (not brag about it). However, I am even more interested in what we can do to thrive. What does moving beyond busy mean?

The opposite of busy is not relaxation, since even in much of our nonwork time we skim and skip between family commitments, social media and digital consumption. The opposite of busy in today's world is sustained, focused attention. It is deep engagement in activities that really matter to us, or in conversations with those we care about. It is taking the time to think, to amble and to plunge into the moment. It is to be found in the way we use our attention, not time; in how we think, not produce; and in how we engage, not acquire.

There are three essential elements to moving beyond busy that emerge from the three faces of busy. They explain how we should rethink our strategies, giving practical and research-based ideas on how we can thrive.

Mastery

To move beyond the frenetic experience of busyness, we have to stop managing our time and trying to get on top through personal organization. Instead we should aim to gain a sense of mastery in our lives. Mastery starts with the willingness to let go of our need for control and with getting much better at making tough choices. It also involves shifting our focus from managing time to managing attention. After all, it is our ability to focus, to think and create, that are our most precious resources professionally—and undiluted attention is the essential foundation of all real joy outside work. Finally, it involves having the necessary tough conversations to negotiate your life back.

Differentiation

This book is not a work-life balance book. A healthy balance is important, but not enough. This book is about rethinking how we succeed in an attention economy. Using lessons from corporate strategy, it explains why differentiation is a better strategy than productivity in competitive markets. It outlines how a strategic focus will maximize the impact you can make with limited resources. It explains how to capture attention through innovation, and hold that attention by communicating a compelling personal brand. Finally, it describes how to gain the confidence to walk your own path, to take risks and to move beyond busy, in the face of the social norm.

Engagement

This section of the book will realign how we are seeking to achieve happiness, addressing three key factors in reengaging with your work and life. First we will talk about redefining success in a way that is more closely connected to your core values—what really matters to you. I'll apply this to relationships in a world where we're connected to thousands of people; I'll discuss which relationships really matter and how to deepen them. Then I'll explain how to replace the transient buzz of busyness with the more nourishing, sustaining joy of deep engagement. Finally, I'll give guidance on how to be happier through doing what you want to do and making the change to move beyond busy.

It's Not Easy

I wrote this book because I struggle with busy. Yes, I thought I had some ideas on the subject; I also believed there was some great research that hadn't yet been pulled together to address what is, for me, one of the biggest blights on modern life. But I really wrote the book to help myself. It is a true "self-help" book. Busy, for me, is a constant lure, a constant challenge. I have to fight to regain mastery, to focus and to engage. I persistently need to remind myself to step away from the herd and follow the subtle call of my individuality. I can't pretend I always win the battle. A bit like an alcoholic who gives up drink yet retains a lifelong dependency, I suspect that for as long as I work, I will battle with busyness.

That may sound wearisome, but the battle with busy is a great one—and this is one of the big insights I've gained while researching and writing this book: beating busy isn't about quick tips. Most of the tips I had initially lined up to be in the book were discarded after I found they didn't help me. Beating busyness is incredibly simple, but not always easy. It is about focusing on the things that matter, on being present in the moment or with people you care for. It's about being you.

To help you make that shift, I have drawn on great research and thinking in psychology. Some of this research is directly applicable to the topic. Most of it isn't. In some cases, it is better to see the research stories as metaphors as much as evidence: I have used the research to highlight underlying psychological processes that I feel are relevant in the fight against busy, to tell stories that illustrate why we do things and how we can respond differently. Mostly, I have used research where I think it helps generate real insight into a better way of responding in the face of too much.

Beating busy isn't easy, but it's a fight worth having. The harder you struggle against the broiling froth of demand, the harder you resist the lure of the immediate, or the call of the ping, the clearer you become about what really matters to you. Active resistance against the norm of mediocrity builds your commitment to your cause.

GETTING STARTED

Too Busy to Read This Book?

The fact that you bought this book implies that you're busy. You're possibly also feeling overwhelmed, like a pressure cooker about to explode. If that is the case, how on earth do you make time to read this book, let alone apply the principles I discuss? So here are ten simple suggestions to let off some of that steam. They will help you to do less, do things quicker, or feel more in control. These suggestions will not solve the underlying problem, but they should help you to create enough space and time to read, digest and apply the deeper strategies that will make a real difference to your life.

1. Use the Word "Because"

There is a magic to the word "because." Research by Ellen Langer, professor of psychology at Harvard University, found that simply using the word "because" in a request doubles the likelihood that you will get what you want.[1] In this study, the word "because" didn't need to be followed by anything meaningful; just including the word "because" makes the listener respond as though there must be a good reason.

Doing less work often starts with influencing people around us. Whether you are saying "no" to a request, or explaining why you will be leaving work on time (rather than at 8:00 p.m.), or asking permission to delay the deadline for a piece of work, if you include "because," your argument will be seen as more rational and acceptable.

2. Switch Off

The brain is not built for constant busyness. One very small but interesting study at the University of London into the impact of being "always on" (via phone and email) suggested that it can reduce IQ as much as smoking cannabis or losing a night's sleep.[2] While we can't draw too many conclusions from the above study, we do know the brain needs its downtime. Gary Small, professor of psychiatry at UCLA, comments that while there can be a short-term buzz from being hyperconnected, long term it can lead to depression and impaired cognition.

Give your brain a break; be deliberate and intentional when you "check in" on mail and messages. Set specific times aside to do it in a focused way, rather than constantly grazing…and certainly don't check email just before bed. (The world will survive without you for a few hours!)

3. Turn Off the Notifier

Research into office workers has found that they hopscotch between tasks, changing activity on average every three minutes.[3] Whenever we switch tasks, the brain needs to reorient itself to the new rules of the game. David Meyer, professor of psychology at the University of Michigan, suggests that jumping backward and forward between even just two tasks increases the time taken for overall completion by up to 40 percent.[4]

One of the biggest culprits for gratuitous task-switching is the email or IM notifier. How many of us can resist the allure of the ping that announces a new message from the world out there? Yet in taking a peek, we distract ourselves and reduce our efficiency. In recognition of this phenomenon, Microsoft has built an internal app called Thinking Time, which allows staff to turn off all their email, IM and VoIP (online calls) for a specified amount of time to allow them to think.

4. Kill a Meeting

Meetings are a major source of busyness. They are on the increase, and have been increasing steadily in frequency and duration since the 1960s. Some surveys show that middle managers can spend up to 50 percent of their time in meetings.[5] Yet, the value of many of these meetings is questionable. One study performed a careful value analysis of 7,000 managers in a major company and found that poor planning and management of meetings was costing the business $54 million annually.[6] American multinational 3M estimated the inefficiency of its middle-manager meetings was costing $79 million annually.[7] Interestingly, there may be additional *indirect* costs: Michael Doyle and David Straus, authors of the bestselling book *How to Make Meetings Work!*, have identified something they call "meeting recovery syndrome"[8]—the time it takes to regain our focus and composure following a (pointless) meeting.

So, do yourself and your organization a favor: kill a meeting this week. Identify at least one meeting that you can either cancel or simply not attend.

5. Think of the Time…and Double It

How do you establish whether you will be able to do something? We think about how long it will take, about all the things we already have on our plate, and we make a judgment, and we get it wrong—consistently. To show this, one study asked college students to estimate when they would finish their thesis.[9] They were also asked to estimate when fellow students would finish, many of whom they didn't know too well. Students massively underestimated when they would finish their own work, but pretty accurately judged the completion date for colleagues. This is something known in psychology as the *planning fallacy*. We overestimate how much we can do, endowing ourselves with greater intellectual and focusing capabilities than we really have, and ignore all the contextual factors that could get in our way.

So, next time you are asked to do something, assess how much "spare time" you have for this task given all your other commitments, then halve it. Next assess how long you think this new task will take, then double it. Now you can make a better-informed judgment over whether to take it on.

6. Watch the Clock

How much work do you get through on the day before you go on holiday? Loads, I imagine. Research shows that when we are more aware of time, such as just before your holiday, we are significantly more productive.[10] So the suggestion is simple: if you want to crunch through a lot of stuff in a short amount of time, make yourself more aware of time. For example, get a very big clock and put it where you can see it easily, or set little alarms for every thirty minutes. It will feel like time is expanding!

7. Finish on Time

Do you have a spare room? Is it empty? The fact is, there is something inherent in human nature that, when given space, we fill it.[11] Giving yourself a clear time to finish (whether a deadline for a project, or a time to leave work) helps in two ways. First, as suggested above, it raises our time awareness, creating a goal. Second, it stops us from creating space and time in our calendars, because things will always fill up that time.

8. Start Quicker

In 1927, a Gestalt psychologist called Bluma Zeigarnik was sitting in a Vienna coffeehouse with a group of friends. They ordered a few rounds of drinks, yet the waiter never wrote down their order. Zeigarnik was intrigued by this, and, after the bill was paid and the group had left the coffeehouse, she returned. On questioning the waiter, she found that he no longer could recall what drinks had been ordered by her group. One way of interpreting this is that the brain works with open and closed "files." Once the bill had been paid, the waiter closed the file and forgot it. This has become known as the *Zeigarnik effect* (and people tend to be twice as likely to remember things in open files than in closed ones).

You can use the Zeigarnik effect to get started more quickly (and procrastinate less) by "opening your file" on a subject early. The things we normally procrastinate over are the big, difficult or creative tasks, but you can overcome this tendency by opening the file on a job a few days before you actually need to begin the work. In practice, this simply involves starting work on the problem for about twenty minutes, possibly in the form of a mind map. Then leave your subconscious to work its magic; when you finally begin the task in earnest, your thinking and ideas will really flow.

9. Clear Your Head

I recently changed my life—well, the performance of my computer anyway! It drives me crazy when my laptop starts to get slower and slower, freezing and crashing. So I wiped the hard drive and reinstalled everything. In essence I cleansed the system of all the unwanted software and cookies. In doing this, I freed up the processor to focus all its power on what I actually want it to do. It's now working perfectly again.

The brain works very similarly. We have a very limited processing power at any time. Any thoughts, worries or ideas that you're holding on to are reducing your processing speed. So don't. I read David Allen's book *Getting Things Done* and the thing that made a real difference for me, was this: create a "brain dump."[12] Find a way of getting things out of your head, of cleansing your system. For most people this means capturing things in either a notebook or their smartphone. There are three crucial elements to this. First, whatever you use to record ideas should always be with you. Second, don't try to analyze or sort things as you capture them (because that's distracting you from your current task)—simply write them down. Third, make a habit of going through your brain-dump list regularly (for me this is once a week). It's amazing how liberating it is to be able to get stuff out of your head, with the confidence it will be dealt with.

10. ...and Smile

Busy is not just a fact, it's also an experience. We get into spirals of activity; we feel under pressure, so we rush, which makes us feel under pressure...The final quick fix is simple: don't take it all too seriously! Wear your life more lightly. There is a ridiculousness to much in ourselves and our lives; we notice this with startling clarity at times of major crisis, but are blind to it for most of our lives. We see only the calamitous consequences of nondelivery in our immediate lives and, as Harvard psychologist Daniel Gilbert has found, we see our possible future through the rosiest possible glasses.[13] So, caught between immediate fear and future hope, we get deadly serious (and a little dull).

Why don't you smile instead? Smiling is good for you: it reduces stress, lowers blood pressure and releases endorphins. As Ron Gutman, founder and CEO of HealthTap, announced in his TED (Technology, Entertainment, Design) talk,[14] a single smile stimulates the brain as much as two thousand chocolate bars, or as much as receiving over twenty thousand dollars. People think you are more competent and remember you better when you smile. You may even live longer if you smile more: In my favorite study, those players in old baseball cards who weren't smiling in their profile photo lived, on average, 72.9 years; those with a little smile lived 75 years, but those who were beaming lived 79.9 years![15]

Yet only a third of adults smile more than twenty times a day (twenty times less than children). No matter how much stuff you have to do, you don't have to take it all so seriously! You may feel less busy if you smile. ☺

Section One

———————

MASTERY

The first face of busy is the experience of racing and cramming—
always on and always juggling—that leaves us feeling
overwhelmed and exhausted. This section challenges the mis-
conception that the best way to respond to our demand overload is by getting better organized and managing our time better.
We have to accept that we will never be in control again; there
are too many demands on our time. Instead we should aim to
gain a sense of mastery in our lives by letting go of our need for
control, by making brutal choices, by managing our attention and
by negotiating our life back.

Chapter 1

Stop Managing Your Time!
(...and Go Surfing)

She calms the bride, settles her father and directs the priest. She adjusts the decorations and a bridesmaid's dress. She puts on her radio mike and effortlessly manages her team, the waiters and the video. When all is ready, she gives the signal, the music plays and the wedding ceremony begins in a church that she has transformed into a flower-filled forest of fairy-tale white. The wedding will be perfect because Mary Fiore is in charge, and she is The Wedding Planner.

There is a lot to admire about Mary Fiore, played by Jennifer Lopez, in the Columbia Pictures movie. Her organizational skills are extraordinary: nothing is forgotten, she is on top of everything, and she is in total control. If any of us was looking for a wedding planner, there is no question we'd want someone with her capabilities. (Assuming of course they didn't fall in love with our fiancé, as Mary does in the movie!) However, characters like Mary or, if you prefer, Danny Ocean from *Ocean's Eleven* are dangerous role models. They make it look so natural; their control is so effortless. They make us realize how much room for improvement there is in our organizational skills. They tap into one of the great myths of modern life: better personal organization is the solution to busy lives. They make us believe that we could get back on top of it all with better time management. It's a fantasy.

Time Management Isn't Helping

There are three reasons why time management isn't helping anymore—it may even be making our lives and our busyness worse.

It Will Not Help You Regain Control

Personal organization can't help you "get on top" of it all, because there is too much to do. Period. No matter how organized you are, you will not be able to time-manage your way back to control. All that happens through better organization is that you do more stuff. Since you are still failing to do most of the things you could, or even should do, doing more things won't help you feel in control; you will just be busier. In fact, a study by Basex showed that 30 percent of knowledge workers were trying to do so much, they had no time for thought at all, and 58 percent had only between fifteen and thirty minutes to think a day![1]

In addition, the usefulness of time management gets less and less by the day as the quantity of information, communication and expectation continues to increase. Rather than spiral into ever more organization-driven activity in search of an impossible goal, you are better off accepting once and for all that you will never, ever be in control again, and that not being in control is okay.

It Will Not Make You Happier

When we search for more and more efficiency, employing the capabilities of our gadgets to the max, we are able to squeeze more things into less time; we are able to juggle more and multitask more. This leads directly to perhaps the biggest single blight on modern life: fractured attention. We think better when we have time to dwell, we enjoy more when we take the time to savor, and we deepen relationships when we stay longer in moments of shared togetherness. These joys are shattered by the staccato rhythm of an overcrammed, busy life. We have mistakenly positioned time as our most precious resource, so by managing it, we fill it to within an inch of its life. The heightened focus on filling our time, in itself, can make us less satisfied with our lives, more stressed. Even sex is less good. This is one of the reasons why Martin Seligman suggests lawyers are the least happy profession:[2] they monitor and bill time by the minute.[3] What is precious, what makes the difference between thriving and existing is not how full our time is, but the quality of our attention. Unfortunately, too many of us are squandering our attention with rabid multitasking and breathless activity. We are losing our moments because we're cramming our minutes.

It Will Not Make You More Effective

In a world of too much, where we can't do it all, our ability to make good choices is essential (as I'll explore in the next chapter). We have to become really good at making tough decisions, and a stronger focus on time interferes with this. Heightened time awareness narrows our attention: We lose perspective, so we fail to see the bigger picture. We get stuck in the weeds, racing to get lots of things done rather than asking whether they are the right things to do. We select the immediate and obvious over what might make much more of a difference. It constantly horrifies me to see how many books and blogs focus on the goal of getting to zero emails or tasks, as if either achievement is at all worthwhile. No organization has been changed by an empty inbox, no family life enriched by it either. We should feel no pride in having a day so full of back-to-back activity we have no time for reflection (or even real work!). If we choose to fill our calendar, we are also choosing not to think, and that can't be effective.

Additionally, as we manage time more closely, we become more aware of time. As we fill our time ever more effectively, we achieve the opposite of the calm, serene control we aspire to; we feel more squashed and time-pressured. This sense of time pressure not only reduces our sense of mastery, but also reduces our performance. Research by psychologists Michael DeDonno and Heath Demaree from Case Western Reserve University showed two things. First, that time pressure reduces performance; second, that it was the sense of time pressure, not an actual lack of time, which reduces performance.[4]

Time for a Change

With the help of time management and all our software and phones, we are more efficient than we have ever been. We consume more information, do more and communicate more than would have been conceivable just twenty years ago, but it's not working. Our tools are not helping us regain control, we are just getting busier; they are not making us happier, just more stressed; and they are not making us more effective, just efficient and more time pressured. We need to fundamentally rethink our relationship with too much.

From Control to Mastery

On August 17, 2000, Darrick Doerner was riding his Jet Ski in some of the roughest, most dangerous waves in the world: Tahiti's Teahupo'o break. Described as a freak of hydrodynamics,

Teahupo'o creates waves of almost unimaginable power and ferocity—pummeling tubes of water that crash onto a shallow, razor-sharp reef. You might think Doerner was nuts, but what about the man he was towing behind him! Laird Hamilton, his feet strapped to a surfboard, was being accelerated onto a wave that was too big and too fast to catch without a tow, a wave that even in the world of big-wave surfing was a once-in-a-lifetime phenomenon. Doerner realized the wave was deadly and turned to shout, "Don't let go of the rope," only to see that Hamilton had already released it.[5]

Hamilton raced down the face of the wave, keeping just ahead of the treacherous barrel. The wave was so potent, he started to get sucked up in it. In the moment, Hamilton improvised, sticking his trailing hand in the water to slow his rise to the deadly crest. As the wave collapsed, Hamilton disappeared, seemingly caught in the explosion, only to emerge, after agonizing moments, still standing.

When a photo of Hamilton on this wave appeared on the cover of *Surfer* magazine, it ran with the simple caption "Oh My God..." Hamilton had just surfed the heaviest wave ever ridden. It is commonly accepted that this ride affected the course of surfing history. It changed the collective perception of what is possible in surfing and secured Laird Hamilton's reputation as the greatest big-wave rider of all time.

What We Can Learn from Laird

Like the waves at Teahupo'o, the information tsunami leaves us feeling insignificantly small and powerless. There was a time, in the not so distant past, when "being on top of things" was not only realistic, but expected. Those days are gone. However, you could gain a sense of mastery by adopting a different mental model. Mastery is less like the meticulous control of the wedding planner, managing everything like clockwork, and more like the experience of a great surfer, skillfully and joyfully carving out a great ride in the face of Poseidon's might. Calmly watching the waves roll by before selecting the best rides, and riding those waves with deep immersion and concentration. The mastery of a surfer isn't about control. Once on the wave, facing the full force of the ocean's power, Hamilton was never going to control that monster, but neither was he overwhelmed by it.

The Laird Hamilton story illustrates the three essential aspects of mastery. First, we have to let go of our desire to be in control, and of the relative safety of responding to everything and everybody. Second, we have to make some tough, even brutal choices. No surfer can catch every wave, so we have to get really good at choosing which wave to catch. Finally, mastery happens when we are able to move from a sense of drowning to one of deep immersion; when we are able to manage and focus our attention, rather than allowing it to be scattered and split.

Letting Go

By letting it go it all gets done. The world is won by those who let it go. But when you try and try. The world is beyond the winning.

—Lao Tzu

Laird Hamilton's ride didn't start, it couldn't start, until he let go. It was the simplest thing to do: all he did was open his fingers. Yet, it wasn't a natural act to let go of the relative safety of a motorized tow to drop into the abyss; it took bravery. Letting go in a world of too much is essential and it is simple, but it takes courage.

It's Not Your Fault

What's the difference between an optimist and a pessimist? One of the biggest differences is the way they explain good and bad experiences and events. For example, the optimist sees bad experiences as being caused by external factors such as chance or other people. Pessimists, on the other hand, would blame bad things on their personal failings (an internal explanation).

When you can't do everything, and you are failing to keep on top, you might feel you are to blame in some way. You might explain the cause of this failure as being you: your lack of time-management skills, effort or ability (an internal explanation). Our organizations help us to reinforce these beliefs (subtly and often not explicitly); it's our fault, we should be more efficient and better organized. I don't agree.

A healthier, more optimistic explanation of this would be to recognize the external explanation for our inability to get on top: The quantity of information, communication and demand are entirely beyond our control; there is too much to do and we can do nothing about it. Full stop.

You are not to blame for too much, so you should let go of your guilt for not doing it all. It's not your fault.

Sloppiness

I work with a senior leader who runs a large organization and is highly regarded. He is also chaotic and disorganized to the point of sloppiness. What I find interesting is that his sloppiness is accepted, even appreciated. It is seen as part and parcel of the fact he is a visionary, big-picture and innovative leader. It occurs to me that I have seldom met a woman who is successfully sloppy. While this book is aimed at addressing an issue equally challenging for men and women, I think the specific issue of sloppiness can be particularly challenging for women.

In her wonderful work on vulnerability, Brené Brown talks about how many of us try to mask our vulnerability with displays of perfection.[6] This clearly applies to men and women, but it's just that I often see women holding themselves to a higher standard of perfection than men, perhaps in direct response to the persistent biases that women, especially mothers, still face. I see brilliant working women tie themselves in knots with impossible expectations. I met a senior leader recently who told me she always felt she needed to be the best prepared person in the room. That's a terrible burden to carry. Deborah Spar, in her great book *Wonder Women* describes the intense pressure women feel across all aspects of their lives to do everything perfectly: to have perfect careers, perfect lives, perfect children and perfect bodies.[7] Since perfection isn't possible, something has to give.

Women or men who feel vulnerable devote too much time and energy to maintaining the appearance of perfection. This is deeply unhelpful. If you want to gain mastery over your life, you will have to accept the fact that, at times, a little sloppiness will slip in. You will drop a few balls, forget a few things and let a few people down. You will be imperfect, and that will be okay. The consequence of maintaining a façade of perfection is too costly on you, your family and your career.

Playing with Sloppiness

Self-esteem and confidence do not come from being perfect, but from accepting our imperfection. Realizing that we are flawed, but that, in all our faults, we are enough. Any mistakes we make are okay, because we are capable, valuable people. Warts and all.

In attempting to retrain yourself to let go, how about some playful experiments in sloppiness and imperfection to see if the sky falls down? How about playing with not getting to zero? Why not play a game to see how many unopened emails you can have at the end of each day, or how many meetings you can miss a week? Or throw away the to-do list, on the basis that you'll remember the important stuff anyway? Let go of some of your "essential tools" that help you get to zero: leave your smartphone at home for a week and leave your laptop at work. I'm not necessarily suggesting these are the right strategies in the long term, but if you're addicted to perfection, a bit of playful detoxing might be helpful.

You are enough.

Beyond Input Dominance

One of the major failings in the way most people try to manage their time is that their focus is driven by the wrong thing. I split things into "inputs" and "outputs." To describe the stuff that comes your way in the form of tasks, information and expectations, I'll use the word "inputs." These include emails, meeting invites and delegated tasks. "Outputs," on the other hand, are the things you actually do. Many of us find our outputs are driven by our inputs. Think how much of your daily activity at work is driven by inputs: you respond to emails because they have been sent to you, you attend meetings because you have been invited, and you join a project because you were asked. Time and again I hear clients describe the causes of their actions (or busyness) from an external perspective. Their outputs are primarily an attempt to get on top of their inputs. This is the wrong approach for three reasons:

1. We have absolutely no control over the demands that hit us, so why should we feel held to ransom by them?
2. The inputs will continue to increase, but your ability to do it all will not. Like the surfer, the quantity of the waves shouldn't worry us. We should simply consider which ones we want to catch.

3. Your inputs are relatively random; unprioritized, they have little or no connection to what you hope to achieve, and so are ineffective guides to what you should focus on.

Mastery is found in what we choose to do—our outputs—not from our inputs. How many times have you arrived at the office, full of ideas and of good intentions to get your teeth into work that will make a real difference? How many times has your focus been dissipated, your intention battered into submission, through the simple act of opening your email? The contents of your inbox are setting the agenda, not because they're the right things to focus on, but because they're in your inbox.

Clearly we shouldn't ignore all demands for activity driven by external causes; I am just suggesting a rebalancing. The starting point, and primary driver for activity, should be internal: "What do I want to achieve?"

I have said that we are not to blame when we can't do it all. We *should*, however, blame ourselves if we allow our output to be externally driven. We are right to feel guilty when we get to the end of a day and have failed to work on what is important. We should feel responsible for an unremitting proactive focus on what we want to achieve, on our outputs. As for the inputs, the endless demands and messages thrown at us by the world, we should respond to these, at specific times of our choosing. But it is you who sets the agenda if you want to feel mastery, not them.

Acting "As If"

Most of us assume that the best way to change our behavior is to learn new things that change our beliefs and intentions. However, in many cases the truth is the reverse: the best way to change your beliefs is to change your behavior. If you recognize a tendency to allow too much of your activity, time and attention to be dominated by inputs rather than outputs, what can you do? No matter how convincingly I've argued my case, I am unlikely to have shifted your deep-seated beliefs or fears, formed and reinforced over a lifetime.

There is a concept in social psychology called *cognitive dissonance* that can help here. It describes our desire for consistency between our beliefs and actions. If we consistently act in a way that is not in line with our beliefs, cognitive dissonance shifts our beliefs to align with our actions, which in turn ensures that these behaviors are sustainable, long-term. Let's imagine you were trying to choose between a Ford F-Series and a Chevrolet Silverado. You carefully weigh the pros and cons of both choices. In the end, you still believe that both pickups are equally suited to you. Even though you have no clear preference, you pick one. Over the coming months, you get into your Silverado every day. This behavior tells your brain that you must have a strong preference for the Chevrolet, so your brain responds: in a short while you find it hard to imagine you ever even considered a Ford!

Following this reasoning, if we want to change behavior sustainably, the place to start might not be changing our beliefs; it might be by changing our behavior! We could do worse than to start acting "as if" we currently held the desired beliefs. What might you do if you were acting "as if" inputs should not drive your daily activity? What would you do differently if you accepted that you couldn't do it all, and that doing it all is counterproductive for your career and your happiness?

When I ask these questions of clients I get some common (and obvious) responses such as:

- I would only turn on my email twice a day.
- I would work from home once a week to avoid distraction.
- I would reduce the number of meetings I go to.

14   Mastery

What would your answer be?

What matters is not the originality of the ideas, but that whatever you identify is simple and that you *do* it—repeatedly. The importance of this might not be obvious straightaway, but by making a commitment, you are slowly retraining your prioritization system away from input dominance.

Building a Sense of Mastery

In a University of Pennsylvania laboratory back in 1967, some unfortunate dogs were being trained using electric shocks. While observing them, Martin Seligman, now professor of psychology and the founder of the field of positive psychology, noticed something unexpected. Typically, you would expect any sensible dog to avoid the pain of an electric cattle prodder if possible. Yet, after repeated shocks, the dogs appeared to give up trying to escape from the pain, even when they had the opportunity: they simply lay down and whined. Why would they do that?

This observation led Seligman to develop the concept of *learned helplessness*.[8] At times, humans, as well as animals, seem to give up any attempt to change their situation. They accept their role as victims and their total inability to do anything about it. I see this attitude in many people I work with today. They recognize they are too busy, that their calendar is too full, their inbox overloaded and their to-do list growing. They feel helpless to do anything about it other than redouble their efforts and get better organized. When I ask them why they are so busy, they will blame it on their organization, on the demands of modern parenting or even on their smartphone. They seldom blame themselves, and therefore they don't recognize the opportunity they have to feel different.

Breaking the Stimulus-Response Cycle

We respond rapidly and emotionally to our environment. Someone does something annoying, you get angry; your task list is longer when you leave work than when you came in, you feel overwhelmed; you bounce from meeting to meeting, unable to address the torrent of email, so you feel helpless. Emotions are natural, but with regard to helplessness, not very useful. Helpless people shrug their shoulders, tell everyone how busy they are ("poor me") and, like a martyr, they struggle on, changing nothing.

There is another way: it's all about how we feel. For example, neuroscientist Amy Arnsten showed that when we feel out of control, the limbic system fires up and we don't think very well: more specifically, our prefrontal cortex—the most important part of the brain for thinking and prioritizing—is impaired.[9] However, when we *feel* mastery, irrespective of the demands, she found the prefrontal cortex continues to function as normal.

Our reactions to circumstances don't have to be automatic; we can change our emotions. Or, more accurately, we can rationally choose an alternative response to the immediate emotional one. This may sound theoretical or academic, but it works in even the most extreme situations.

> *Everything can be taken from a man but one thing: the last of the human freedoms—to choose one's attitude in any given set of circumstances, to choose one's own way.*[10]

These aren't the words of some modern-day, pampered, so-called guru. They are the words of Viktor Frankl, a psychiatrist and a survivor of some of the worst brutality ever inflicted by the human species: the Holocaust. Frankl made this comment while reflecting on his experience as a prisoner of war at Auschwitz and Dachau (among others). He observed and experienced unimaginable horrors in the death camps. He also noticed that different people responded differently to their situation. Some gave up hope and "ran into the wire" (the camp term for committing suicide by running into the electric barbed-wire fence). Others became aggressive and animalistic; he tells of how many of the most brutal people in camp were the *Kapos*, prisoners who assisted the guards in maintaining order in the camps. Yet many prisoners took a different path: they seemed to go inside themselves, to a heightened inner life. He tells of how on a march to a day of relentless manual labor, frozen to the core, swollen feet bursting out of his boots, and half starving, his friend brought up the topic of their wives. For the rest of that day he actively maintained his wife's image in his head, imagining talking to her, hearing her laugh. He escaped from the horror of the moment into the joy of the past and the hope for the future. He tells of how, in the depths of their horror, they would rush out of their huts just to see a lovely sunset, gazing in wonder at the skies, drinking in the beauty. Even in a situation where death was likely, life was horrible and the future seemingly hopeless, the prisoners still retained one area of their life where they could feel some mastery: their thoughts and feelings. He came to the conclusion that, no matter the scenario, we never lose the ability and the freedom to choose our response.

Choose Your Response

Your emotions ebb and flow throughout the day, even when you are extremely busy. While they may seem ever present, your feelings of being overwhelmed or of impotence are not constant, but in reality spike at some times, fading into the background at others. A key to building a sense of mastery is to spot the triggers for these spikes. The very act of noticing extreme emotions can start to give us distance from them, and we can start to move beyond the automatic stimulus-response cycle; we can begin to insert mastery into the process by choosing an alternative response.

Take the story of a friend of mine, Simon, who was struggling with persistent traffic on his commute. Day after day his car would come to a standstill on over-congested roads. Each time he came to a stop, he could feel his tension rise and his blood begin to boil. For him, these weren't simply moments of irritation, they were emblematic of a life that wasn't living up to his expectations. They were the emotional epicenters of his feeling of despair.

Clearly he could do nothing about the traffic jam, nor did he want to change his job, and, for family reasons, he didn't want to change his home. This all left him with one option: he had to change his response to the inevitable. Following a number of conversations and a few experiments, Simon ultimately came up with a solution that worked for him: He would use his traffic-jam time as a chance to do two of the things that had been hanging around in his "should" list for years: learning Spanish and practicing the harmonica. During his morning journeys listening to Spanish lessons, a little extra time in the car due to traffic jams improved the conjugation of his verbs. On his return home, each time he ground to a halt he'd snatch up his mouth organ and play the blues (appropriately!). Trivial though this may sound, he'd chosen a different response to an unavoidable situation that, through practice, gave him a sense of mastery again (as well as some new talents).

Reverse Your Motivation

Have you ever noticed that you can have completely different reactions to the same experience from one occasion to the next? An invitation to dinner at a friend's house can be relished one day and dreaded the next; a looming deadline can trigger energy or fear.

Reversal theory,[11] developed by the British psychologist Michael J. Apter, explains that these differing reactions to identical scenarios are a result of opposing motivational states, which drive how we respond to situations and experiences. We fluctuate between states, flipping or reversing our motives and thereby changing how we respond to situations. The interesting thing about reversal theory is how easy it is to flip from one motivational state to another once you recognize what is going on.

Two motivational states that are relevant here are "serious" and "playful." When we are operating with serious motives, we are focused on goal achievement and working toward longer-term ends. When things are going our way in this state, we feel calm and relaxed. When they are not, we feel anxious or even fearful. By contrast, when we adopt a playful state, we look for in-the-moment fun and arousal, and we will either feel excited and energized, or bored, depending on whether our motives are being met or frustrated.

Busyness comes from being too heavily focused on the longer term; we feel too busy when we're taking it all too seriously. Reversal theory demonstrates that in every serious situation there is an alternative response—if we recognize that we are operating with serious motives, we can flip our motivations and see the ridiculousness of the scenario, the lightness of the moment; we can aim to have fun.

A number of years ago I was asked to run a big event for Microsoft. It was possibly the biggest event of my career at that point. It was in Seattle, with 120 senior, high-potential leaders. I was also leading a team of twenty experienced external facilitators. In the run-up to the event, I put in months of preparation;

I had designed and redesigned the event scores of times. I was taking the whole event very, very seriously. Halfway through the event, a wise colleague and friend, Bobbi Riemenschneider, took me to one side and gave me some feedback. She told me I hadn't smiled once through the entire event; she told me I was taking it all too seriously and that I should "play" a little more. What I hadn't realized was that my very determination to get it right, my work ethic and earnestness, was making me less present with the group, less fun and less flexible. In my seriousness I was a less effective facilitator.

Over the years, I have identified my tendency to take it all too seriously. I have also learned that I am at my most impactful, creative and engaging when I am in a playful mood. The ability to flip into a playful motivational state has become an essential tool in helping me to think and perform better; it also helps me enjoy the ride more. I'll often ask myself how I could go about what I'm doing in a more playful, mischievous way. As a facilitator, what is interesting is that the ideas that emerge for me in a playful state are nearly always more risky; they are also more striking and innovative.

It isn't hard to change your state. Three things help me to trigger a change in state: music, movement and the word "playful." There is nothing like a blast of music to move into a more present-oriented, less serious state. To encourage movement, I put a massive great whiteboard on the wall of my office; I find that I can break out of my seriousness by jumping up to my whiteboard and starting to kick around my ideas with multicolored pens and images. Finally, simply thinking of the word "playful" triggers a change for me, as I remember the feedback from Bobbi.

We can all feel more mastery by spotting seriousness and, when appropriate, triggering a reversal into a more present, playful state.

THE BIG MESSAGES IN "STOP MANAGING YOUR TIME!"

Think of yourself as a skilled **surfer**, carving a great ride across the face of too much. Your job is not to control the demands made on you; it is to **gain a sense of mastery**.

Time Management Isn't Helping
- Time management will not help you **get in control**; because there is too much to do, it will only **make you busier**.
- Time management will not **make you happier; it fractures attention** and destroys our moments.
- Time management will not make you more effective. It reduces our ability to prioritize; it **makes us more efficient, but less effective**.

From Control to Mastery
- **It's not your fault** you can't do it all—there is simply too much to do.
- **Get sloppy.** Perfection is an impossible façade to maintain that masks vulnerability; the cost of perfection is too high.
- You **can't control the inputs; mastery comes from your outputs**. Let the inputs wash by you and focus on the outputs you choose to make.

Building a Sense of Mastery
- Busyness can be a form of **learned helplessness**, but we don't have to feel that way.
- **You can choose to feel more mastery**—you can choose how to respond and how to feel in almost any set of circumstances.
- **Flip seriousness into playfulness**—a state of busyness comes from being too serious; change your motivational state to have more fun, be more creative and engage people better.

Go-Do

Act "As If"

Sit down and identify one thing you would do differently if you genuinely believed your outputs are more important than your inputs, for example leaving your email switched off for most of the day. Then do that thing, daily.

Choose Your Response

Identify one of your triggers: at what point in the day, or what activity makes you feel most overwhelmed? Think about how you currently respond, and design a better response that will help you to feel more mastery.

Experiment

Get Sloppy

Play with imperfection. Don't empty your inbox, don't tidy your desk, rip up your to-do list and leave your phone and laptop at work. Go on, I dare you! See if the sky falls down.

Reverse Your Mood

Identify what will trigger a switch in mood from a serious to a playful mood. This might be music, environment or trigger words. Experiment with it and get good at the flip.

Chapter 2

Make Choices
(Fighting Fish and Terminal Consumption)

The Siamese fighting fish (known as the betta fish in the US) originates from the paddy fields of Malaysia and Thailand. In the early nineteenth century, the king of Siam collected them for their aggression, wagering large amounts of money on male-versus-male conflicts. Today, they have become popular with aquarium owners because of their beautiful colors and large, flowing fins. What I find interesting about these fish is their appetite. Owners have to limit the fish's food because, given the chance, they will quite literally eat themselves to death. Unlike most living species, they mindlessly consume what's in front of them, not seeming to recognize when enough is enough.

There seems to be a parallel to busyness here. For the whole of history and beyond, we have inhabited a world of scarcity. The resources and opportunities open to us were limited by our environment. These limits restricted our lives, but they also protected us. Now, in our world of too much, the limits have been removed. We are exposed to almost limitless knowledge, communication and stimulation. With this explosion of information has come opportunity, but also increased expectation and work.

To put the speed of the switch from informational scarcity to excess in context, think of it in evolutionary terms. The first of the *Homo* genus, our ancestors, appeared in Africa about 2.3 million years ago. Informational excess has only been with us for the last twenty years. If we view our evolution as a single calendar year, excess didn't arrive until four seconds before midnight on New Year's Eve! We haven't adjusted to this new world of limitless abundance yet. We're still operating as if we lived in scarcity: we're consuming what we can. The Siamese fighting fish see food and eat it, not stopping to consider how it will affect them. We too are getting dangerously close to a terminal case of consumption. We see email or texts or voice mails; we consume them. We don't seem to realize when enough is enough.

Did you ever actually *decide* to be really busy—to race from task to task? Is this the life you planned and hoped for? Without making tough choices, we feel helpless and overwhelmed. We may also feel like heroic victims, stoically facing a universe of demands. Yet, from a psychological point of view, busyness could also be seen as the easy choice. There *is* too much to do, but that's not why you're busy. You're busy because you haven't made the right choices.

When there are so many options and so much work, an ability to make tough choices is a muscle we need to build like never before. Without these choices, it is incredibly easy to overload your palette with too much color. Given the finite size of your palette, the risk is that the colors will start merging together and, as we all know, if you mix too many colors together, you don't get a rainbow, you get gray. To paint a vivid life, to have a vivid career, you need less color rather than more.

The truth is, every choice has a consequence. Each time you choose something, you unchoose something else. So when we try to do everything, we are unchoosing things. When we choose busy, we are unchoosing thinking, creativity and focused attention. We are unchoosing interesting and impactful careers. We are unchoosing quality time, relationships and the joy of deep engagement. Instead, we should be consciously and deliberately choosing not to do things, killing off options in our lives and work to allow a greater focus on fewer things. Instead of choosing more, we should choose less, and instead of gray, we should choose color.

This chapter aims to insert a great big question mark into your work and lifestyle choices. I want to show you how to better the betta fish: how to avoid mindlessly choosing more busyness, how to resist the temptation of the easy choice that leads to the gray life of busy, and how to recognize when enough is enough and set limits on too much.

Beating Mindlessness

Have you ever noticed that if you are watching TV, or playing cards, and there is a bowl of chips or pretzels in front of you, you keep eating until they're gone? You don't stop to think, have I had enough yet? We just mindlessly consume. Brian Wansink, professor of marketing and applied economics at Cornell University, wondered if this would still apply to food that wasn't so appealing.[1] He gave moviegoers buckets of five-day-old popcorn. One participant described the popcorn as "like eating Styrofoam." He gave some participants a medium bucket and some a large bucket. Those with big buckets ate 53 percent more popcorn than those with the smaller bucket, even though they didn't like it. Afterward, when confronted with the evidence, most denied the size could have affected their choice. One person said, "Things like that don't trick me." He was wrong.

System One and System Two

There is mindlessness in lots of our daily behavior. We make choices, and reach constantly for more just because things are there in front of us. The reason for this is energy conservation. The brain has developed a smart way of managing the energy required for decision-making. It has to do this because, although your gray matter only accounts for about two percent of your body weight, it uses about 20 percent of all the energy you consume. It's the 4x4 of your organs. The worst offender of all is the part responsible for decision-making, the most recent part of the brain to evolve: the prefrontal cortex. This isn't just any old 4x4, it's a 6.6-liter Hummer! This means that making rational choices is hard work, so the brain does all it can to avoid the effort.

Psychologists, such as the Nobel Prize–winning Daniel Kahneman, have split our thinking into two forms: System One and System Two.[2] System One is fast, automatic and unconscious; System Two is slow, effortful and conscious. Both systems are always on while you are awake. System One automatically and effortlessly responds to experiences, generating immediate impressions, intentions and feelings. The more energy-sapping System Two prefers to take things easy when it can, spending most of its time coasting along, vaguely scanning what is generated by System One. On the whole, System Two accepts System One's impressions, which become beliefs; it accepts intentions, which become actions. By doing this, humans have evolved into an incredibly energy-efficient thinking machine: only about 2 percent of all mental activity is effortful and conscious. It's like having a hybrid car that runs silently and cheaply on battery power for 98 percent of the time!

This works fine most of the time, but in a world in which the default behavior and social norm is frenetic busyness, we are mindlessly drifting to toxic levels of activity and consumption.

The only choice any of us seem to be making is for "more." We reach out, mindlessly, for more stale popcorn, and we grab our smartphone, mindlessly, for more empty activity.

Justifying Mindless Choices

The first thing we have to accept about mindless choices, is that we are not aware of how mindless they are. If questioned, we genuinely believe we are making rational choices. An example of this comes from the world of education. In one study, five professors rated the attractiveness of 885 economics students (with an even gender split) on a scale of one to five (five being most attractive). Those who were rated a four achieved a 36 percent better mark than those rated a two.[3] This is an example of what's called the "attractiveness halo effect." Now imagine asking these eminent professors why they gave the "twos" such low grades. They will point to flaws in the student's work, they will give a strong rationale, and they will remain oblivious to the effect attractiveness had on their grading.

If I asked you why you are busy, you would be able to give all kinds of rational explanations. You might describe the state of the economy or the fact that your business is short on staff at present, you might describe a demanding manager or a demanding project, or you might explain your commitment to the children's extracurricular activities. The point is, you *will* have a justification for your busyness. You will have a story you tell yourself and others. All I ask from you at present is to accept the possibility that some of your busyness has come from dumb, irrational and mindless choices.

The Power of the Default

Imagine you have just started in a new job. One of the attractive benefits being offered is an employee 401(k) retirement plan. It is universally accepted to be a good deal, with your firm matching your contributions: it's virtually free money. Would you join? You probably think your answer to this question would be most influenced by the details of the plan, the quantity of money at stake or your current financial situation. However, it is likely that the biggest factor in your decision-making on this important financial question is whether you had to fill out a form or not. In one study, economists Brigitte Madrian and Dennis Shea found that when employees had to opt into the scheme, only 20 percent joined in the first three months. In contrast, when membership was automatic—the default condition—initial enrollment was 90 percent.[4]

The Default of "Busy"

One of the most common forms of mindlessness involves defaults. In the context of busy, they are particularly relevant since busy is the default, standard condition. The default for all communication is to ingest (read or listen) and respond. Let's take emails for instance. How many emails do you get a day? Let's say you currently receive 200 emails a day, a figure that has doubled in the last three years. At what point do you need to fundamentally question the value of reading and responding to all these: when they get to 400, 1600, 12,800? At some point we need to take a stand in favor of thinking instead of mindless reactivity.

Many people moan about the number of meetings they "have to" attend, how time poor they are, and how disruptive it is to their day. Yet I find very few people with a solution. One of the issues is that it is so easy to invite people using Outlook or Gmail. Given that the inviter can see your calendar, can see you are free, there becomes something of a default expectation that you will accept. Acceptance is a click; opting out requires an explanation. This is especially evident in the curse of all office life: weekly meetings. These meetings happen whether there is a purpose or not, but since they are regular, by default, you are expected to attend—and another hour is lost.

How are defaults shaping your life at present? What are the unspoken assumptions and expectations that are driving a large amount of activity for you? Some of these defaults may serve you well, some will not. Collectively they are strangling you.

A Reimagining

If you were to redesign your working life from scratch, what would it look like? Reimagine your work in order to maximize your capability, to rekindle your excitement and harmonize it with your personal life. You probably imagined a working life free of a lot of the unhelpful defaults. Choose one default that's getting in the way of a more satisfying working life, and redesign how you respond. Choose to be less mindless.

The Lure of Social Norms

How would you persuade people to recycle towels in hotels? A famous study by Robert Cialdini into social norms revealed that the standard environmental plea persuaded about 30 percent of people to recycle.[5] When the wording was changed slightly to state that *most guests* choose to recycle at some point in their stay, 26 percent more people recycled. When the wording was made even more specific, stating that most guests staying in *that particular room* had chosen to recycle, the percentage increased by 33 percent. This influence doesn't happen at a conscious level, but we are affected by the social norm. The reason the more specific hotel card worked even better is that the more similar people are to us, the more their behavior influences us.

The quantity of work you do, and your perpetual busyness, develop because that's what everyone else is doing.

The effects of social norms are even more powerful when we compare ourselves to people we actually know. Everyone we come into contact with is incredibly busy. The fact that they are frantically juggling too many things powerfully shapes our expectations and behavior and makes it difficult for us to rationally assess how busy we should be.

What's wrong with the norm? There is nothing, in principle, wrong with going with the herd, if the herd is going in the right direction. In the case of busy, the herd is definitely not going in the right direction. We need to find our own unique responses to our challenges; we need to create a better way of communicating and delivering. The answer does not lie with the herd.

Awareness of the Norm

When you compare your busy behavior to those around you—what do you do that is just the norm? Remember, "the norm" isn't the degree to which you have an intellectual rationale for your behavior; you always will. It is the degree of similarity to those around you. If it's similar, it's probably driven by the norm, in which case, it is not *your* behavior. You didn't choose it; you are simply acting out the collective pattern like a faithful worker bee.

Choose a Different Role Model

When was the last time you met someone who explained how unbusy they are? When was the last time you traveled to work on a train not filled with people tapping away on laptops, phones or tablets? Think about how their behavior might be affecting your own feelings of busyness.

To combat this, identify the behavior you most want to change and find people in your organization, in your personal life or in your family who model good alternative behaviors. Spend time with them, and build relationships with them. Ask them about what they do, observe closely how they behave and how they think about busyness. Do all you can to start making *their* behaviors *your* norm.

Be the (Different) Norm

Just for the fun of it, next time you're in a conversation and the other person has just described how busy they are, say you've decided not to be busy. (I dare you!) Say you've decided that you want to create time to think, instead of endless, mindless busyness. You'll get different reactions—alarm, pity or envy—but you'll get a reaction.

Step out of the herd (or even lead it).

Busy Is the Easy Choice

How do you behave at a buffet table? If you're anything like me, you pile your plate high with all kinds of weird and wonderful flavors and end up with something you would immediately send back to the kitchen if a chef served it up. We would have a far better meal if we chose better. More specifically, we'd have a better meal if we asked the right question.

When we see the chicken korma we ask "whether or not" we'd like it. We then ask the same question when faced with sweet-and-sour pork and with steak pie. For me, the answer to all three of these questions is usually "yes," and so I end up with a culinary disaster. The question I should have asked is "Which would I prefer?" The thing is, "whether or not" is a much easier question to answer than "which." The price I pay for not choosing "which" is a terrible meal.

Busyness is buffet table madness. We make the easy choice of "whether or not" we should do this or that, and end up overwhelmed as we pile too much on our plates. By choosing the easy option, we choose busy. Mastering a world of too much involves making the tougher "which" choice more of the time.

The Perils of "Whether or Not"

Paul Nutt, business school professor at Ohio State University, was keen to understand how businesses made important decisions. He looked at how companies went about making the decision to buy another company. Corporate acquisitions are costly, complex and risky. When he looked at how 168 acquisition decisions were made, he found that only 29 percent of those decisions involved more than one option. For the other 71 percent of the companies, the only question being asked was "whether or not" they should buy the company in question. When Nutt then followed up on those decisions, he found that 52 percent of the "whether or not" acquisition decisions failed, as compared to only 32 percent of those decisions where they asked "which" of two or more alternative options were better.[6]

In their book *Decisive*, Chip and Dan Heath use this study and a number of others to show two things: that more often than not, we slip into "whether or not" choices and that "whether or not" choices are ineffective; they fail to take the broader implications of the decision into account.[7] This is all too true in the case of busyness. However, I think there are two additional reasons we should be especially mindful of "whether or not" decisions when it comes to fighting busyness. The first is, as with the buffet, the answer will be "yes" much more often than it should be. When deciding "whether or not" to check your email, or attend that meeting or sign your child up for another after-school class, since all of these activities are worthwhile, why would you respond in any other way than yes? And so we become busier. Finally, the more busy we are (or the more we are focused on managing our time) the more narrowly we'll think—the more likely we are to narrow choices down into "whether or not" decisions, rather than see the impact of these choices.

Chip and Dan Heath describe "whether or not" choices as

one of the "Villains of Decision Making"; I would add that they are one of the villains of busyness too.

Opportunity Cost

Dwight D. Eisenhower was effective at making tough decisions. To avoid the perils of "whether or not," he reminded himself and others of the true consequences of his choices, of the alternative options. For example, in his first term of office he explained "The cost of one modern heavy bomber is this: a modern brick school in more than thirty cities." Everyone, in the early years after the war, would say "yes" if asked whether or not the government should buy more bombers. But were they more important than thirty schools?

Dwight D. Eisenhower was aware of the *opportunity cost* of his decisions. Opportunity cost is a concept from economics that describes what we miss out on, or lose, through making a decision. If I buy a new laptop, I might no longer have the money for that trip to Vegas, or to buy a new grill and throw a neighborhood barbeque. A quality decision involves choosing "which" alternative is the highest priority (since they may all be attractive).

In a study into opportunity cost, Shane Frederick told participants about a movie containing their favorite actor or actress. He explained it was available at a special sale price of $14.99. He then gave them two options:

a) Buy this entertaining video
b) Not buy this entertaining video

Perhaps unsurprisingly, 75 percent of people opted to buy the video. He then changed the wording of option b slightly to "Not buy this entertaining video. Keep the $14.99 for other purchases." Clearly, to any sane adult, the additional words are obvious. However, this simple reminder of the opportunity cost of the decision meant that the number of people who decided *not* to buy the video doubled.[8]

"Whether or not" choices are dangerous in the case of busyness. They are too likely to lead to a "yes" decision. The opportunity cost in the case of busy might be time to think, or focused attention, or precious moments with loved ones. The cost of the "yes" decision may be less immediate and obvious than its benefits, but there is always a cost.

To combat "whether or not," simply ask yourself the following questions whenever you are considering saying "yes" to more work, activity or stimulation:

- What am I giving up by making this choice?
- What else could I do with the same amount of time or attention?

Good Choices Take Energy

Jonathan Levav, professor at the Stanford Graduate School of Business, and Shai Danziger, psychology professor at Tel Aviv University, reviewed more than a thousand parole decisions made by judges in the Israeli prison system. After hearing each case, judges decided whether to parole or not. In this situation, the tougher decision was to release, since the parole board needed to make a complex choice between the relative priorities of prisoner freedom, risk and cost. On average, each judge approved parole in about one in three cases. However, a very strong pattern occurred: Of those prisoners who appeared before a judge early in the morning, 65 percent were paroled; of those who appeared late in the afternoon, only 10 percent were paroled![9]

The explanation for this shocking, but very human, lack of consistency is something called ego depletion. We have only so much mental energy to go around. When our brain gets tired, we begin to avoid decisions altogether or make the easier choice, like the judges later in the afternoon.

High-Energy Decisions

The working day in a typical office places a lot of strain on our brain; we get rapidly ego-depleted. In this state, we will be a lot less likely to try to make tough "which" decisions about relative priorities. We have to accept that at certain times of the day, we are going to be pretty poor at making clear, strategic choices about the best use of our time.

"Which" decisions are demanding on the brain and so are most effectively done when the brain is fresh, normally first thing in the morning. Give yourself time each day, before diving into the treadmill of activity, to think clearly about which task will deliver the most value, and make the necessary brutal choices on where you will place your attention. In addition, the study above did not find a gradual decline of parole (difficult) decisions through the day. They found that after each break or lunch (where food and drinks were served) there were spikes of higher parole levels. The boost in glucose levels increased the likelihood that the board would make the harder choice. So, take regular breaks, and have a small snack during each break to replace some of the glucose. Then, when your brain is refreshed, review your progress and reprioritize.

Loss Aversion

When a friend took up kite surfing, I felt a kind of pain inside. It wasn't envy or resentment. It was a sense of loss. My life wasn't allowing me to kite surf (or skydive or even play golf). One of the reasons we load our plate up so high is that we hate losing out on things. We hate narrowing our options.

In one of his experiments, Dan Ariely had people play a game. In it, there were three rooms people could enter by clicking on a red, blue or green door. Once inside the room, further clicks would be rewarded with money. In total, participants had one hundred clicks. Each room had a different range of payouts, so the challenge was to find the room that gave the highest average payout and spend the rest of your one hundred clicks in that room. Then they added a twist. When subjects were not using a room, the door to that room would start closing. After twelve successive clicks, if a door had not been clicked, it would close forever. As you will realize, the rational strategy here is still to find the highest paying room, and stay there—to let the other options close. Yet that is not what people do. Ariely found people tended to get into something of a frenzy, desperately racing from room to room to avoid the loss of a closed door. In doing so they earned, on average, 15 percent less (and had a much more frenetic game).[10]

Close Some Doors

Overwhelm and overcommitment are just as applicable to our nonwork life as to our work life. We pile our plates high with after-school activities for the children, with hobbies, with worthy causes and with personal learning projects. We have to accept that not only can't we do it all, but also that we shouldn't.

This takes us right back into "which" decisions. Which outside-of-work activity will you kill? How will this help you to focus more on the rest and to reduce the general frenzy?

When Enough Is Enough

In another Brian Wansink experiment on mindless eating, participants were invited to eat bowls of Campbell's soup.[11] What they didn't realize is that each bowl had been tampered with so that, as the person ate, the bowl secretly refilled. An awful lot of the participants just continued mindlessly eating; they didn't notice when they'd eaten enough. Ultimately, it was the experimenter who, out of concern for his subjects, put an end to the experiment. We can be a bit like betta fish, unless we get better at noticing when enough is enough.

Recognizing When Enough Is Enough

Nassim Nicholas Taleb, an economist, explains how many things in our life are nonlinear. Take traffic, for example. When the roads are very quiet, a small increase in traffic makes little difference. Increases in the number of cars and trucks continue to have minimal impact on the flow of traffic, until the roads start to get more congested. After this, any small increase in traffic leads to much worse jams and gridlock. Taleb describes this relationship as a concave relationship.[12] Small increases at the start make little difference, but as you go further up the scale, additional traffic has an increasingly larger effect.

I think the relationship between the quantity of stuff we do and our experience of busyness is also concave. When we have little going on, a bit more demand makes scant difference to our busyness. However, there comes a point when any small additions to your demands can send shock waves of panic through every fiber of your being. You may feel you're already there! If you get too far up the curve, your ability to absorb new demands and to adapt will be decimated.

The Busy Footprint

So here's a practical tool I've developed to help us notice when we are approaching our limits. It's called the Busy Footprint. As we move up the demand curve, and things start to get too much, our behavior starts to change, subtly. These changes happen without conscious thought and are idiosyncratic, but they are consistent in individuals over time; a unique "busy footprint." The simple idea is that if you can recognize your

Busy Footprint, you can use it like an early warning system and take timely steps to readjust your activity levels, preventing yourself from tipping into complete overwhelm.

For example, when I start to come close to turning the corner into crazy busyness, I start drinking more tea, and adding sugar to it. I stop reading. I get colder, and need warmer clothes. I want baths rather than showers. I lose things. I stop listening. Your signs will be different. Over the years, I've found it really helpful to notice these behaviors for what they are: warning bells that adjustments need to be made.

What is your Busy Footprint?

Managing Boundaries

At one of my events, I had a corporate vice president at Microsoft come to speak to us about leadership. His opening few lines gripped the room: "I have never missed my wife's birthday or the birthdays of any of my three children. I have never missed the first day or the last day of any school term. I have never missed my wedding anniversary. I have never missed the opening night of a school play." This was just a small part of the list he reeled off. The room was full of senior leaders, all of whom had missed many of the type of special events listed by the CVP. They all wondered how it was possible for this man, running a billion-dollar business, in a global role, to be present for all those moments.

So we asked him. He explained the understanding that he and his family had come to: that while they accepted that demands on him would rise with his increasing seniority, certain moments were sacred and irreplaceable. He accepted he would travel a lot and he accepted he would work hard, but he would not accept missing these moments. They were one of his ways of harmonizing his work and his family life. In always being present for those moments, he demonstrated to his children, his wife and himself where his priorities lay. He also explained that this value of his was part of his "Rules of Engagement" with any manager. Before he agreed to take on any role, he would negotiate certain agreements with that manager. He would not take a job if a prospective new manager was unwilling to agree to his Rules of Engagement.

Be Specific

What really hit me as I listened to the CVP was how wonderfully specific he was about what he wanted. His role required him to make tough decisions each day, not only about his business but also about the way he worked. He had been able to identify very specific moments that allowed him to feel connected to those he cared most about; they could accept his absences, confident in the knowledge that he would be there when it mattered most.

We can't do or have everything. When setting boundaries, we have to accept that some things will have to give as we negotiate with our manager or partner. What's important is that we are clear about those things that really matter to us, and build boundaries around them.

Use your answers to the following questions as the basis for negotiating your boundaries:

- What do you (really) want when it comes to your work or your life? (Be specific.)
- What are you willing to let go of in favor of those things that are truly important to you?

The Preemptive Strike

The other aspect of boundary setting is what I call "the preemptive strike." Let's imagine our CVP gets a call from his manager telling him that a real issue has arisen and he needs to attend a meeting with the CEO of Microsoft on his daughter's birthday. Most of us might grumble during this call, but it would be followed shortly after by an apologetic conversation with our daughter.

Now consider the case of the CVP. When situations like this occur, all he needs to do is remind the manager of their prior agreement. Both people are clear about the values of the CVP; both people are clear of the Rules of Engagement. The discussion rapidly shifts to a workaround solution to this issue; the refusal to attend this critical meeting poses a challenge, but is not a problem.

Prior agreements demonstrate how important things are to you, where your values stand. We respect individuals and leaders who have clear and strong values. The preemptive strike sets out your ground rules and allows you to manage your boundaries, but defuses difficult conversations in advance.

What are your Rules of Engagement? How clear is your manager about your Rules of Engagement?

THE BIG MESSAGES IN "MAKE CHOICES"

You didn't decide to be endlessly, frenetically busy, it just happened, one email at a time and, like the Siamese fighting fish, you're in danger of a terminal case of consumption.

Beating Mindlessness
- Most of the "choices" we make are made on autopilot.
- Even if we can justify our actions, a lot of our **busyness is irrational**, driven by the **default condition** or **social norms**.

- In the absence of proper choices, the only choice we make is to mindlessly reach for "more," without considering the consequences.

Busy Is the Easy Choice

- Too many of our decisions are **"whether or not"** choices, which are too likely to be answered "yes" and drive more busyness. To move beyond busy we have to make **more "which" choices**.
- When our brain is tired, we're more likely to do the thing that requires less choice. The busy, **depleted brain is less able to make the tough choices** to step beyond busyness.
- We make **great choices when we're "cold,"** but in the grip of temptation (when we're "hot") all our best intentions disappear.

When Enough Is Enough

- We are not good at spotting when enough is enough, so we need to be more aware of the early warning signals of approaching overwhelm.
- Boundaries can protect us and stop the color in our lives from bleeding into gray; they work best when they are specific and negotiated in advance.

Go-Do

Prioritize, Cold

When you're fresh, first thing in the morning, take out a clean sheet of paper (it's better to do this the old-fashioned way, so you don't get tempted by email, etc.). Write down all the important things you want to work on today. Now choose the three most important of those. On a Post-it, write down those three important activities (and only those), in priority order. Stick it where it is visible to you all day. Before you even turn on your computer, get started on the first item.

Unchoose

Identify one thing you need to choose *not* to do in order to focus on the above tasks today. Do this every day and you'll get better at focusing on what's important.

Experiment

Social Norms

Identify people who seem to be better than you at managing a particular aspect of busy, and spend more time with them.

Outcasting

Be the outcast: Play with never saying "I'm busy." Find more interesting responses, and look at the shock and horror in other people's faces!

Chapter 3

Manage Attention
(How to Use Our Blobby Tissue Better)

Your brain consists of just two to three pounds of a blobby tissue. It doesn't look like much, but it is considered by scientists to be the most complex object in the universe. It contains about 100 billion neurons and a trillion support cells. To put that in context, you have as many neurons as the total number of people born in the entire history of the world! Now, to understand how much messaging is happening inside this blobby tissue, imagine every person that ever lived is also fanatical about social media and has seven thousand friends on Facebook (each neuron is connected to an average of seven thousand other neurons) and sends between five and fifty status updates every second!

The brain is amazing. However, it wasn't designed for the modern working environment and all the challenges, distractions and stimulations of life today. The brain evolved for a different world: a world of simple choices, of limited information and distraction—a technology-free world. For example, our ancestors needed good memories to be able to recall if this or that animal would kill them, or how to find the way home after a hunting expedition. They didn't need to be clever and think about weighty problems of global economics, but they did need to spot signs of danger in the environment, and respond quickly. In other words, we've got pretty good memories, we're bad at thinking and we're distractible.

While biological evolution is very slow, cultural evolution can be astonishingly rapid. Our brains aren't much different from those of our ancestors thousands of years ago, yet our culture has evolved, bringing with it new tools and technologies that change everything as far as the brain is concerned. We no longer need a good memory: When was the last time you tried to commit a new telephone number to memory? On the other hand, we have never thrown as much information and complexity at our brains with as much speed. We have never pounded our poor, overloaded neurons as hard and as relentlessly with so much distraction. We have never maintained a state of alertness as consistently as we do today, aided by our multiple pings and rings.

It's About Attention, Not Time

Edward M. Hallowell, expert in attention deficit disorder (ADD), describes the experience of ADD like this: "People with untreated ADD rush around a lot, feel impatient wherever they are, love speed, get frustrated easily, lose focus in the middle of a task or a conversation because some other thought catches their attention, bubble with energy but struggle to pay attention to one issue for more than a few seconds…feel they could do a lot more if they could just get it together…feel powerless over the piles of stuff that surround them, resolve each day to do better tomorrow, and in general feel busy beyond belief."[1]

Sound familiar? That description would apply to many of us in our daily lives. Hallowell, in his book *CrazyBusy*, explains that being busy is more akin to attention deficit disorder than many of us would like to accept—and that's a problem. In her insightful book *Distracted*, Maggie Jackson describes attention as the bedrock of society. Our willingness and ability to think deeply, to ponder the complex rather than the superficial, to be focused rather than diffuse, are critical not only to our thinking but also to our morality, our happiness and our culture. She worries that, culturally, we are losing our powers of attention: that our lives of distraction are reducing our capacity to create and preserve wisdom. She believes this could have dire consequences: "We are on the verge of losing our capacity as a society for deep, sustained focus. In short, we are slipping toward a new dark age."[2]

Whether or not you believe we are moving to some kind of intellectually dumbed-down, cultural dark age, I think we'd all accept that the multiple sources of information, stimulation and demand hitting our brains today scatter our attention horribly. We can get so used to being buffeted by each and every attraction, our ability to stay focused on a single task drops. In fact, many otherwise healthy people who need to focus are looking for chemical assistance. Many are reaching way beyond coffee and Red Bull. The latest trend is "cosmetic neurology": to self-prescribe drugs for ADHD or narcolepsy to support fading powers of concentration. In a significant study of over 1,800 students, 34 percent had taken drugs like Ritalin and Adderall illegally to help them concentrate![3]

I would argue that attention management is far, far more important than time management. We can put in lots of hours at work, or put lots into our hours at work, but our impact starts, our breakthroughs occur and our real relationships are built when we get the best from our attentional systems. After all, our ability to think is our most valuable capability: to prioritize the wheat over the chaff, to solve complex problems and to create new ideas. Our ability to be fully present in the moment is our most rewarding capability, allowing us to find real joy, to cherish moments and experience connectedness. We cannot hope to thrive and achieve all we dream of unless we manage our attention better.

Focusing Attention

Busyness is bad, but that doesn't mean full and active lives are bad. Many of us have a lot of things we want to achieve, which will only be delivered with hard work. However, there is a huge difference between deep focus on an important activity, and hopscotching busyness. It's not a quantity thing, it's a quality thing. Days and lives crammed with deep immersion in projects, interactions and experiences that are truly meaningful to you, are the juice of life. That is mastery.

One Thing at a Time

Have you ever noticed that if you are walking while talking on your mobile phone and someone asks you a tough question, you stop moving while you think? You stop because you intuitively want to divert all your paltry mental resources to your prefrontal cortex. In fact, it was shown by the scientist J. C. Welch in the late 1800s that thinking makes us physically weaker! Welch asked people to squeeze a lever as hard as they could, and measured the force they applied. Then the test was repeated, this time giving people a mental task to complete simultaneously. When people were thinking really hard, the physical force they could exert reduced by as much as 50 percent![4]

The converse is also true. Harold Pashler, distinguished professor of psychology at the University of California, had people perform simple physical and intellectual tasks in tandem. He found that performance dropped significantly when the subject attempted to do more than one thing at a time, even though they were different kinds of tasks.[5] Pashler would argue that part of the reason for this is *dual-task interference*: our brains are not designed to do two things at once, to multitask. Multitasking, it seems, can drop the performance of a Harvard MBA student to that of an eight-year-old.[6] The only way to work around this is to focus on one thing at a time.

Get It Out of Your Head

Two Buddhist monks were walking together when they came to a river. Next to the river was a beautiful woman. She turned to the monks and asked them to carry her across the stream so she didn't spoil her dress. The first monk, knowing that touching women was not allowed, apologized but said no. The second monk, without pause, picked her up and carried her across the river. They walked on for many hours and miles. Then the first monk turned to the second and asked why he had carried the woman. To which, the second replied, "I carried her a few steps across that stream; you have carried her many miles."

In the opening I talked about the Zeigarnik effect and how a few minutes on a topic, left unfinished, opens the file so that the brain continues to work on the topic in the background. This is a great strategy to accelerate your ability to solve that problem quickly the next day. However, the Zeigarnik effect has a less than positive side. All open files demand attention from the brain. Open files clutter the brain and redirect energy; they reduce our thinking power, they distract our attention. The second monk was only able to get into the Zen of his walk because he had closed the file relating to the woman.

In his book *Getting Things Done*, David Allen describes the effect of carrying lots of open files as the "monkey mind"[7]— when our thoughts leap from task to task, from idea to idea. Anytime we have "a lot on our minds," we are carrying lots of thoughts, worries or tasks in our heads. The *executive network*—the part of the brain's attention system particularly tasked with focus—doesn't know where to direct attention. A monkey mind struggles to focus.

In *Getting Things Done*, Allen suggests a simple tool for getting things off your mind that I mentioned in the opening. It's so valuable I just want to expand on it here. I referred to it as a brain dump; Allen calls it a *collection bucket*. A bucket is something you throw stuff into. A bucket isn't a to-do list of actions; it just collects stuff. That's the beauty of it. There is no categorization happening at all when you decide what goes in the bucket: big and small, urgent and important, shopping items, creative insights and actions. The important thing is that you always have your "bucket" with you. You may be "old skool" and use a notebook as your bucket, or you may prefer to use your smartphone. Whenever a task, important thought or action comes to mind, don't try to remember it—capture it in your bucket. You are not trying to do anything with it at this moment, you are just getting it out of your head to free up your prefrontal cortex to think better.

Buckets only work if we have confidence that we will respond to them. To make a bucket work, we need a habit of emptying it on a regular basis. If not, the brain will soon learn it can't relax. Most people I've worked with review their bucket daily, at specific chosen points. It's important to remember, when you review the bucket, that it isn't an action list. It is likely to represent the intellectual flotsam and jetsam of your mental meanderings. Seeing these items listed allows you to stand back and make rational choices. You will find that many items can simply be deleted, many you will put in what Allen calls a "Someday/Maybe" file, and others you will choose to do. I have found my "bucket" to be a simple discipline that helps to get stuff out of my head, confident I will address what should be addressed. Doing this allows me to step back into the moment, focus and think better about the things that really matter.

Externalize Your Thinking

Have you ever tried to play chess only in your mind? It's really hard, because not only do you have to decide the next best move, you also have to remember the positions of all the pieces. It's much easier to play when you can physically see the board. When you have a board, you free your brain from the task of remembering where all the pieces are; it can focus all its intellectual capability on making clever moves. The same applies to our thinking at work: anything we can do to externalize our thinking will free up more intellectual horsepower.

One of the most important intellectual tools I possess is my humble whiteboard. Time after time, when I'm getting a little stuck or entrenched in my thinking, I leap up and grab a pen. I write all the elements of the problem on the board, then I start playing around with what I've written. The reason this really helps is that when we're trying to think through a complex problem, we're trying to do three things at once. We're trying to hold all the different parts of the problem in our head, we're trying to manipulate the concepts and organize them in a sensible way and we're trying to solve the problem, all at the same time. My whiteboard frees my mind of the burden of holding all that information in my working memory. I organize it externally too, which allows all of my intellect to focus on solving the actual problem. My whiteboard makes me cleverer!

From Drowning to Immersion

When Laird Hamilton let go of the rope and dropped onto that wave, he wasn't worrying about his inbox, or his board-shaping business, or what he would buy for dinner that night. He was focused, 100 percent, on the moment, on the task at hand. The single biggest concern of sports psychology is help-ing athletes to get into that state of peak performance called "the zone." When an athlete is "in the zone," they are operating at their best because they are entirely focused and immersed in the activity. However, this is not always easy to achieve: athletes, like all of us, get distracted easily.

So how do we get more immersed more frequently? How do we get into the zone? Dr. Daniel Gucciardi and James Dimmock, associate professor at the University of Western Australia studied this in professional golfers. They asked one group of golfers to focus on three specific aspects of their swing such as "head," "shoulders," "knees" (...and "toes"?); they asked another group of golfers to focus on a single, all-encompassing aspect of their performance that they wanted to achieve, such as "smooth" or "effortless." When not under pressure, both groups performed strongly. (They were professionals after all!) However, performance differed greatly when the distractions were increased in the form of cash prizes. The pros who were concentrating on three aspects of their swing started faltering; those with a simpler focus continued to perform well.[8]

Focusing on multiple aspects of the swing, we might think, would help us stay immersed by keeping our attention on the activity. However, when we are under pressure or distracted, this requires too much cognitive effort, and we stall. We get lost in the mental jump between "head" and "shoulders." We think of too much, we start drowning and we lose immersion.

To remain fully immersed in what you're doing, you need to maintain a simple focus. This can take a number of forms. Most obviously, it's about focusing on one thing at a time. However, it's also about maintaining a focus on the "how." Thinking about a single aspect of your performance within a task, one that stretches you, appears to be just enough cognitive demand to accelerate you into the zone. In the same way the golfers focused on "smooth," I have often found single word

challenges help me get in the zone. When approaching a complex task like designing a presentation or writing a proposal, if
I set myself a challenge to make it "surprising" or even "beautiful," I find I become more immersed, more quickly.

Stop Churning

One of the things that prevents us from becoming immersed in
what we're doing is the churn: the relentless washing-machine
spin of fears and concerns. It feels terrible, it's exhausting and
it won't surprise you to know that all those open files reduce
your thinking power. As I mentioned earlier, you might capture
these concerns in your bucket list, but when they are more
emotive, that often doesn't help. It's easy to mistake this churn
as a natural consequence of having too much to do—a consequence that won't go away until we're back on top, having
done it all. In fact, that's not why we churn. More important,
there is a simple cure for churning.

A graduate student from Florida State University, working
with psychologist Roy Baumeister, came up with an interesting
little study.[9] He asked some students to think about their final
exams and others, the control group, to think about an important party at the end of term. Among those who thought about
the exam, half were also told to make specific plans for their
study regimen. Nobody was given any time to actually study.

He then tested the students to see if they were churning.
He gave each person word fragments to complete. For example, subjects were asked to complete "ex**" and "re**" to make
four-letter words. Each of these could be completed to form a
study-relevant word (exam, read), but could also be completed
to form a totally different word (exit, real). We would expect
more study-relevant words from those people who had begun
churning over their exams. This was very much the case: those
with exams on their minds identified a lot more exam-related
words than those who had been tasked with thinking about a

party. However, those who had thought about the exam, but subsequently made a study plan, showed no evidence of the churn; the words they identified were no more exam-related than anyone else's.

The starting point to massively reducing your churning is to catch yourself doing it—and stop. Take a few minutes to write down a plan of action. Additionally, rather than waiting for the churn to hit, many people I work with develop a discipline to write a plan at certain times of the day, the most common being when they arrive at work or just before they leave. Writing a simple plan doesn't take long, but it's the most powerful technique we know to free your mind from the churn, to allow you to immerse yourself in the task at hand.

... or Just Reschedule Churning

Ad Kerkhof is professor of clinical psychology, psychopathology and suicide prevention at Vrije University, Amsterdam. For thirty years he has studied the events and the thoughts that lead up to a person taking their life. He found that, before committing suicide, people experience a period of extreme rumination on their life. He has developed simple, effective techniques, based on cognitive behavioral therapy, which really work. One of these strategies worked so well he was tempted to try it on people who weren't in the least bit suicidal; people who were simply churning or worrying. His evidence showed that this strategy worked on people with relatively mild cases of worry too.

Kerkhof suggests we should actively and deliberately worry, just not all the time. Instead we should set aside a couple of slots in the day, fifteen minutes in the morning and fifteen minutes in the evening, as our "worry time." During that time we make a list of all our concerns, and think about them. When the fifteen minutes are up, we stop worrying.[10] Whenever we feel a worry enter our head at other times of the day, we tell ourselves that we will worry about this, just not now. In effect, we procrastinate our worrying! If this sounds a little weird, it might be, but there is a wealth of empirical evidence to show it works. As Tom Borkovec, professor of psychology at Penn State, says, "When we're engaged in worry, it doesn't really help us for someone to tell us to stop worrying...If you tell someone to postpone it for a while, we are able to actually do that."[11] This technique has become known as *stimulus control*. By compartmentalizing our churns, we take control of them, leaving us free to think unfettered by the chains of concern.

Maintaining Attention

As I sit here at my desk I have the world at my feet. In a way that wasn't available to even the richest rulers in recent history, I have instant access to a world of information, a world of television shows and a world of weird videos of tightrope-walking dogs. Our executive network is all that stands between a healthy, productive psychological existence and a meaningless life dissipated on a wave of information consumption. It's just that we are evolutionarily primed to spot novelty. Managing our attention is more than the ability to focus deeply; it's also the ability to maintain attention on a singular task for longer.

Reduce Switching

Multitasking can mean performing two tasks simultaneously, but the most common type of multitasking involves switching rapidly from task to task. Each time we move between tasks, the brain takes a little time to reorient itself to the rules of the new task at hand. The time taken for this reorientation creates what is called a "switch cost." As mentioned at the start of the book, professor David Meyer has found that even if the cost of an individual switch of attention is small, the cumulative cost of regular switching is significant. He suggests multitasking, in the form of switching backward and forward between tasks, increases the overall time needed to complete the tasks by 40 percent.[12]

Big Chunking

The simple message of this is that we achieve more if we stay focused on tasks for longer. The more we switch backward and forward, the harder the brain has to work, and the slower we think. I call this strategy "big chunking" to suggest that we chunk our time into big chunks of activity, not micro-slices of tasks. For example, Teresa Amabile, Edsel Bryant Ford professor of business administration at Harvard Business School, found, in a study of nine thousand people in the creative industries, that subjects had more breakthroughs when they worked on a single project for a major chunk of the day.[13]

This might sound obvious, but it doesn't feel that way. In fact, quite the reverse: A small amount of dopamine (a feel-good neurotransmitter) is released when we switch, helping us feel potent, effective and efficient. The more we bounce between report writing, phone answering and email reading, swatting tasks away, one by one, the more effective we *feel*. As the velocity of the demands increase, so does our dopamine. We have to learn not to mistake the buzz we get from multitasking for a rightly earned sense of effectiveness. This buzz perpetuates our illusion of efficiency; we delude ourselves into mistaking our ability to machine-gun disconnected tasks for working well. In fact, Jonathan B. Spira, an analyst at the business research firm Basex, highlighted the scale of the multitasking illusion. He estimated that the increased inefficiency and ineffectiveness of multitasking was wasting 28 billion hours of knowledge workers time a year in the US alone.[14]

Break your day into big chunks of activity. The more complex the task, the bigger the chunk of uninterrupted time it needs. Of course, life will intervene at times, the director will tap you on the shoulder and distract you, but your goal should be to maximize chunks of focused time.

...And It's Not Just a Question of Practice

If you're reading this and thinking quietly to yourself, "Okay, I get the general point, but I've multitasked for years...I'm an expert," then I would ask you to think again. Multitasking is one of the few areas, intellectually, where practice does not make perfect. Researchers at Stanford University split people into those who were typically heavy media multitaskers, and those who multitasked less frequently. They expected to find that those with more practice in multitasking would have developed a greater capability in this area. Surprisingly, they found the exact opposite.[15] Those people who multitasked a lot in their day-to-day lives underperformed on a test of multitasking ability. The reason for this is that serial multitaskers were less able to separate the wheat from the chaff; they got more distracted by irrelevant and unimportant information. The more you multitask, the more distracted you'll be and therefore the worse you'll be at thinking. So go ahead if you want to continue, but don't say you weren't warned: multitasking is reducing your intellect and performance.

Avoiding Distractions

How often do you switch tasks at work? Whatever the frequency you just guessed, I would wager you are underestimating it. A Boston College study, published in the fantastically named journal *Cyberpsychology, Behavior, and Social Networking*, found that people underestimated their frequency of distraction by a factor of 10.[16] When working on a computer with a TV in the room, researchers monitored eye movements between the two screens. The participants estimated that they switched the focus of their attention every four minutes. In actual fact, their eye movements showed their attention switched every fourteen seconds! One study of office workers showed that people tend to hopscotch between activities every three minutes.[17] This is worrying since professor of informatics Gloria Mark at the University of California found that workers took an average of twenty-three minutes to recover from interruptions like phone calls or answering email, and return to their original task.[18]

Some distractions are unavoidable. A lot, however, are self-induced. In fact, Mark found that 44 percent of all interruptions were self-initiated.[19] If we're really honest with ourselves, a lot of the hopscotching isn't driven by necessity, it's because the novel is more exciting and the simple is more attractive than a more intellectually demanding activity such as deep thinking. So we flip into our inbox, triggered by the ping of a new email; we flop into a chat instead of persisting in thinking through tough challenges.

It would be better to avoid the distraction in the first place. First on everyone's list here should be the email notifier in Outlook. Turn it off, or even better, turn off Outlook while you're working on a big chunk. You might turn your phone to silent or at least put the text notifier on silent. You could remove visual temptation. For example, my friend was regularly getting complaints from his wife about the degree to which he was "present" when they were together—his smartphone was always there, luring him away from her. He agreed that when they ate out in restaurants he would no longer place the phone on the dinner table. It worked; he was less distracted.

What distractions might you avoid and how will you go about avoiding them?

Machine-Gun in Bursts

To allow yourself to focus properly on chunks of activity, you also need to create the opportunity to address email and the simple tasks on your to-do list. I call this machine-gunning. This may sound extreme, but I like to imagine blasting through email and messages, killing off these distractions, before returning to my key priority areas for chunks of time. I seldom find much that will change the world in my daily inbox; however, that doesn't mean I can afford to ignore it.

I have three rules for machine-gunning the inbox and other tasks:

- Choose a time. Machine-gun at certain, specific points of the day. For the rest of the day, the email is off and the task list goes unaddressed. You don't need a to-do list to tell you what's most important: you know that already (or, if you don't, it's not important).
- Time-limit the blasts. The nature of micro-tasks is that, if you are trying to get through them all, they can easily swamp your day. Give yourself a deadline, or even better, put a clock in front of you. This not only protects your time for the important stuff, it also creates urgency to your blasting.
- During these periods, follow David Allen's two-minute rule: if there's any item in your inbox or on your task list that will take less than two minutes, do it straightaway. Otherwise the cost in organizing or filing it anywhere will exceed the time required to actually do it.

Refreshing Attention

Muscles are designed for bursts of intense activity followed by periods of rest. You will realize how useless muscles are at continuous effort if you have ever held your arms outstretched for as long as you can. It gets pretty uncomfortable pretty quickly. The brain can be thought of as being like a muscle: it works best in pulses of activity. For an image of the most optimal way to use your brain (or body for that matter), picture a heartbeat monitor. Yet our busy lives these days are anything other than pulses of activity. For many of us, our experience from the moment we rise to the moment we sleep is one long, steady state of busyness—like a flat line on a heart monitor.

Perhaps the biggest challenge to our ability to think well in today's world is what Linda Stone would call *continuous partial attention*.[20] We pay partial attention to everything, continuously, because we don't want to miss anything. We constantly scan the environment for information, messages, stimulation and threat. We are always alert, constantly connected, and continuously trying to optimize efficiency.

In the size of doses we serve ourselves, continuous partial attention is fragmenting, stressful and empty, and compromises our ability to think and focus. To gain mastery, the last thing you need to do is stay alert and immersed 100 percent of the time. Instead you need to think of your days as being intense pulses of focus and stress, followed by recovery.

So what is the right balance of focus and recovery? One recent study by the makers of the time-tracking effectiveness app DeskTime suggests that the optimum balance is 52 minutes of focus, followed by 17 minutes away from your desk. They found this through electronically monitoring the behavioral patterns of the top 10 percent most effective workers.[21] I'm not suggesting you follow a 52/17 schedule rigidly, but that your day is a pulse. Intense activity is punctuated with recovery periods, allowing your body to relax and your attentional systems to regroup.

Involuntary Attention

Given the importance of attention, how do you refresh it when it gets tired? How do you increase your ability to focus? This was a question asked by psychologist Stephen Kaplan. He developed the *attention restoration theory* (ART),[22] which splits attention into two types: directed and involuntary. Directed attention is effortful and focused, in which the executive network deliberately brings all our attention to bear on the project at hand. Involuntary attention is when inherently interesting things, such as the beauty of a sunset, naturally capture our attention. ART suggests that, as involuntary attention takes hold, it gives the parts of the brain associated with directed attention a chance to recover and replenish.

Given the importance of our ability to focus, Marc Berman, John Jonides and Stephen Kaplan decided to test what types of breaks would refresh the brain best. To do this, they had subjects take a walk. Some walked through a busy city; others walked through a wood. The results showed that the woodland walk significantly improved cognitive performance; the city walk didn't.[23] The reason for this is that, to avoid being hit by speeding taxis, directed attention could totally switch off. The pleasant sights and sounds of the woods, on the other hand, attracted involuntary attention, and gave directed attention a full break.

The moral of this story is not that we need the woods and trees, but that to replenish our ability to direct our attention we should find ways to trigger our involuntary attention. It does little to cognitively recharge us if we switch our attention from our work onto WhatsApp, the TV or Angry Birds; they all require focus.

Schedule Recovery

Hardworking consultants from the Boston Consulting Group were practically forced to take planned breaks. They committed to taking one night off a week, no matter how busy they were. Even this small step caused alarm in the consultants; they were afraid that they would disappoint clients, that their work would pile up or that it would have an adverse effect on their careers. Instead, the results showed increases in satisfaction, in career success, in development and in the value they felt they were contributing to their clients.[24] The trick was scheduling these breaks, so they were more likely to be taken. How could you schedule your breaks?

Get Out of Your Head

As an information worker, it can sometimes be easy to forget we are not just a brain. Our work, our interests and our distraction involve us being relatively sedentary, staring at screens and thinking. However, in case you need reminding, you also have a body. To refresh your attention, you need to refresh your body. For example, you might start by breathing! Linda Stone found that 80 percent of people don't breathe properly when they are typing (a thought that horrifies me after all the hours I've spent typing this book!). She called this *email apnea*.[25] So get up, get moving and start breathing! Make sure there is aerobic exercise built into your routines, but even a slight increase in your breathing patterns (from a walk up the stairs, for example) will refresh attention.

Optimizing Breaks

You haven't got much time to spare, so how do you make your breaks most effective? Here's a little reminder of the four things you should build into your breaks to maximize their impact on your attention. If it helps you to remember them, use the acronym FAME.

Fuel	*Attention*
Boost your energy with water and food. About half the population walk around with mild to chronic levels of dehydration so make sure you drink some water. You should also try to eat low glycemic foods, such as nuts and beans, which release energy more slowly.	Think of attention as being of two types: focused, intentional attention and meandering, mind-wandering attention. If you have been focused, in your breaks you should de-focus. If you have been staring at your screen, turn away (switching to Google, Twitter and Facebook gives the brain no chance to recover).
Movement	*Emotion*
If you have been physically passive during your period of activity, move. Change your actual pulse; get out of your head and into your body for a few minutes. Walk, do some stretches, climb some stairs. Anything that puts your body into motion and makes you breathe more deeply.	A great way to recover quickly is to change your emotional tone. Use music, conversation or activity to change your vibe. (See *Reversal Theory.*)

...And Sleep

Cheri Mah, from Stanford, had basketball players keep a normal sleep schedule for a few weeks. Then she asked them, for five to seven weeks, to get more sleep: to take more naps and try to get ten hours of sleep a night. When they slept more, their three-point and free throw shooting averages went up by 9 percent![26] Sleep matters; it refreshes our attention and so it raises our performance. In fact, a lack of sleep due to our frenetic lifestyles is estimated to be costing the US economy $63 billion a year.[27]

Take naps when you can. Of course, as a resident of Spain, I love a siesta! However, one suggestion I love from Arianna Huffington, a passionate sleep advocate, is to set an alarm...to remind you when it's time to go to bed!

THE BIG MESSAGES IN "MANAGE ATTENTION"

Your brain is possibly the most complex object in the universe; it's amazing, but it's not designed for the level of demand, distraction and stimulation you're throwing at it.

Our effectiveness and our happiness are both entirely dependent on our ability to be focused and present. For this reason, it's much more important to manage your attention than your time.

There are three aspects to our attentional systems: the executive network, which helps us to focus; the orienting network, which spots novelty and distracts us; and the alerting network, which determines the quantity of attention we have.

Focusing Attention

- When we do more than one thing at a time, dual-task interference drops the performance of a Harvard MBA student to that of an eight-year-old.
- Do one thing at a time by getting things **out of your head** and **externalizing** your thinking.
- **Immerse yourself deeply by giving yourself a single-word focus, like "surprising" or "beautiful."**
- **Free up your mind by coming up with a simple plan to stop churning.**

Maintaining Attention

- Switching regularly between tasks makes you 40 percent slower, even if you feel productive.
- Cut down on the number of times you switch your attention between tasks by working in bigger chunks of time, and minimizing distraction.
- Practice does not make perfect: Heavy multitaskers get more easily distracted.

Refreshing Attention

- The brain is like a muscle; it works best in pulses of focus, with periods of recovery.
- When we maintain **continuous partial attention**, constantly scanning for information, we never give our focusing powers a chance to regroup and recharge.
- We regain our ability to focus best through unfocusing, through periods where we don't exercise our directed attention.

GO-DO

Big-Chunk Your Time

From today, create uninterrupted chunks of time so you can stay on task for longer. To help with this, cut off distractions by disabling the email notifier and your IM.

Machine-Gun Emails

Choose certain slots in the day to work through your emails and messages. This tends to be low-demand work, so choose times when you are not at your most alert and save your freshest moments for the important things.

EXPERIMENT

Sleep

Set an alarm to remind yourself when it's time to go to bed!

Churning

Next time you're churning, grab a pen and a piece of paper and devise a cunning plan. Not only is this helpful, it also gets the churning thoughts out of your head.

Chapter 4

Negotiate for Your Life
(To Keep Those Missiles at Bay)

In 1962, the world stood perilously close to Armageddon. The Soviets had dispatched a shipment of nuclear missiles to Cuba. These were approaching the island country where they would be trained upon the US. President Kennedy couldn't allow this to happen. He had three options: let the missiles arrive in Cuba and just accept the threat to the US mainland, retaliate by bombing Cuba and launching an invasion, or start seriously negotiating. Sensibly, he chose not to ignore the threat. Thankfully, he chose not to launch an invasion since, unbeknownst to him, the Soviets had 40,000 troops in Cuba, and the Cubans had 250,000 well-trained troops ready too. Instead, he chose to talk. Through skillful negotiations on both sides, a nuclear war was narrowly averted.

We all have a choice as we face shipload after shipload of missiles, all pointing at us. We can, as most of us have been doing, accept the busyness. Alternatively, we could retaliate: we could hand in our notice or say "to hell with this." Or we could start talking. People are often remarkably resistant to talking and negotiating. They worry that they might lose out in the process, or that somehow starting to talk about an alternative response to busyness is revealing their dark secret: that they care about life beyond work. They worry that talking might place them in opposition to the needs of the business. But they pay a high price to avoid talking: they put up with way too much.

This applies at home too. How do you agree with those you love on the best balance of your time and energies? Is it better to put a few extra hours of work in, do homework with your son, go to your daughter's soccer game, or go to the gym? Other members of your family can't fully understand your burdens, nor will you ever fully understand their perspectives. Many of the conversations resulting from a more imaginative response to a world of "too much" will be difficult.

However, at some point, if you want to find a way forward that doesn't involve the ineffectual drudgery of busyness, or doing something drastic, you're going to have to start talking. When you get to that point, the rest of this chapter will help.

Negotiate Beyond Busy

An immortal Monty Python sketch from *The Life of Brian* involves a desperate Brian trying to escape from a group of Roman soldiers who are chasing him. He goes to a market stall where he selects, and tries to pay for, a false beard as a disguise. The market trader can't understand Brian's behavior and says, "Wait a minute, we're supposed to haggle." When a gourd gets thrown into the bargain, the market trader asks for another ten shekels. When Brian agrees to the price, the trader says, "No, no, no, no. It's not worth ten. You're supposed to argue! Ten for that, you must be mad!"

The sketch, funny and weird as it is, does point to two standard beliefs about negotiation: you're supposed to haggle and you're supposed to argue. Roger Fisher and William

Ury, founders of the Harvard Negotiation Project at Harvard Law School, would disagree (in a nonargumentative fashion, obviously!).[1]

Imagine a business executive returning from a business trip. She has attended a "Life Balance" seminar and, inspired, has decided she wants to improve her health and fitness. She walks into the house and announces to her husband that she's off for a long run. Her nearest and dearest—who has been single-handedly managing the home and children in her absence—reacts to this, expressing (in no uncertain terms) his desire for a break, immediately; he is off to meet his friends. Since that would leave no one to mind the children, both of them can't get what they want. The most common thing to do here is to haggle (or argue like cats and dogs).

In their book *Getting to Yes*, Fisher and Ury suggest an approach that results in two winners from the negotiation process. I find that this is the best approach for the tricky lifestyle negotiations that are needed to move beyond busy. Their approach is called *principle-based negotiation* and is built upon two foundations: focusing on underlying needs and seeking agreements.

Focus on Underlying Needs

In any negotiation, we have certain needs or principles we want met, and, in approaching a negotiation, we will identify ways to fulfill these needs. These are called our "positions." The negotiation, then, becomes a debate and trade-off between our respective positions. In the case of the business executive coming home from the seminar, her position is to go for a long run—right away. Her husband's position is that he needs a break—immediately. Clearly both positions cannot be maintained. There will be a winner and a loser, or a compromise (two losers).

Principle-based negotiations are based on building agreements founded on underlying needs. For example, if the business executive, instead of focusing on wanting to run immediately, talked instead about her desire to improve her work-life balance, her husband would almost certainly agree with that desire and be supportive. At the same time, if her husband talked about how he had been run ragged by the children and had felt caged in the house for the last few days, she would recognize those feelings and understand his need to get out of the house for some adult company.

Once an agreement is reached around underlying needs, the magic can happen. The wife and husband are no longer competing, pushing for their positions to be met. They are working together to find solutions to needs they both agree with. In the end, the couple above might agree to go out to the park together, with the children; they take a soccer ball, and have a game (exercise need fulfilled). In the evening, they get a babysitter, and go out for dinner together (break need fulfilled). The fact is that most needs can be satisfied in multiple ways. If we start our discussion from the need, we can get creative, together, to identify solutions that fully meet both parties (instead of only partially meeting both).

Seek Agreements

Have you ever played devil's advocate? When we play devil's advocate in normal conversations, we argue a case just for the sake of the debate. Let's say, for example, someone is arguing that Babe Ruth was the greatest-ever baseball player. You may be relatively neutral on the subject but, for the sake of a conversation, you argue the case for Barry Bonds. What happens next is interesting: the longer, and the more strongly, you argue for Bonds, the more you begin to convince yourself that the famous left fielder for the Giants really was the greatest baseball player ever to play the game. This isn't because of your brilliant arguments either; in fact, your opponent is becoming more convinced than ever that Babe Ruth was the best. This is because of cognitive dissonance: when we argue forcefully for something, our beliefs start to come into line with our argument. We're more likely to persuade ourselves than our opposition!

When you apply this to a negotiation, the risk is that the very act of arguing or "negotiating" based on different opinions, can actually drive both opponents further apart, thereby reducing the chances of reaching a workable agreement. Instead you should seek to find *agreement* in your negotiations to give you a better chance of finding a solution that will work for both people involved.

Let's say that you are about to renegotiate your boundaries. You want to spend more quality time with your friends and family. It's not that you want to do less work, it's just that the hours you work, the journey you make and the constant emails through the evening and weekend mean you are barely present at home anymore. You could storm in and ask for a finishing time of 4:30 p.m. (a position), given you have a long journey. Your manager will then have two options: yes or no. If she says "yes," then you're okay; you're better off, providing your manager didn't feel backed into a corner and irritated by your request. If she said "no," where can you go? "I want to finish at four thirty...[no]...But I have such a long journey...[no]... I'm hardly seeing my children...[no]...Don't you care about children?" It's a road to nowhere. You start off disagreeing, and get further apart as the argument gets more and more heated.

On the other hand, if the conversation is framed in much broader terms, in terms of needs, you can build on agreements. "My work and my family are both important to me...[agree]... I want to find the right balance...[agree]...Will you help me find a solution that works for you and me?...[agree]..."

So, in order to negotiate your boundaries in a positive, productive manner, you need to do the following:

- Make sure you are really clear in your mind about your underlying needs and how they differ from any positions you currently have in mind.
- Start by describing your needs. Don't forget to use the magic word "because" (as mentioned in the opening of the book).
- Seek to understand their needs.
- Look for agreement before trying to find a solution.
- Once agreement is established, get creative. Together, generate solutions to meet both of your needs.

When Compromise Can Help

Williams-Sonoma is a cookware company that makes high-quality cooking utensils. After having the same bread machine on the market for a while, they decided it was time to make an improved version. They released the new and improved bread maker at a premium price to reflect its higher quality and additional features. What happened next was unexpected: almost immediately, sales of the original bread maker doubled.

Researcher Itamar Simonson explains that this happens because consumers tend to prefer "compromise choices."[2] The new bread maker attracts your attention; it would be wonderful but is too expensive. You then recognize that the original model still makes good bread, and appears cheap compared to the new one; it suddenly becomes an attractive option. It makes you feel that you are making a sensible choice.

So let's imagine you have a burdensome report to do each week, which you feel takes more time to do than it warrants. You might put a proposal to your manager, offering three options: the first is to keep producing the same report, the second is to produce a substantial but significantly scaled-down version, and the third is to take a bare-bones approach. Positioned this way, your boss is more likely to choose the middle option, which will still meet their needs but save you a huge amount of time. This approach is likely to reduce your burden, while simultaneously satisfying your manager; after all, it was your manager who chose that you should do less.

A Foot in the Door

Would being asked if you are likely to vote actually make you more likely to vote? The answer, according to social scientist Anthony Greenwald, is yes. He asked this very question on the eve of an election. Those asked to make a prediction of their behavior were 25 percent more likely to vote than those not asked (86.7 percent versus 61.5 percent).[3] This effect occurs because we're motivated to behave consistently over time. So, if we act in a particular way, or agree to something small, we become much more likely to act consistently with that action later.

If you want to make a change in your behavior at work, and you want your boss to agree to it, start by making really, really small requests that would be difficult to disagree with. If these are accepted, your boss will be much more likely to agree with your real, and bigger request. If you do want to work from home one day a week, you might simply start by asking to work from home on a single, one-off instance. That will pave the way for a larger request.

Time to Say "No"

Would you kill someone with a lethal electric shock if a man in a white lab coat asked you to? Or would you say "no"? In one of the most chilling psychological experiments ever, social psychologist Stanley Milgram began studying the effect of authority on people's actions back in 1961 (soon after the beginning of Adolf Eichmann's war crimes trial began in Jerusalem).[4] The subjects were told that they would be "teachers," and they should administer small electric shocks to the "learner" if they got answers wrong. Each time the learner gave the incorrect answer, the voltage was increased by 15 volts (so the subjects were told—though no actual shocks were administered). The subjects were told not to worry; they were not responsible for any consequences. Despite hearing increasing screams and requests for the experiment to stop, 65 percent of all subjects continued to do as they were told, up to the maximum shock: a massive 450 volts! They never said "no."

Work provides us with authority figures in abundance, all of who can dictate our actions. Authority can reduce our need to take responsibility for our actions: being told to do something removes our need to decide. Additionally, saying "no" to anyone, let alone someone more senior, is really hard. At some point though, you'll need to use that two-letter word if you want to set boundaries and avoid the drudgery of the perpetual "yes."

The Power to Say "No"

Before we look at what to say, let's look at how you feel. In one of the most popular TED talks ever, Amy Cuddy described her research about the effect of our body posture on our confidence. She had students "stand powerfully" for just two minutes, which increased their levels of testosterone by 10 percent (associated with confidence) and decreased their cortisol (the stress hormone) by 25 percent. When offered the chance to place a bet, those who had adopted a high-power pose were about 50 percent more likely to gamble than those in the low-power posture. All this in just two minutes![5]

So what is a high-power pose? Just make yourself big. Open your arms and legs, shoulders wide and head up. My favorite is the "Wonder Woman" pose. Remember how she stood: tall, feet shoulder-width apart, both hands on her hips. You may feel completely ridiculous doing this, but that's no bad thing if it lightens your seriousness before saying "no." Find a private place to go and "stand big" for a couple of minutes, then go and say "no," powerfully.

The Truthful "No"

In 1901, Harry Houdini was handcuffed and locked inside an oversized milk can filled with water. Trapped, he had only a limited time before he ran out of breath and drowned. After much wriggling, he emerged triumphant to cheers from the crowd. This became one of his most iconic escapes. There's something about saying "no" that brings out the escapologist in all of us. Being requested to do something puts us on the spot. After much wriggling and squirming, hopefully, we find our escape.

Let's imagine you've just been asked to attend an important business conference over the following weekend. What do you do? Do you tell your boss "no" because you want to spend time with your family, or do you get creative? Our desire to escape can be so strong that we entirely fabricate a convincing-sounding story to demonstrate that we certainly cannot say "yes": "My long-lost school friend, who was with me in 'Nam, is visiting with his three-legged Chihuahua, who has canine leukemia, so it might be my last chance to see her." We can feel an almost irresistible urge to create excuses to get out of things. Our primary goal is to escape. This can help us escape from an awkward situation, but leaves us open to similar future conversations: "Will you stay late to help me with my report tonight?" "Oh, I'd really love to [lie], but [excuse coming...] I'm taking my budgie to the vet." "Ahh, that's a shame; how about tomorrow?"

While I'm all for creativity, when it comes to saying "no," the truth is best. Escaping can help us to get out of awkward situations and is often an attempt not to damage the relationship, but it can lead us down a dead end. The truth may feel more challenging to say, but it can help to set boundaries and clarify your priorities.

Oh, and by the way, don't say "I'm busy" as your excuse. It may be true, but it's not sufficiently explicit; it just sounds like a rude brush-off.

The Thoughtful "No"

One of the things that can prompt us to either say "yes" when we want to say "no," or to make up excuses, is the feeling that the spotlight is on us. When we get an unwanted request, a request to which we might want to say "no," we can often say "yes" simply because we can't think it through quickly enough. When the pressure is on, we default to the safest option and say "yes." It might be that we need time to think through our response based on all our other commitments. It might be that we already know we want to say "no," but just want time to think through our delivery. Either way, get out of the spotlight. Say "let me think about it" or "give me five minutes." Then go and reflect in a cool, rational manner on your response. Assertiveness is not the same thing as quick thinking. Take your time, make the right choice, then have the conversation.

The Positive "No"

The starting point for saying "no" effectively is saying "yes." The "yes" is the big reason behind your "no." Having an important "yes" makes saying "no" a whole lot easier because it provides you with your reason for saying "no." It also provides you with the motivation to say "no." When you say "no" to busyness it's not because you want to stop being busy, it's because you want to become more immersed, more effective, more energized and more connected. Find your big "yes" and you'll find your "no."

In his book, *The Power of a Positive No*, William Ury suggests thinking of your "no" as a tree.[6] The origins and the strength of the "no" come from your big "yes," the roots. This is where you start in preparation and in articulating your "no." This is followed by the trunk, where you say "no" clearly, simply and unemotionally. Finally, the tree branches out. The final part of the "positive no" is to reach out to see if there is a solution, to try to make a positive proposal.

To be clear, this isn't a proposal to soften your "no." Your delivery should be consistent with your big "yes" and your clear "no." It shouldn't offer false hope either. Your "no" can often be presented in the form of a third option. Let's say you're being asked to develop a staff survey to assess training needs. Your role has nothing to do with training, but you do have some expertise in surveys. The reason you want to say "no" to the project is that you are working on a major project launch (your big "yes") and don't want to be distracted by survey development. After explaining your big "yes" and stating your "no" clearly, you want to close with a "yes," a third option. You could say, "Look, I'd be happy to act as an informal advisor on this. If you put your objectives and ideas together, come and see me and I'll give you my perspective. Would that help?"

The Project Management "No"

In project management, they have something called the Triple Constraint Triangle. There are three fundamental constraints on any project; change one of these and it will immediately affect the other two. The model is shown below.

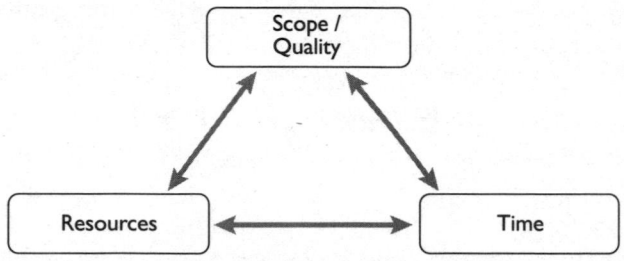

Imagine you're building a new sports stadium for the next Olympic Games. If the scope or quality is increased, e.g., someone decides "Let's put a removable roof on the stadium," it will have an impact on either the budget required or on the overall build time—or both. Given that there is a fixed delivery date for the Olympics, any changes to either scope or quality will have an instant impact on the resources needed (e.g., "We'll need to get a lot more people on the job, quickly") or vice versa.

In the context of busyness, we might often be saying "no" due to the overall press of work. You are saying "no" to unrealistic expectations due to the other challenges you are facing. The "project management no" involves explaining the implications of a "yes." It means saying "no" to the demand as it was positioned, but leaving open a conditional "yes" if the other person agrees to adjustments to the other constraints. For example, say you have been asked to prepare a presentation on your department's marketing spend in the last fiscal year by Friday. You may realize that this is not possible. However, you might say that you would be able to do the presentation if the scope were scaled down, the presentation were a week from Friday instead of this week, or if you get support to help you with this (or with your other work). This allows the "no" to return back into a rational negotiation.

THE BIG MESSAGES IN "NEGOTIATE FOR YOUR LIFE"

We can't go on forever accepting more and more, doing more and more. At some point, for the good of our families, for the good of our work and for the good of ourselves, we will have to start negotiating.

Negotiate Beyond Busy

- If you want to negotiate, **don't haggle**! Discuss your **underlying needs**, and the other party's. Build **agreement**, and from that agreement start to **identify creative solutions** that work for both of you.
- Don't just offer one option, but three; more often than not, people will choose the middle "compromise" option. People like to act consistently. So, ask for a little and you make it much more likely, when you ask for something bigger, that you will get a "yes."

Time to Say "No"

- The **authority** of a man in a lab coat persuaded normal people to give someone a lethal electric shock, just because they didn't want to say "no." **Learn to say "no"** or suffer the consequences!
- The **truthful "no"**: honesty is the best policy. If you make **creative excuses**, you may hang yourself!
- The **thoughtful "no"**: we often say "yes" because we can't think of a good way to say "no." **Give yourself some time to think**. Figure out what you want to say, then go back and say it.

- The **positive "no"**: behind every "no" should be a big "yes." Focus on the **positive reason you are saying "no."**
- The **project management "no"**: In every project there are three constraints—the **time** taken, the **resources** needed, and the **quality or scope** delivered. The project management "no" doesn't involve the word "no" at all. It simply involves a negotiation around constraints: If one changes, the others will need to change to compensate.

Go-Do

Renegotiate
Meet with one person in your life with whom you need to renegotiate expectations. Focus on underlying needs and find a fresh, more healthy agreement.

Say "No"
Over the next week, say "no" to at least one request you would normally say "yes" to. See how it feels. Practice makes perfect.

Experiment

The "No" Toolkit
Play with different ways of saying "no." Which gets the best response? Which feels most authentic?

Offer a Compromise
Try negotiating a better work-life balance by offering a compromise or by starting with very small agreements.

Section Two

DIFFERENTIATION

This section addresses the second face of busy, which sees busyness as a success strategy. We wrongly assume that we will make more career progress through working hard, reacting fast and delivering without pause. Our perception is that if we can do more, we'll achieve more. We will never escape busy unless we can transform our implicit view that the path to success is through personal productivity. Corporate strategy explains why we need to shift our focus from getting things done to making an impact, and how, in an information economy, we will only succeed if we differentiate ourselves.

Chapter 5

Stop Being So Productive!
(Become More Strategic)

In the 1980s, Japanese companies seemed unstoppable. They had developed fantastic improvements in productivity that helped them churn out products faster, more cheaply and to higher standards. Yet, after a decade of irresistible global domination, the tide started to turn for Japan. By the '90s, Japan entered a recession that lasted more than a decade, with zero growth, rising unemployment, and deflation. Other countries around the world had copied the best practices of Japanese manufacturing and destroyed Japan's competitive advantage.

Productivity can provide important advantages over competitors, which can increase profitability, but it will rarely keep you ahead in the long term. Investments in new technologies can increase productivity, but best practices spread quickly, and the immediate gains in output are soon shared by competitors, so no competitive advantage is gained, meaning no increased profit. In fact, what tends to happen is that as all competitors get ever more productive, the investment cost in making further gains gets larger, and this eats into profits. It becomes an arms race in which everyone loses.

As individuals, our productivity has increased enormously with the arrival of each of the following: the computer, the laptop, the mobile phone, the Internet, the smartphone and the cloud. Each of these raised performance levels by allowing us to produce more. This has impacted our careers in three ways: First, we are all able to produce a lot more. So we do. This creates an ever-increasing amount of work for us all to do. Second, as we all use the same technology, our ability to differentiate ourselves on the basis of our productivity gets harder and harder. Finally, any further increases we want to make in our productivity in the hope of achieving ever-smaller advantages over our competition come at an increasingly large cost (especially if we remember Nassim Nicholas Taleb's concavity).

The "More" Game

In the Industrial Age, the primary goal was production: given a set level of quality, the more you could produce, the better. As time passed and production processes improved, managers started to realize the thing that was slowing output the most was the human factor. They needed their people to work harder and more efficiently. Enter Frederick Winslow Taylor and his approach called *scientific management*. Taylor analyzed employee activity with time and motion studies to find out where efficiencies could be made. Ever since then, the core focus of most management teams has been to get their people to produce more.

In a curious parallel to the Industrial Age, a recent study has looked at what is holding back the effectiveness of computer systems today. A research group at Carnegie Mellon University claims that the limiting factor for computers today isn't the processor speed or memory size or network capacity, it's the human factor again. We are the limiting factor to progress. But this time, it isn't our efficiency or hard work that is slowing advancement, it's our (lack of) ability to focus and think.[1]

In our mania to squeeze ever more efficiency out of the workforce, ever more connectedness, ever more output, we have neglected the fact that our brains are not machines. In doing more and more, we are thinking less and less. Which is curious because in an information age, it is our cognitive abilities that matter: the collective intellect, imagination and problem-solving capability of our people. In other words, the very capability that our businesses need to cultivate is being damaged, day by day, by "more." Floundering under the avalanche of corporate communication and demand, our poor brains struggle to do anything more than flit from micro-task to micro-task. We are productive but dumb; our battered and distracted attentional systems are slowing the entire system, and eroding corporate progress.

"More" Is Career-Limiting

From an individual perspective, we see that management wants productivity, and so realize that the more productive we are, the more valuable we are. So we all play the "More" game. The rules are simple: the people who produce the most (and are seen to be producing a lot) win. You work hard, you work long and your bosses notice you seem to be more motivated than your colleagues. Management starts giving you more to do: more work and more responsibility.

The "More" game *can* still work. If you are working with people who are much less hardworking than you, your extra efforts and productivity will be noticed and rewarded. Typically though, this only happens at the very start of our careers. At some point, it stops working. Then, we get to a point where we are no longer competing against the unmotivated; we find our fellow workers are also career-minded and playing the "More" game too! Then, the arms race starts, with email response time, working hours and the sheer quantity of stuff produced being the criteria for success. When the "More" game doesn't bring results, we redouble our efforts trying to squeeze ever more activity, ever more output and ever more responsiveness out of our tired brains. The quality of our thinking drops, our imagination fades and our energy dwindles. Ever so slowly, we fade into the background.

Email: The TV of Work

One of the most obvious domains in which rampant productivity is demonstrated is our response to email. One study of two thousand UK workers found that 77 percent of them would consider "a productive day in the office" to be clearing their inbox.[2] Jonathan B. Spira found that reading and processing just one hundred emails (who only has one hundred emails!) uses up half of a knowledge worker's time.[3]

I think email has become the TV of work. It offers little, but it asks little too. So rather than do the big work that will make a difference, we turn on the email and pass the time (productively of course).

Transforming Our Success Strategy

We may not want to be busy, but few of us are willing to let our career aspirations die to achieve a calmer existence. So if our desire to succeed remains as strong as ever, what alternative do we have to the "More" game? I think the answer lies in the hard-bitten world of corporate strategy. There's no fluff in the strategic world. Strategies either work or they don't, and the game is scored in dollars. Strategy is about delivering success.

More than that, corporate strategy is a great place to look for lessons on how to operate in a world of too much for two reasons:

1. The central problem that business strategy addresses is how to succeed in a competitive market with limited resources. No company can do everything. They have limited resources of money and workforce capacity. To survive, they have to make tough choices on where they can focus their resources most effectively. On an individual level, we have limited resources of attention and time. In the last section we discussed how we have to make choices because we *can't* do everything. Michael Porter, one of the world's leading strategists, would say we have to make choices because we *shouldn't* do everything. If we want to succeed, we have to maximize the impact of our limited resources, and that means focusing our efforts on a limited number of areas.

2. To succeed in today's crowded marketplace, companies have to capture the attention of consumers who are frantically busy and overwhelmed with choice. To do that, they need to be different; they need to stand out. The people who are making career-altering decisions about us are also distracted and overwhelmed. In an attention-scarce economy, corporate strategists have shown the route to success isn't productivity; it's differentiation.

This whole section is about changing your success strategy. It will show you how to succeed through a strategy that will differentiate you. This has two broad components: focusing your efforts more effectively to make the most impact with your scarce resources, and capturing the attention of your distracted and overwhelmed consumers. This chapter looks at the first of these.

Strategic Focus

In 1993, Continental Airlines launched its new, low-cost airline, Continental Lite. It opened to great fanfare as a specific move to compete against highly successful low-cost competitors, such as Southwest Airlines. Continental had many advantages: It had a large and wealthy parent company; it was offering some of the cheapest fares in the industry; it could meet the frequency of other low-cost airlines; it could allow passengers to transfer between flights without having to collect their bags; and seats were pre-allocated. It sounded perfect. Yet two years and $300 million later, Continental Lite flew its last flight. Partly as a result of this disaster, the parent company, Continental Airlines, came under hostile attack from Delta and Northwest Airlines. Ultimately, Northwest closed the deal that allowed Continental to maintain its brand, but all power transferred to the Northwest board.

Why didn't this promising new airline, with so many advantages on its side, become successful? Michael Porter, in perhaps the most famous *Harvard Business Review* article ever, "What Is Strategy?"[4] attributes the failure to a lack of strategic focus. In the face of stiff competition, Continental struggled to do both full-service and low-cost. The company relied on travel agencies for its full-service business, but couldn't afford them for its low-cost option, so it cut agency commissions on all flights. Continental couldn't support the frequent flier benefits on its low-cost version, and so it reduced perks to members on all journeys. Flights were also frequently delayed at hub airports due to baggage transfers that other low-cost providers didn't have to worry about. The result: irritated agents, disappointed customers and late flights. Porter described Continental Lite's approach as "straddling strategic positions." It failed because they said "yes" to too many things. Continental paid a high price for its loss of strategic focus.

Where Will You Focus?

Porter gives the example of IKEA to demonstrate strategic focus. IKEA serves young furniture buyers who want style at a low cost. This isn't unique in itself. What is unique is the way they choose to do it. You wander the showroom by yourself, with only a catalogue for reference, so there are no expensive showroom assistants to pay for; you collect your selections from the warehouse yourself, saving transport costs; and you build your own furniture when you get home, saving in storage. These various savings allow IKEA to focus on delivering the maximum in style for the minimum in cost. In addition, since its target audience is young and in full-time work, the stores are open long hours and often contain free child care services. IKEA is different, not because its furniture is different, but because it has adopted a different strategic position in the market. Where rival firms are competing only on the quality or value of their furniture, IKEA has focused its efforts differently. In strategic language, it has taken a different strategic position. In so doing, it has gained a sustainable competitive advantage.

When we try to compete by being productive, we do similar things to the competition, but try to do more of them, faster or more efficiently. Competitive strategy, on the other hand, is not about "more," it's about being deliberately different. It's about doing *different* things than your rivals, or doing the same things in *different* ways.

A strategic position describes the activities you choose to focus on, the problems you choose to solve for your customers. Developing a strategic position allows you to bring real focus into the way you can add value. For example, IKEA chose not to focus on cash-rich, time-poor over-forties, even though that segment of the population is a lucrative one. The over-forties would want speed, service and ease. If IKEA had chosen to meet the needs of both young and older, the speed and service it would offer would require sacrificing design quality or increasing prices. Both of which would have disappointed young furniture buyers. It would be doing what Continental did. In focusing only on young buyers, IKEA can go way further than simply providing cheap, quality furniture; it can properly understand its target audience. It can add extra services like long hours and child care, because it knows they are valuable to its audience. In this way it differentiates itself.

Clarifying your strategic position helps you to shift your prioritization away from getting things done, and onto something more proactive and intentional. You start choosing how you will maximize your limited resources, by focusing on just those things that will help you deliver the most impact. It also helps you to differentiate yourself, by identifying how you can make your offer more unique.

Your Strategic Position

I talk to my clients about the four options from a career perspective: everything-everyone-based positioning, cost-based positioning, product-based positioning and audience-based positioning. Only the final two, for most people, are attractive.

Everything, Everyone

A restaurant I know had developed a good reputation for the quality and creativity of its food. Flush with success, it moved to larger premises. In the first week it became clear that the demand in its new location was strong. But then it all started going wrong. To meet the demand, the restaurant decided to hire cooks from a well-known, low-quality, high-turnover restaurant. Rather than accepting a need to restrict client numbers while training new staff, it filled the restaurant, and the kitchen staff simply did their best. In addition, not all their new clientele were appreciative of the innovative haute cuisine, so the menu was "dumbed down." Rather than sticking to its formula of quality, interesting food, the restaurant tried to do every-thing for everyone. In a few short months, what had seemed like the glorious beginning of a very bright future was a dis-tant memory. The restaurant lost its position in the market and failed to satisfy its customers; it closed shortly afterward.

Trying to do everything for everyone is no strategic posi-tion at all. The business or person that adopts this approach spreads themselves thin and ends up delivering very little of real impact in the business. This approach is the most common position of those who focus first on productivity—those with serial busyness.

Cost-Based Positioning

A valid, and often effective, corporate strategy is to be the low-cost option. This also applies to careers. This doesn't mean that what you do, the service or product you produce, is low quality; it simply means that you sell it for less than others in the same market. For example, I know many consultants who work independently, or who work for small consulting firms, who offer a high-quality service. However, that's not why they get their work; it is only how they keep their clients. They get work because they offer the same service as big-name consultancies at a significantly lower cost. This model can work for them, since they have fewer overheads.

This is a valid strategic position, but I won't dwell on it, since few of my clients get very excited about this strategic option (for some reason!).

Audience-Based Positioning

This strategy was called a "needs-based" position in Porter's *Harvard Business Review* article. It involves offering a wide range of products or services to a very specific group of cli-ents. Take the example of a private bank that specifically tar-gets a small selection of wealthy individuals. In targeting a small group of people, they gain a deep understanding of their clients' needs and build strong relationships. They offer the customer a one-stop shop of integrated products, all catering to people with very similar needs. A company basing its strategy on audience-based positioning aims to beat its competition by using a deeper insight into the customer, individually tailoring to the customer's needs and building a trusting partnership.

Could you differentiate yourself by identifying a specific target audience and seeking to understand it better than others, having stronger relationships and offering them unexpectedly bespoke solutions for their needs? For example, Frank is a sales manager in a large media organization. He had clients spanning a wide range of spend with his business, but the majority of his business (a bit over half) was coming from 5 percent of his clients. When he reflected on the way he spent his time, he realized that his time allocation bore little relation to client spend. He had been allowing the requests and queries of his various clients to determine how he spent his time; he needed a strategy.

He made a deliberate choice to make a radical shift in how he spent his time, spending more than half of it on the 5 percent. He didn't do this because the 5 percent were asking for more time, but because he saw the 5 percent as his biggest opportunity. He met with them more, not to sell, but to really understand their business and to build personal relationships. He started to understand how he could support them better. His partnerships with his clients helped him to recognize that their advertising needs were being met by individual media owners offering relatively narrow, standard products. Based on his insight into their needs, he developed an award-winning solution by pulling together an airline, a travel agency, a TV company and a newspaper. He became the first person the 5 percent would call, not just when they had advertising to buy, but also when they had an idea or a problem. Frank transformed his effectiveness: his sales increased, his clients loved him and he differentiated himself in the eyes of his employer.

If you think this is the game you should play, reflect on the following questions:

- If you were being really targeted about your core audience, who would they be?
- How well do you really understand your target audience's needs?
- How could you bring much more focus toward your target audience?
- What are the problems you could help them solve, which they are not even discussing with you at present?
- How could you strengthen the relationship with your target audience and build a stronger partnership with them? How can you make their lives easier?

Product-Based Positioning

This strategy is all about creating a narrow range of products or services that will appeal to a wide population of people. Economists Kjell Nordström and Jonas Ridderstråle argue that there are only two effective strategies: to be "fit" or to be "sexy."[5] "Fit" means meeting a specific customer need better than anyone else. "Sexy" means producing a product or service that has an emotional appeal—that stands out from the crowd because it is cooler, more desirable. Product-based positioning can come from either strategy. Henkel, the German company, invented the glue stick to allow people to easily and cleanly glue paper. Henkel released Pritt Stick in 1969, which fit a need (we didn't know we had) in schools and offices; by 2001 they were being sold in 121 countries. Apple is the obvious example of sexy. At the time iPods were becoming dominant, there were many other MP3 players, but none were so cool. It's about doing very few things really well, so that they stand out from the competition in a crowded market.

How could you differentiate yourself through what you do? What capabilities or areas of expertise could you develop that would truly set you apart? What service could you develop or offer that uniquely fits a specific need in your organization or market, or that's just downright "sexy"?

Amy works for a multinational food company that has grown through a strong sales culture and a capability to acquire and integrate other businesses. Due to the turbulence of the food industry, and the acquisitive nature of her organization, Amy noticed that there were a lot of change initiatives. As someone who had a low boredom threshold she felt working in change would suit her. Amy decided to get involved, but...she worked in finance.

Amy started to volunteer for any change initiative, which started to get her noticed. She demonstrated real commitment and not a little talent on these initiatives. With her manager's blessing, she completed a master's degree in change management. She wrote a couple of articles for the internal newspaper and then in the trade press. She was proving herself to be increasingly useful and became recognized in the business for her ability to offer insights into organizational change backed up by sound financial understanding. Her breakthrough came when she was given a business (rather than financial) leadership position at a factory due to be closed. She turned the factory around through a change program involving all the staff and a series of tough decisions to stop the production of long-established products. Next she worked with the CEO on the biggest acquisition in the company's history. She is now a managing director, not because she was a good accountant or because she worked hard, but because she differentiated herself through a persistent focus on delivering change. It was her expertise in change, alongside her financial skills that made her stand out.

If you think this is the game you should play, ask yourself the following questions:

- What makes you uniquely useful to your business? What capabilities, expertise or experiences do you have that are most valuable?
- What can you do that no one else can?
- Which of your capabilities are most in need—or admired—in the business at present? In the future?
- How do you build a track record of success that demonstrates your strength?
- What particular products or services will you develop or deliver?
- How is your capability driving innovation and change in the business?

Still Undecided?

When it comes to you and your career, strategic questions like this can be quite hard. Organizations can take years to really clarify their strategic position, and many never do. My strong recommendation is that you ditch the "everything and everyone" strategy and get a clear idea of where your focus should be. It should be either audience-based or product-based. Once you know that, you can be more specific about the particular audience or product you will focus on. Once you can define your strategic position, differentiating yourself is much easier.

Play to Your Strengths

I meet people all the time whose primary focus and concern seems to be responding quickly, producing stuff and keeping everyone happy. These are talented people, with great capability, crippled by a desire to execute in order to get it all done. They judge themselves, and feel they are judged by others, only on their efficiency and productivity—on how much they do and how fast they do it. It feels like judging a Ferrari on the basis of its fuel consumption.

What are you great at? Every corporate and career strategy should be grounded in the core capabilities of that business or person, not just the market need. Your strategy could be as simple as finding a way to double the percentage of time that you are involved in the activities that you do best. Gallup found that only one in three people in large corporations use their core strengths every day;[6] that's a ridiculous waste of our abilities. Find ways to use your core strengths a lot more, then figure out how to deal with all the other stuff that has been filling so much of your time to date. It is only our core strengths that allow us to make our greatest contribution—to our organization, to our families and to the world.

Trade-Offs

I remember watching a documentary about Ryanair, a successful European low-cost airline based on the model of Southwest Airlines. The program was made in the early days of Ryanair. It was designed as a shocking exposé of the terrible customer service provided by the airline. It revealed passengers receiving little or no support from Ryanair after being stranded in obscure airports when their flights were canceled, unexpected charges and fines, and rude and militant staff. It was quite shocking. At the end of the show, the investigative reporter got a short interview with Michael O'Leary, the chief executive, to see how he would respond. His answer was brilliant. He said, more or less, we don't do customer service; we do cheap flights. For me it was one of the strongest examples of clear strategic thinking I'd ever heard: he understood that there is a cost to customer service—a cost that might increase fares. His strategic trade-off was clear: fly with us and you might not get the best customer service, but you will certainly get a cheap flight. Ryanair's position doesn't appeal to everyone, and even upsets some people; that is the risk it takes. But it *really* appeals to the airline's target audience.

Frank and Amy had to make trade-offs to allow them to focus on their strategies. Frank had to manage the other 95 percent of his customers as he deliberately reduced the time he spent supporting them. Amy had to find time for her change work, even if that took time away from her pure accountancy. We don't have unlimited resources, so if we want to succeed in a competitive workplace, we have to make some tough decisions. Making choices is a strategic activity. It is only those choices and trade-offs that allow us to focus and differentiate ourselves.

What trade-offs do you need to make?

- What should you stop doing, to allow you to focus on your core strategy?
- What should you do less of?
- What risk or loss do you have to accept to stay focused on your strategy?

Less Is More

We are the most focused company that I know of or have read of or have any knowledge of. We say "no" to good ideas every day. We say "no" to great ideas in order to keep the amount of things we focus on very small in number so that we can put enormous energy behind the ones we choose.[7]

—Tim Cook, Apple CEO

Succeeding in a world of too much is not about producing "more"; in fact, it is about doing less, better and with more impact. It's about focusing on fewer, bigger things with enormous energy. Like Apple. Here are some practical tactics to help you to do this.

Do the Big Stuff First

There is a little experiment Stephen Covey used to do with rocks, gravel and sand. You take a big jug and fill it with big rocks. When you can't get any more in, you add the pebbles until you can add no more. Finally, add the sand. Empty the jug and do the same thing in reverse. Add the same amount of sand, then the gravel, then the rocks. You will notice, try as you might, that you will only be able to fit a small number of the big rocks into the jar this time.

This is a well-known time management demonstration that conveys a simple, profound and seldom-followed principle: focus on the big stuff first and fit the little stuff around it. When we think about managing our time or being productive, we often think about what we will do, or when we will do it by. We don't tend to think much about the order we will do it, but the *sequence* matters. It matters because we get tired, we get distracted and we often don't get through all the items on our list. The things we choose to do first, we are much, much more likely to get done.

It is too easy to adopt the "if" or "when" mentality: *if* I get on top of my emails I'll give some time to my strategic work; *when* I have more time I'll be more strategic. You will only deliver real impact through persistent focus on your strategy, or the big rocks, over time. If you want to differentiate yourself in this world of too much, do the big rocks first, then the sand and gravel.

Tracking Important Practices: A Balanced Scorecard

Robert S. Kaplan and David P. Norton introduced the concept of the balanced scorecard to the business world back in 1992.[8]

At the time they were concerned that focusing solely on financial measures of performance was driving the wrong behavior in organizations. In essence, the balanced scorecard helps organizations track what really matters. It accepts that people will seek to deliver what is being measured. So by starting to measure a more balanced set of things, you get a more balanced and sustainable set of business practices.

Things have moved on since the early '90s, but the need for a broader view of performance has never been more important. What about for individuals? We naturally track whether we have an empty inbox, are delivering everything on time, clearing our to-do list, etc. We track these because they are so visible, so noticeable. These might be valuable things to track, but this does not provide a very balanced view.

Most balanced scorecards have four areas they track, one of which is financial performance. I keep a balanced scorecard on myself to keep reminding myself of where I want to focus. It has four elements. One is Delivery, my day-to-day business; one is Writing, which incorporates research and thinking; one is Relationships from a work perspective; and the final one is Energy, which focuses on two areas: emotional energy from quality time with family and friends, and physical energy. I am truly succeeding when I focus on, and make significant progress in, all four areas over a month.

What would your four be?

Focus on "Horizon Two"

Mehrdad Baghai and his colleagues from McKinsey and Co. introduced the concept of three time horizons in which to think about corporate strategy.[9] Horizon One is short-term: managing the business over the next year. Horizon Two is middle-term: identifying and putting in place the next generation of high-growth opportunities. Horizon Three is long-term: incubating the germs of new ideas that will sustain the business long into the future. You need to focus on all three horizons in order to succeed.

Horizon Two, the middle-term, is a dangerous middle ground. It's quite nice for executive teams to go for off-site meetings and dream up bold, wonderful-sounding visions and long-term strategies. Back at work, these same executives enjoy getting embroiled in the heart-pumping, adrenaline-fueled thrill of the day-to-day. Somehow what gets lost is the middle term. For example, failed companies such as Kodak, Sun and Xerox, all invested heavily in Horizon Three; and they all continued to run their businesses effectively day-to-day using Horizon One strategies. The problem was, they failed to translate these long-term ideas into concrete realities. They failed to pay sufficient attention to Horizon Two.

How true is this for many of us busy folk? Horizon Two has none of the emotional appeal of long-term Horizon Three dreams or activities such as signing up for that MBA. They also don't have the adrenaline-fueled payoff of the immediate Horizon One. Yet most of the strategic impact you will make will be from Horizon Two initiatives.

I define Horizon Two activities as three- to six-month concrete initiatives. They may be projects, process changes or activities to your network. Often, Horizon Two activities are initiated proactively, based on your view of where you can contribute most. They are not broad intentions, but specific sets of activities designed to deliver a result, typically within two quarters. As a result, Horizon Two activities require substantive focus, but deliver substantive results.

- What Horizon Two activity will make the most impact on your strategy?

- What Horizon Two activities are you not focusing enough on?
- What can you do to stop getting sucked into endless Horizon One work?

Bigger Picture Beats Detail

We know that we can improve our performance by coming up with a plan, but what kind of plan is best? In a carefully controlled study, researchers were keen to understand how to help students improve their study skills through planning. Students were put into one of three groups. One group was instructed to make daily plans for what, where and when they would study. A second group was asked to do similar plans, only month by month. A third group made no plans. Monthly planners performed best in terms of improvement in study habits, grades and in retention of the good habits: a year later the monthly planners were still getting better grades than the daily planners (though both groups beat those who didn't plan at all).[10]

It turns out that having a broader view of what you mean to accomplish is more effective and motivational. Focus is often lost when we're too close to the detail. So when it comes to your Horizon Two initiatives, develop broad plans, and get on with them.

How Many Horizon Two Initiatives?

A psychologist asked a bunch of US army generals how they managed their affairs. A battle-hardened general, the only woman in the group, summarized her approach: "First I make a list of priorities: one, two, three, and so on. Then I cross off everything from three down."[11] I mentioned the value of a balanced scorecard earlier, with four focus areas. This works well in directing attention to the key areas of your performance.

However, when it comes to substantive Horizon Two initiatives, the general's steer is useful: one or two at a time is enough to focus on.

THE BIG MESSAGES IN "STOP BEING SO PRODUCTIVE!"

Productivity is not the way to sustainable success. Any small improvement we make soon gets matched by others. Since everyone is working hard, it's a fool's game to try to outwork everyone else.

The "More" Game
• In the Industrial Age, productivity was the way to succeed. The core capability since then in management teams is how to make people work hard.
• In that context we assume that the "More" game is the route to success: work hard, produce a lot, get noticed and succeed. It no longer works (apart from early in careers).
• You *can't* do everything and **you shouldn't do everything** if you want to succeed in your career. You need to focus with a strategy. Business strategies are useful because they are based on how to **succeed in competitive situations with limited resources**.

Strategic Focus
• A much better strategy than **productivity** (the "More" game) is **differentiation**.
• There are four strategic positions we can take: **Everything, everyone** is the most common, and it's useless. **Cost-based** is valid and works, but is often less appealing. **Audience-based** differentiation means serving the unique needs of your key stakeholders; **product-based** differentiation means developing unique capabilities or expertise.

- **Focus on your strengths**: Build a strategy that allows you to spend a lot more than 20 percent of your time using your greatest strengths.
- **Trade-offs**: Choosing not to pursue great ideas in order to go deep on others is hard, but that is strategy.

Less Is More

- We will achieve more by doing less, by choosing fewer, big, important things to focus on. Like Apple.

Go-Do

Strategic Position

Take a view. What is your strategic positioning: audience, product or cost? Once you're clear, draft an annual strategic plan to bring greater focus into your core strategic areas.

Your Balanced Scorecard

Identify the four key things you will focus on and measure regularly.

Experiment

Trade-Offs

Stop doing things that are not core to your strategy. Some of these will cause problems; many of them will go unnoticed. By doing this you'll build up a clear idea of the real essentials.

Big Things First

Practice starting every day with the big things. Leave the little stuff to take care of itself, and fill in the gaps when you're tired later.

Chapter 6

Impact Through Innovation
(Don't Be the Invisible Man)

In his Father Brown series of detective stories, G. K. Chesterton included a short story called "The Invisible Man." The essence of the story is that all those involved (apart from Father Brown) are flummoxed by a murder that has been seemingly committed by an invisible man: no one was seen entering or leaving the house where the murder took place. The case is solved when Father Brown realizes that the usual and expected often becomes invisible—in this case, the postman. When observers insisted that they hadn't seen anybody, what they really meant was they hadn't *noticed* anyone. The postman, because he was so entirely expected, was tuned out and forgotten.

The essence of the career strategy I am suggesting in this section is differentiation. This chapter continues to explain how you can differentiate yourself through innovating—in big or small ways. Innovations are critical to business survival, and so are inherently valuable. They are also, by their nature, novel, and so they capture attention and make you stand out. In an attention economy, we can't expect to be noticed simply because we're doing a good job or working hard. All those busy people making decisions about our careers are distracted and overwhelmed. We have to capture their attention through making an impact with a strategic focus (as explained in the last chapter) and through innovating in our department, our organization and our society. If we do this, we'll stand out from the crowd and so we'll succeed.

The Innovation Imperative

In the Agricultural Age, competitive advantage came through ownership of land. In the Industrial Age, it came from productivity. In the Information Age it came through information, and the ability to capture and analyze it. My hunch is that the Information Age is now over, because information is no longer valuable. In fact, information is so ubiquitous it has become a commodity, or even free. Wikipedia has killed off paid-for encyclopedias such as Microsoft's Encarta and *Encyclopaedia Britannica*. Twitter is replacing paid-for news feeds as the quickest and most reliable way to hear breaking stories. Music and movies are free to a large percentage of the consuming world. The old assumptions that information had a value are being challenged in every domain.

If information is now a commodity, what is valuable? In a word: innovation. This is true for three reasons. First, the markets are so competitive, products and services have a shorter and shorter shelf life before being copied. Second, technology is evolving so quickly; the way we live, the way we consume and what we expect are also changing more rapidly than ever before. A product that is the height of cool today will be obsolete and forgotten in a few months or years. Finally, consumers are overloaded, and their information channels so bloated, that they struggle to focus on anything. So unless companies are doing interesting, novel things, like the Invisible Man, they and their products will fail to capture any attention, and therefore any consumer dollars.

The Nomura Research Institute, a highly regarded economic research organization, suggests we are now entering the fourth era of economic activity.[1] They call this new period the Creative Age. In the Creative Age, the only sustainable source of competitive advantage for any business is the ability to innovate faster than the competition. Innovation has never been more important commercially. It has also never been more important from a career perspective for the same reasons as above: our post-recession organizations have been stripped of any excess, making them lean, competitive places. To keep pace with market and societal changes, our organizations are having to change and adapt quicker than ever before, and there is that recurring theme of a lack of attention. Businesses are crying out for innovation. Yet inside those businesses, the inbox rules, meetings abound and people leap from task to task. Everything businesses do internally encourages drone-like behavior. By focusing on innovating as a career strategy, we can demonstrate and deliver real value; we can stand out and differentiate ourselves.

This chapter provides practical suggestions on how you can innovate more. You don't need to be "creative" to innovate. Most innovations are small and few would fall into the category of breakthrough ideas. However a persistent focus on innovating, big or small, will not only have a major impact on your business, but will help you to capture attention. Here's how.

Becoming Creative

Ever fancied a piano...made of concrete? Or a concrete picture frame, bath or wardrobe? Making just about everything from concrete was the brainchild of perhaps the most brilliant inventor of all time, Thomas Edison. His concrete obsession developed when another project of his failed: extracting iron ore using magnets and massive crushing rollers. He was left with a village full of heavy machinery ideal for making concrete. So he started another project, the Edison Portland Cement Company in 1899 (a company that went on to supply the cement for Yankee Stadium). Despite lots of investment, in 1906 his cement production was losing money hand over fist. So he decided to create his own demand. In an after-dinner speech in New York City, he proclaimed to the world that he was inventing concrete houses. These could be made from a single mold, and would sell for just $1,200 each—cheap enough for everyone, even those in slums. They would come with bathtubs and picture frames, and yes, even pianos. They would never need repainting, and additional stories could be added with a small adjustment of the molds.

Does it sound too good to be true? It was. The early proto-types proved disastrous, and though molds could be reused, the initial investment for a builder would have been $175,000. In truth, why would anyone want to live in a house that had been nicknamed the "salvation of the slum dweller?" Today, only twelve of Edison's world-changing concrete houses remain.

When we think of Thomas Edison we think of the light bulb, the phonograph and the motion picture. But for me, what's more inspiring about the Edison story than his big successes, is the sheer scale of his creativity. He was an idea machine! Edison registered an incredible 1,093 patents for items he'd invented, even though many were failures! He was constantly on the lookout for new ideas and ways to do things better. He was constantly questioning things and always experimenting. Not all his ideas worked but in the end Thomas Edison didn't just have a successful career, he changed all of our lives.

Choosing to Be Creative

New ideas won't appear if you don't have permission within yourself.

—Marc Benioff, CEO Salesforce[2]

I often hear people say "I am not creative," and it worries me. It's not so much the words that worry me, but the full stop. It's a big one. People label themselves uncreative, and that's that. They leave the job of being creative to those who were good at painting at school. Yet thinking differently and creating new ideas is a core business imperative for every department. I believe "creative" is an activity not a label; it's a verb not a noun. This is at the very heart of the "creative"/"not creative" divide: people who define themselves as creative are much more likely to consciously try to come up with creative, alternative solutions.

Neuroscientists have carried out brain scans of people as they approach a problem. They then compared the participant's mental activation prior to tackling the problem with the quality of the solution they generated. Those who ultimately produced a sensible, somewhat obvious, answer to a problem had beforehand activated different parts of the brain than those who came up with more creative solutions. Those who ultimately came up with creative solutions entered the problem with their anterior cingulate cortex activated. They were open to playing with options and switching approaches; they were primed for creativity.

Creativity starts with the decision to try to create. We can all make that choice.

Plan C

My father-in-law taught a design course. When he gave students a project, they would typically produce their first attempt fairly quickly. On completion, he would approach them and ask if they were happy with their design. Irrespective of their answer he would reply, "Good. Now put that to one side and create a Plan B"... and then he'd push for a Plan C. Inevitably the student would groan and moan. Also, almost as inevitably, Plan B would be better than Plan A, and Plan C better yet.

As Emile-Auguste Chartier said, "Nothing is more dangerous than an idea when it is the only one you have." I have seen too many teams, working on complex business problems, come up with a possible solution relatively quickly, then spend the rest of their time together thinking about how to implement it. Which is crazy. Coming up with ideas is relatively quick; implementing those ideas can take months and even years. Surely it makes sense, when a great Plan A is on the table, just to pause for a few minutes to search for a Plan B and C before racing into implementation. Once there are three options, you can then rationally choose the best. The worst that can happen is you lose thirty minutes. More often you will save yourself months of pain.

Borrowing Ideas

Sometimes the solution to a problem can come from unexpected quarters. Devi Shetty is India's leading heart surgeon, but his skill couldn't help him achieve what he wanted to. He was overwhelmed by the sheer quantity of patients needing care. There was also the issue of cost: a typical heart operation costs $20,000–$100,000 in the US. He couldn't see a way of meeting the need while keeping it affordable. Many surgeons would have gotten "realistic" here, recognizing the fact that heart operations all over the world are expensive. Devi Shetty didn't accept the full stop. He looked outside of his industry and profession for ideas.

Shetty recognized that Henry Ford had faced a similar challenge in the early 1900s, and had solved the problem with the assembly line. Shetty pioneered a new medical approach by applying Henry Ford's principles of mass production to open heart surgery. For example, training heart surgeons is normally a very lengthy and costly business; heart operations are complex procedures. However, in Shetty's model, each surgeon performed only a small piece of the overall operation, making it much quicker and cheaper to train them, and allowing them to rapidly gain very specific expertise. Using this approach, forty cardiologists were able to perform six hundred operations per week, for a tenth of the cost incurred by equivalent Western hospitals, but with the same success rate.[3]

Shetty didn't try to come up with a brilliant new idea; he just borrowed one from elsewhere. He simply asked, "Who else has solved a similar problem?" Next time you're stuck for an idea, just ask yourself who you can borrow from.

From Idea to Innovation

In 1959, Henry Kremer offered a huge prize for the first team to produce a human-powered plane that could fly across the English Channel (equivalent to $2.5 million in today's money). Team after team took up this challenge, and team after team failed. It looked impossible.

And so it looked for the next sixteen years, until the American engineer Paul MacCready decided to have a go. He quickly realized something surprising: everyone was solving the wrong problem! Everyone believed the problem to solve was how to build a human-powered plane. As a result, they would spend months developing theories, designing the plane and testing it. Only to have it destroyed on the first flight—the first failure.

MacCready's insight was that the only way to solve the problem would be through deliberate trial and error, learning what worked and didn't. Looked at this way, the problem wasn't "How to design and build a human-powered plane," it was "How to build human-powered planes that could be rebuilt in hours not months."[4]

The planes he built could be repaired so quickly and cheaply, he could often do four flights (and crashes) a day. Eighteen years after Kremer had posed the challenge, Gossamer Albatross successfully flew over the channel. MacCready had succeeded after only eighteen months (and many more than eighteen crashes!). The starting point of innovation is that we solve the right problem.

Solve the Right Problem

Between 1990 and 1995, Mihaly Csikszentmihalyi, then a professor of psychology at the University of Chicago, led a team to study ninety-one exceptional individuals, including fourteen Nobel Prize winners. All ninety-one were chosen because they were generally considered to have made major contributions in their field. In particular, he was interested in understanding how it was they achieved their great breakthroughs. What he found was counterintuitive (at least to business today): finding the solution was easy; the hard part was finding the right question. Once the question had been discovered, ideas flowed freely.[5]

Mike Marquardt is an inspirational colleague, professor and one of the leading lights in the world of Action Learning, a process for solving complex strategic problems. When working with Action Learning groups, there is one question he asks repeatedly that always has a profound impact: "What is the problem we are trying to solve?" The question addresses the very heart of the issue: We spend loads of time and energy trying to find a solution and a plan; we spend almost no time trying to understand the problem.

At certain points in the discussion, he stops the debate and has every person in the group independently write down the problem they think the group is trying to solve. It is astonishing how often people within the same debate are still unclear on the problem, or trying to solve different problems. Even after hours of debate! This question stops people in their tracks, but nearly always leads ultimately to better, more innovative solutions.

*   *   *

Think of an area of your work or life where you are repeatedly struggling to make progress. Ask yourself: Am I solving the right problem?

Trial and Error

We are surrounded by living proof of a system for innovation that has served the test of time: evolution. More specifically, what works is variation and selection. Stuart Kauffmann, a complexity theorist, has shown that evolution isn't just a sensible way to attempt to solve complex problems, it's the best possible approach.[6] Sexual reproduction and genetic mutation produce a lot of variation. Of these variations, some fail, some survive and some succeed spectacularly. Repeated over millions of years, great solutions emerge that would never happen through careful planning, but they work.

As Tim Harford, author of *Adapt: Why Success Always Starts with Failure* explains, when you're manufacturing any detergent, the design of the nozzle is critical.[7] Unilever was struggling to get this right. They called in the experts, but without success. In the end, they tried running a series of experiments. They built ten different nozzles and tested them. They then took the best of these, and created ten variations of that design, and tested again. After forty-five further experiments, each time selecting the best nozzle and designing ten further variations of that design, Unilever found a brilliant design: one that no expert in the world could ever have designed.

The lesson from Edison is that the way to innovate is not through genius and coming up with a single, world-changing idea. If you want to innovate, learn from evolution: experiment. Do different things. Some stuff will work; some stuff won't. Select the stuff that works and discard the stuff that doesn't, and then vary things again.

*   *   *

What aspect of your work isn't working? What are three alternative, untried approaches? Try them and keep the most effective.

Survive the Failures

Chris Rock is one of the most successful comedians in the world today. He came to prominence performing on *Saturday Night Live* in the early 1990s, has appeared in a wide range of movies, and was voted the fifth greatest stand-up comic of all time by Comedy Central. Chris is constantly trying to come up with new jokes but, like most comedians, can't accurately predict which ones will be funny and which will fail. To remain successful, he constantly tries out new material at small venues, where his reputation will survive a few bad jokes.[8] The stories and jokes that work, that have been tried and tested, are the ones he successfully uses on the big stages.

If you want to innovate, ask yourself how you can experiment on a small scale. How can you test your idea in a way such that failure is not a major issue?

Learn the Lessons, Objectively

A Dutch charity, International Child Support (ICS), wanted to fund a school assistance program in Kenya.[9] Like any charity, they had limited resources and wanted to make the maximum impact. They selected twenty-five schools at random and supplied them with textbooks, and tested the impact. When compared with the non-selected schools, the textbooks made little difference. Rather than giving up, ICS ran a second experiment. Again they chose twenty-five further schools randomly and this time gave them illustrated flip charts. For a second time, the results were disappointing. Finally, ICS gave the schoolchildren tablets to treat intestinal worms. Worm tablets turned out to be a great success, boosting height, reducing infection and cutting absenteeism. They were then ready to make a much larger investment, confident that it would make a real impact.

It's not always possible to run random trials and control groups for everything. However, it's remarkable how often what we do in work and in life is untested. Ernest Hemingway once said, "Write drunk; edit sober." We have too much to do to waste time on ideas that aren't working. Try new things, but then get sober and look at the evidence. Success doesn't result from making the right guesses in the first place; it comes from trying things and then, in the cold light of day, identifying what works and what doesn't and then responding accordingly. Keep moving. Try stuff out. Keep discarding the things that aren't working, to allow you to try new things. Find the stuff that has real impact. When you find what really works, put all the resources you can into it, confident in the knowledge that you are investing wisely. To misquote the great Muhammad Ali, *you have to float like a butterfly to be able to sting like a bee.*

THE BIG MESSAGES IN "IMPACT THROUGH INNOVATION"

We are in an attention economy. To succeed we need to capture the attention of very busy people by actively differentiating ourselves. We do this through strategic focus (as discussed in the last chapter) and actively innovating.

The Innovation Imperative

- The ability to consistently deliver innovation is the only sustainable source of competitive advantage due to the speed of the markets, the rapid shifting of consumer trends and the limited attention of customers. All of these principles apply equally in our careers.

Becoming Creative

- Innovation starts with a choice to be creative. "Creative people" aren't genetically endowed with ideas; they simply have the habit of looking for alternative options.
- Multiply your new ideas by always asking for the Plan B and Plan C and borrowing ideas from other industries.

From Idea to Innovation

- Take the time to make sure you are solving the right problem in the first place.
- Not all ideas will work. Don't be too attached. Like evolution, try things and discard those that don't work.
- Make sure your failures are small and survivable.

Go-Do

Plan C

Stop that big piece of work you are doing right now for a moment and ask yourself, "Is there an entirely different way of doing this?" Continue to challenge yourself on every big piece of work: Is what you're doing differentiating? Have you taken the time to identify Plan B and a Plan C?

Borrow Ideas

Look to completely different industries and environments. Who else has solved a similar problem? What can you learn from them?

Experiment

Killer Question

Try using this killer question in meetings and discussions: "What problem are we trying to solve?" It can have a profound effect.

Fail

Practice failing constructively, to learn and remove your fear of failure. Deliberately choose an activity or project you think you are likely to fail at; enter it with an intention to learn.

Chapter 7

Busy Is a Terrible Brand
(Develop a Better Brand)

All twenty tables contained three glasses, one marked A, one B and one C. Each glass contained a different beer: Budweiser, Coors and Miller. Damian Horner, a brilliant marketing strategist (and source of many of my best ideas on branding), and I asked the participants at each table to taste the beer and tell us which beer was Budweiser, and we held our breath. The truth was, we'd never done this experiment before, and we were doing it with 140 senior managers! We didn't know if it would work, but we had read the research on this test. One by one the tables gave us their responses. Four chose correctly, seven chose incorrectly, and the other nine thought it was a trick: they thought all the beers were the same! The experiment had worked. (Phew!)

In the United States, almost 50 percent of all beer sold is Budweiser: an astonishing dominance with so much choice available to consumers. If you speak to many Budweiser drinkers, they will imply they'd rather cut off a limb than sully their taste buds with the likes of Miller or Coors. Yet, in all the research, and in our own blind taste test, the majority of

Budweiser drinkers cannot tell these three beers apart and certainly cannot recognize which is Budweiser.

People choose Budweiser because it has a great brand.

The Importance of Brands

You're in a major supermarket such as Target or Walmart, and you're choosing a soup. In front of you are three hundred options. Following economic theory, choice is a good thing: it allows you to use logic to identify the best one for you. So you carefully scrutinize the labels, the contents and the prices to make a rational decision. Three hours later you move on to the breakfast cereal aisle and start again. Of course you don't.

An Easier Way

It's amazing, really how seldom we are stuck when faced with complex decisions. Occasionally you might be asked to do some long division when you don't have a calculator on hand, but most of the time, we breeze through our decisions. There are two reasons for this: The first is that when faced with too much choice, we simply move on and don't make a decision at all. The second reason we are seldom stumped was identified by Amos Tversky and Daniel Kahneman early in their work together. When faced with a hard question, we simply substitute it with a much easier one. The following experiment shows this nicely. German students were given a survey including the following questions:

- How happy are you these days?
- How many dates did you have last month?

When the responses were analyzed, there was virtually no correlation between the answers given for these two questions.

However, when the questions were reversed, so that the "How many dates?" question was asked first, the correlations between the two sets of answers were extremely high. In asking the "dates" question first, the experimenters had conveniently given the students an easy question to use as a substitute for the harder question "How happy are you these days?"[1]

Back to the Supermarket

So, we've established that you don't spend three hours rationally evaluating the best soup on the basis of predefined criteria. What happens instead? One of two things: either we walk on, deciding we don't want soup today, or we substitute. Instead of answering the question, "Which soup would be the ideal choice for me (and my family) based on my taste, health and price preferences?" you ask, "Where's the soup I bought last week?" or "Which has the nicest label?" or simply, "Where's the Campbell's chicken soup?" Brands work by helping us make these mental substitutions; brands make decisions easier and simpler. It is for this reason that brands matter.

You Have a Brand Whether You Like It or Not

The same is true in our careers and our performance. First, people don't have enough information about you. Very few people have a real and accurate understanding of your day-to-day performance; they just don't see you at work enough. Yet, every day, these people are making decisions about you that shape your career. These may be big decisions, such as whether they should offer you a job or what performance rating to give you. They may also be much smaller: whether to invite you to a meeting or onto a project, to turn to you for advice or, indeed, what to say about you when you're not around. These decisions matter. Given that they haven't got the capacity to make full and objective decisions, they substitute a difficult question for an easy one. They make their decisions not on your performance but on your brand. Whether you think this is right or wrong morally, whether or not you like this idea, it makes no difference: your brand already exists in the minds of those around you. Your brand is already influencing your career, and will do so increasingly as people get ever more busy. Your choice is not "do I want a brand or not?" but "do I want to intentionally build my brand or not?"

Busy as a (Terrible) Brand

Busy isn't just a fact of life; busy is also a brand. In hundreds of ways each day we strive to demonstrate how busy we are, and we tell people about it. Which is weird. There is nothing that can possibly be noteworthy, memorable or differentiating about busyness, since everyone is busy. It is not cool, it is not interesting and it is not effective. Yet, because we see it as a success strategy, the biggest message many of us are communicating about ourselves is that we're really, really busy.

Which is a real shame, because whenever we have people's attention, it seems a real waste to squander the opportunity by describing our inability to achieve mastery. Instead what I suggest is that you build a brand that is based around your strategy, how you want to differentiate yourself. Your brand helps you convey, clearly and simply, what you want to be known for; your key contribution.

Identifying Your Brand

Who would you invest in? A company listed on the New York Stock Exchange with the three-letter ticker symbol of "KAR" or one listed as "RDO"? It turns out, if you said KAR you would make 9 percent more money than if you chose RDO.[2] This is an example of a phenomenon called *cognitive fluency*. Cognitive fluency is the ease with which we can process something: the degree to which a mental or perceptual task is easy or hard work. The brain likes simple. However, that enjoyment of the simple has a halo effect: we feel all kinds of positive things about things if they are cognitively fluent. For example, if we read two pieces of writing, we think the writer of the piece that was simpler to read and understand is more intelligent; if a phrase is simple to remember, we believe it more.[3] We remember, prefer and trust more cognitively fluent information.

This plays out commercially too. When Procter & Gamble reduced the number of varieties of Head & Shoulders shampoo by half, sales per item more than doubled.[4] When Zurich Insurance Company simplified their life insurance brochures, stripping out technical information and replacing it with easy-to-understand client stories, sales increased by 7 percent.[5] The brain likes simple, so we choose simple.

A Brutally Simple Brand

One of the ways brands work is that they make something very complex into something much simpler to understand. When we think about Volvo, we don't try to remember all the different models and all the different features in all those models. We don't run a detailed comparison of all these models with their nearest competitor. Instead, we hear the word "Volvo" and think "safe." When the brand is simple to understand, more cognitively fluent, we remember, like and trust the brand more.

A good personal brand should be brutally clear and simple. It should make it easy for extremely busy people to make sense of you, to understand you, to trust you, to explain you and ultimately to position you correctly for the right opportunities.

So if you are worried about dumbing all your skills and expe-riences down into a single word or phrase, get over it! Your audience hasn't got the spare attention to understand all your richness and complexity; they want, and will choose, simple.

To bring this alive, I was once leading a session in Singa-pore with a bunch of high-potential leaders. During the day, two senior leaders came to speak to the group. The first leader spoke about his role and the lessons he'd learned. At three dif-ferent points during his presentation he said, "I make the com-plex, simple." Each time his comment was relevant to what he'd been saying, a kind of summary of the point he'd just made. He wasn't bragging either, just stating a fact. The next leader spoke clearly and eloquently, but at no point did he include a personal summary.

I was intrigued by the difference between presenting styles. At the end of the day I asked the group what they remembered from the two presentations. I asked about the second speaker first. The group remembered a variety of things, but there was little consistency. I then asked about the first leader. Without pause, and almost simultaneously, the group called out, "He made the complex, simple." That leader had just landed his brand with the group. The group also remembered other things he had said as well, perhaps more than the second speaker, but underlying everything they remembered was an understanding of his core value to the business, they "got" him. I suspect even if they'd met him months later, they'd remember his brand.

You, but on a Really Good Day

Berocca is a type of multivitamin produced by Bayer. One of their advertising campaigns shows a man in a suit get on his bicycle (one of those folding travel ones), don his helmet, and start riding to work. Instead of the normal, monotonous pedal-ing to work, the cyclist starts doing tricks: he wheelies, jumps and spins his way to the office. The advert then says, "Berocca. You, but on a really good day." This is also what your brand should do for you: it should capture you at your best, not simply summarize everything you do. Your brand should be a completely true and accurate reflection of you, but on a really good day.

Think about times when you have been amazing. Reflect on these occasions and ask yourself what made you so great at those times. Look for the common themes that made those moments really stand out.

Keep these themes in mind as you go into the exercise below. They will help you clarify a brand that doesn't just summarize your strategy, but captures your core contribution to the organization.

So What Is Your Brand?

Circle the five words in the table below that best represent you and your career strategy.

analytical	entrepreneurial	perceptive
assertive	expert	positive
big picture	farsighted	practical
clarity	firm	problem solver
clever	flexible	productive
client-focused	focus	purposeful
commercial	frank	quality
connect the dots	friendly	quick-witted
conscientious	helpful	realistic

cooperative	honest	reliable
courageous	humorous	results driven
determined	imaginative	risk taker
direct	innovative	self-reliant
disciplined	insightful	sincere
dynamic	logical	straight-talking
easygoing	methodical	team member
effective	motivated	tenacious
efficient	on time	thorough
energetic	organized	thoughtful
enthusiastic	original	unconventional

Why do these five words best represent you and your strategy? Write a short sentence, or even a single word, that describes the essence of your brand. Don't worry about making it perfect, just have a go. I call this first attempt your "brand hypothesis." Once you have written it, leave it somewhere so you see it regularly, talk about it with friends and colleagues. See if it works for you and them. Sleep on it, mull it over regularly, play with alternatives. You will probably find, over the coming weeks, that you get much clearer about what is right and not right about it. Then adapt it, refine it and, when you've got it right, start using it.

If it helps, here are a few examples of brands my clients have come up with:

- "I join the dots." This person was great at connecting people and ideas.

- "Clarity." This person was brilliant at bringing clarity to discussions and projects.
- "No problem!" This client simply used the nickname he was given in his business. He persistently said, "No problem!" His colleagues jumped on his turn of phrase, since it captured his can-do attitude. At the beginning of the process, he had come up with boring words like "can-do" and "helpful" before finally realizing his nickname was a great brand.

Build Your Brand

I start this section aware that you don't have very much spare time to market yourself. You may have even less desire to start promoting yourself and elevator-pitching any unsuspecting executive to the point of submission. No matter how valuable you believe branding to be, you haven't got loads of time to do it, nor the appetite for bragging. So I will share a few simple ways to build your brand without killing your calendar and annoying those around you.

Market Research

Imagine two colleagues came up to you. One told you he was brilliant at closing deals; the other asked you what you thought he was good at. Which person do you prefer? I'm guessing you said the latter. We prefer to be asked our opinion than told anything.

No one will ever mind being asked for their opinion on your brand, on how you contribute best to the organization. Most people will mind being told, without request, what you think you're good at. Once you have your brand hypothesis, start asking people for input. Ask for their opinion, and when they ask, tell them what you think your brand is. Get their feedback. In so doing, not only will you have some great feedback, you'll also have landed your brand with them.

Living Up to Your Brand

Was Einstein good at organizing?

The simple answer is, I don't know and I don't care. I do have a hunch though: How can anyone with hair like his be organized? His contribution to the world wasn't because he was good at lots of things, but because he was great at one thing. History will not record his punctuality, or his ability at darts or his panache at throwing a party (by the way, I just made all these up, I have no idea if he was any good at them), it will remember him for his physics.

One of the best and most authentic ways to build your brand is also one of the biggest benefits you will receive from having a clear brand. The best form of communication is action. You build a brand by living up to it. By striving in the way you focus, innovate and interact to be true to your brand, you contribute in the way you have decided you can contribute best. This probably all sounds a little circular as an argument but that's because it is, and that's the genius of it.

For example, imagine your brand is "clarity." Once you have decided to make this your brand, you can constantly challenge yourself to live up to it. Look for chances to innovate by making business processes more clear, or run a project to identify how to make the decision-making process of clients more clear. (You might even call that project "Clarity!") All your presentations, meetings and emails can be designed in such a way that they provide very visible clarity. Your emails become short and to the point, starting with the main point at the top and in the subject line. In meetings you become the person who summarizes the chaos, saying, "So, for clarity, the three key points so far are…"

Your brand describes your greatness, and in living up to your brand, you become greater.

High-Leverage Signals

The small things matter as well as big things. If you consistently do really small things that reinforce your brand, people will remember them and infer that the big things are true as well. These small things are called "high-leverage signals." One client I worked with from Shell had a brand around reliable, on-time delivery. He wanted a very simple way to consistently reinforce this brand. So he changed his voice mail message to say "Leave a message and I'll call you back in three working hours." Most importantly, he always did. I remember whenever I called him I couldn't help glancing at my watch as I left my message. I was timing him. Every time he called before the deadline, he reinforced his brand. Every time he returned that call on time, he built confidence that if you gave him a multimillion-dollar project to run, he would deliver it on time.

Be playful with this. For example, I had one person who wanted to show that despite being a serious corporate executive he was creative and a bit of a maverick. He started wearing bright red socks under his company-standard pin-striped gray suits. I saw the business card of a divorce lawyer who wanted to show he could manage these serious affairs with humanity and, at times, humor. His business card had perforations down the middle (so it was easy to tear in half!).

What could your high-leverage signals be?

THE BIG MESSAGES IN "BUSY IS A TERRIBLE BRAND"

Since we are using busy as a success strategy, the only real message we are transmitting to the world about us is that we're really busy, which is a real shame. It says nothing about us, and it certainly doesn't differentiate us (it's also dull).

The Importance of Brands
- We are all overwhelmed with too much information and choice these days. Brands help us make decisions by substituting a difficult decision with an easier one.
- Brands influence choice and preference, especially when people are busy.
- You have a brand whether you like it or not; your only choice is whether to manage it or not.

Identify Your Brand
- Keep your brand brutally clear and simple.
- It should describe you at your best (and be in line with your career strategy).

Build Your Brand
- We build our brand best through living up to it, in all our interactions and activities. In doing this, it is authentic and it brings out our best.

Go-Do

Clarify Your Brand

Develop your own brand statement based on your strategy and understanding of your core contribution to your organization.

Market Research

Once you have your first hypothesis, speak to five people who know you well at work, and get their feedback on your brand. Reflect and adapt it.

Experiment

Live Up to Your Brand

How could you make the next email you write, or the next report, or the next meeting you attend a chance to live true to your brand?

High-Leverage Signals

What creative ideas could you come up with to subtly reinforce your brand?

Chapter 8

Walk Your Own Path
(Fixing Radios by Thinking)

Richard Feynman became one of the greatest theoretical physicists of the twentieth century and won the Nobel Prize. As a twelve-year-old, he set up a little lab in his room, bought his first radio and, rather than listening to it, he took it apart. He soon became quite good at fixing radios. This was in the early 1930s, during the Great Depression, so a boy who could fix radios cheaply was useful. On one occasion, he was picked up by a client who seemed far from convinced that this boy wouldn't be a waste of his time and money. He kept on asking Feynman how a boy could know anything useful about radios until they arrived at the client's poorhouse. Feeling pressured, Feynman turned the radio on. It started wobbling, then gave out a terrifically loud roar for a few minutes before quieting and playing correctly. Feynman was confused. He had never encountered this before. He shut the radio off, began pacing around the room and thinking. The client was entirely unimpressed. He wanted action, he wanted to see the boy working, and he wanted to know Feynman knew what he was doing.

He started protesting to Feynman, asking him to stop wasting his time and get on with fixing the radio, or leave.[1]

Despite the heckling, Feynman kept on thinking. He wondered how any radio could make such a noise. Most radios failed because of faulty equipment or loose wiring; he wasn't convinced it would be either. After a while, he came up with a theory: Radio sets in those days were made from a series of tubes. If he took them out and reversed the order, the vibration and noise may disappear. Now, at last, Feynman was ready to act. He changed the tubes and turned the radio on. It worked perfectly. The man was astonished. He became one of Feynman's biggest advocates, telling everyone he knew of the boy who "fixes radios by thinking."

Under pressure to perform, most of us would have dived into activity to demonstrate how hard we are working and that we know what we're doing. We would have prioritized action over thought, and in doing this we might have got so caught in the detail of the wiring, that we missed the bigger possibilities. Feynman had the confidence to do his own thing. He recognized playing around with wires would look right to the client, but everything he knew about radios told him that the wiring wasn't the problem; he needed to think about other options. We can learn a lesson from Feynman here: even if we recognize the value of thinking, of focusing on our strategy or of innovation, we still have to face up to the daily pressures and expectations for activity. He had the confidence to do what he felt was right; we need that same confidence.

Walking Your Own Path

I don't think there has ever been a better time to be employed. There are more opportunities for autonomy, innovation and flexibility than ever before. We have never had so many options in our lives, so much capability to achieve great things and so many ways to connect and have rich relationships. There has never been a better time to live, but whether you experience it as a world of overwhelming busyness, or one of amazing opportunity, depends on your approach.

It would be hard to find someone in a modern organization who didn't accept that they should focus on more important things, that they should find more time to think, or even that they are too busy. Yet somehow, day after day, that intention does not translate into action. Why is that?

I think it's for two big reasons: avoidance and anxiety. To walk your own path and create your own possibilities takes the self-control and confidence to resist the temptations and pressures to conform and get busy. All the strategies in this section will not work if they stay as good intentions. However much you are clear about your strategic position and your core focus areas, it will all come to naught if you allow persistent busyness to prevent your taking action. However many great ideas you have, you will fail to innovate or change if you are afraid to take the risk.

We can choose to stay victims of the demand avalanche or take a more positive approach to our careers. To walk our own path, to differentiate ourselves, we have to deal, headfirst, with what actually stops us from doing the things that we know will make a difference. We have to stop avoiding the big stuff, and we have to stop being so defensive. After all, as the poet Ted Hughes said, people's biggest regret is not living boldly enough. This chapter will outline how.

Busy Is Avoidance

The *Oxford Concise Dictionary of the Christian Church* defines "acedia" (slothfulness) as "a state of restlessness and inability either to work or to pray."[2] I would put that definition in a modern work context and say acedia is "a state of restlessness and inability to focus and think." In other words, acedia is busy, or busy is sloth. I have discussed the importance of focus, prioritization, problem solving and innovation. Each of those activities is critical if we want to move from a career strategy of "More" to one of differentiation. However, each and every one of those activities is hard. All four of those activities push the prefrontal cortex to the max, and our brains are lazy (or at least energy conscious). In simple terms, given the choice between easy and difficult tasks, your brain will opt for easy.

This is the temptation of busy. It allows us to avoid doing hard work. However, don't be fooled into thinking that the temptation I refer to here involves goofing off on Facebook or YouTube. The bigger temptation I see is the lure of the simple tasks over the complex activity. One of the greatest things about the world of too much, is there are always so many small things to do; we never have to do anything big ever again, and we'll still feel productive. The endless stream of electronic chatter and our horribly full agendas service our need to feel useful, and our desire to appear hardworking, but they are also wonderful opportunities to procrastinate from doing the hard thinking. This was confirmed by Gloria Mark, who found that people were happiest doing mundane, rote tasks that asked little of the person's brain, preferring this work to more complex tasks, where the stress levels rose.[3] Rather than work on that big project, we flop into email, arrange a meeting or knock a few tasks off our list. Overwhelm is a price we might be willing to pay for not stretching ourselves.

If you are serious about wanting to make more of an impact, what can you do? In my view, there are two things you need to address. The first is to figure out ways to avoid the temptation of the simple task. The second is to procrastinate less by getting better at starting the big tasks that will differentiate you.

Avoiding the Temptation of Busy

Wilhelm Hofmann, professor of psychology at the University of Cologne, led a study into temptation. He and his colleagues monitored a group of 205 men and women in Germany, using beepers that went off at random. On hearing the beep, each participant had to record whether or not they were in the grip of a desire or temptation at that precise moment. They found that these people spent about 25 percent of their waking hours actively resisting temptations. These temptations ranged from desires for food, sleep or sex to more modern desires such as checking email and surfing the web. It turns out that the attractions of busyness—checking email or the Internet—were harder to resist than food and sex! They failed to resist 50 percent of all busy temptations in that area.[4] Against our will, we can't help succumbing to our desire for a quick fix of stimulation, a quick glance at the phone.

Self-control has been shown consistently to be one of the biggest predictors of success at school and at work, in sport and in marriage. People who are able to keep their focus on the big stuff when faced with a multitude of technological temptations will achieve more, connect more and live more. But how do we resist the lure of the ping or ring?

Don't Resist–Avoid

In an analysis of many studies of self-control, researchers were interested in how good those with strong willpower were at resisting temptation; it was assumed they would excel. Yet, that wasn't what they found. Those with strong willpower had more self-control because of the strength and effectiveness of their habits.[5] In other words, strong willpower helps you to set up good habits; it helps you avoid temptation, not resist it. They didn't eat healthily by resisting plates of chocolate cake when offered, but by making sure their fridge was only full of healthy foods.

This is very true for busyness and the distractions that pull us back into its embrace. The trick is to identify the temptations that are likely to lure you away from your important work, and to develop preventative habits. In an extreme example from another study by Gloria Mark, an organization agreed to switch its email off for a week. That one change meant that at the end of the week, the workers were less stressed, switched tasks less, and they stayed focused on the big stuff for longer.

I've said it before, but I'll say it again: if you want to be more focused, switch off your email notifier on your computer; better yet, just switch off your email while you are working on the big stuff. Do the same with your texts and even the phone. Or work from home one day a week, or even better, work from a place with no Wi-Fi coverage. Or use an app like "Freedom," which blocks your access to the Internet for up to eight hours at a time. What you need is not iron willpower, but great habits.

Eat the Frog

I am always attracted to simple ideas. That's why I love Brian Tracy's "Eat that frog" strategy.[6] It is one of the simplest techniques for avoiding the temptation of the small task that I've ever encountered. Once you've adopted it, it's so obvious. The concept is that if you eat a frog first thing in the morning, anything else you do that day won't be too bad! Essentially Tracy is suggesting that, before you open your inbox or voice mail, set aside a slice of time to work on the biggest, scariest, most important project you are facing at that time.

One of the reasons this idea works so well is that, before starting work, we have a kind of emotional distance and therefore a better perspective on what matters. We are in a cold, rational state and are more able to make good choices about the best use of our time and attention. When we arrive at the office and turn on our email, etc., suddenly the temptations of the small, the urgent, send us spiraling away from our main purpose. The habit of not turning on your email for a short time each morning, and using that time to focus unwaveringly on those areas you identified in your cold state, really works.

How long could you last before turning on your email? I recommend the first hour of your day be distraction- and email-free, but if you can only manage thirty minutes, you'll still see a big difference in your focus on what matters.

Monitor Yourself

Why do male prisoners get fatter in jail? It's unlikely to be because of the rich food, and options for exercise are normally available. Brian Wansink believes it's because they don't wear belts![7] Since they don't have belts or tight-fitting clothes, they are not getting regular feedback on the growth of their girths. One of the simplest and most effective ways we can improve our ability to resist temptation is through regular monitoring. That is why further research by Wansink shows that dieters who weigh themselves every day lose a lot more weight than those who step on the scales less often.

It appears that one of the purposes of self-awareness is to boost our self-control. Even putting a mirror in front of people changes their behavior; they tend to act more honestly and diligently. RescueTime, for example, is an app that tracks your computer usage. The program has turned up data that the average person uses sixteen different computer programs, visits forty websites and is interrupted every 5.2 minutes by a message every day. The founder, Tony Wright, was depressed to find he spent nearly a third of his day on "the long tail of information porn" (his words not mine!): visits to sites not related to his chief work.

There are some brilliant apps out there for monitoring your behavior. Or, you could simply time yourself. If you're about to start a big piece of work, start the stopwatch! See how long you last before being distracted. Keep your time, and practice trying to beat it! Add a bit of fun and gamification to your focusing efforts. Get measuring, get focusing, get differentiating.

Stop Procrastinating!

Procrastination goes hand in hand with busyness. In fact, I would argue that an awful lot of busyness *is* procrastination. We tell ourselves that we don't get around to doing all the things that will make a real impact *because* we are so busy, instead of recognizing that we are busy *because* we are avoiding and procrastinating.

Big, important work is hard to start, but it is often less hard to continue. Once you get into that work, your mood can flip from "I can't be bothered" to a state of deep enjoyment and engagement called "flow" (which we'll explore more in Chapter 10). Even if you don't get into a flow state, a sense of satisfaction kicks in as you make progress; you realize you are working on the right thing, and that feeds your motivation. It's a bit like those evenings when you feel you *should* go and exercise, but can't be bothered. If you do manage to drag yourself to the gym, more than likely you'll enjoy yourself and feel great after. In fact, in a study involving 12,000 diary entries, Harvard's Teresa Amabile found that making progress on important work was one of the biggest motivators at work. In fact, making progress on meaningful work was a key feature of 76 percent of all peoples' best days. She called this the *progress principle*.[8] So, one small change we can make that will produce a big change on our impact, and our motivation, is to reduce our procrastination by getting better at starting the big stuff.

Procrastination DIMs Your Visibility

In this section we've talked a lot about capturing attention and making an impact. Procrastination on a daily basis will kill all that. It will DIMinish your impact and DIM your visibility. Here, in my view, are the three causes of procrastination: D.I.M. It is likely one or another will affect you more. Notice it, deal with it and make an impact.

Dependence: This is dominated by the word *when*: "I'll do it *when* I'm on top of my inbox"; "I'll do it *when* I have heard back from Angelina"; "I'll do it *when* I have all the information."

Inertia: It's a physical law that it is hard to get moving. This is especially hard for those who set unreasonably high expectations for themselves. The higher the bar people set for themselves, the greater the inertia.

Mood: "I'm not in the mood." Too many people, too often, wait to be in the right mood before getting started at all.

Before we move any further, which of these causes affects you most? I will start by addressing inertia, because I think that's the biggest issue for most of us.

Inertia

Inertia "is a power of resisting by which everybody, as much as in it lies, endeavors to preserve its present state, whether it be of rest or of moving uniformly forward in a straight line."

The above quote comes from Sir Isaac Newton's seminal work, *Principia Mathematica*, which became the cornerstone of classical physics. His first law of motion, in that work, was inertia. It's rightfully first, because without the ability to overcome inertia, nothing will move or change. Inertia applies to objects, but it also applies to getting started on anything, and it can cripple our effectiveness. Perfectionists struggle the most with inertia; it might be because of fear that their work will not be up to scratch, or it may just be that their expectations overwhelm them into passivity. Either way, these people seem to magnify big tasks into huge ones, and the bigger the task, the greater the inertia.

To overcome inertia we need to create momentum (Newton's second law). Start moving, and procrastination evaporates. One way of building momentum is to create the impression that you have already started. Alia Crum and Ellen Langer were interested in exercise at work. They looked at the working habits of hotel maids, and how many calories they burned. It turned out they were dramatically exceeding the daily dose of exercise recommended by the Surgeon General. Crum and Langer then asked those maids if they thought they were exercising enough. Of these, two-thirds felt they weren't, and more than a third thought they weren't exercising at all.[9]

These maids were split into two groups. Both were told about the benefits of exercise. One group was also told how much actual exercise they were doing already in their daily work, including the fact that, for example, they burned one hundred calories after half an hour of vacuuming. The other group wasn't told. Four weeks later, the first group had lost nearly two pounds in weight; the second group had lost no weight at all. Knowing they were exercising already created momentum for the first group, it was easier to do a bit more because they were already in motion.

I was totally stuck and uninspired recently. I had to write some publicity for a keynote speech I was going to give. I couldn't think what to write, so I couldn't generate the energy to get started. In the end, I dealt with the inertia by going to my files and pulling out all the previous publicity pieces I had written. All of a sudden I wasn't starting from the beginning; I had text to work with and my procrastination evaporated. If you need momentum, start by remembering and finding what you've already done (or others have done) before you start to produce. Pretty soon you'll be in the flow and off.

Inertia and Thin Slicing

Marla Cilley, or, as she calls herself, "FlyLady," is a self-help guru focused on housekeeping. She talks of the dread some of her clients experience when facing disastrously messy, dirty houses. It is overwhelming. Sure we want our homes to be immaculate and tidy, but we are stuck in neutral as we consider the scale of the challenge. She developed a policy of the "Five-Minute Room Rescue": You enter the dirtiest, messiest room in the house with a kitchen timer. You tidy and clean like fury, but only for five minutes—then you stop. What tends to happen is that people, since they're already in motion, keep going. Success in this task has shifted from overall task completion, to completion of an allocated time—a much easier demand.[10]

I am a huge believer in regular, short bursts of activity to get momentum going. For me, five minutes is too short for intellectual tasks; I tend to go for thirty minutes. However, big projects can be a lot easier to start in thirty-minute chunks every day—especially as the Zeigarnik effect means you'll be thinking about the project all day!

How to Get in the Mood

Sometime, a barrier to starting is your mood. I hear people talk about "not being in the mood" to start on big things, waiting till they feel right or are in the right environment before they make progress. Rather than leave yourself hostage to your moods, there are a few things you can do to get started, despite how you feel. First, you can use reversal theory as discussed in Chapter 1 to change your motivation (flip between "serious" and "playful") and so get "in the mood." For me, movement, chocolate, music and play are the best ways. When I'm not in the mood for that big piece of work, I'm probably taking it too seriously. I put on upbeat tunes, get some chocolate (or the next best thing), grab my markers, and I start playing on the whiteboard with ideas I want to work on. I change my goal from a serious, future-focused one, to one about enjoyment and playfulness. I ask myself, what would be really cool? (Even though I know that is such an uncool thing to think!) Moods are transient; we don't need to be held captive by them.

Or, if you can't shift the mood, decide what aspect of the big task you feel you *could* fruitfully make progress in, and start on that. Some of those pieces will require intense concentration and activity from the prefrontal cortex; others are more practical, easier. For example, if you were faced with analyzing an enormous data table that was causing your head to spin, you could begin playing with the table, hiding columns that don't seem essential, reorganizing the columns, etc. You may not be doing the big stuff, but you're preparing the ground— and that means you're moving forward.

The Chemical Side of Mood

Amy Arnsten discovered that the degree to which the prefrontal cortex is operating effectively depends upon the right balance of two chemicals: dopamine and norepinephrine.[11] Without enough dopamine you feel lethargic and bored, but too much and you feel scattered and restless. Without enough norepinephrine you lack urgency, but too much and you feel stress and anxiety. If you feel "not in the mood," what kind of "not in the mood" is it?

Chemical levels	What you can do
Not enough dopamine	Use reversal theory. Shift the goal to having fun rather than task completion.
Too much dopamine	Switch off all distractions.
Not enough norepinephrine	Scare yourself (a little)! Visualize what could go wrong if you don't deliver on time.
Too much norepinephrine	Break the task into manageable chunks. Come up with a concrete plan of execution...and breathe.

Dependence

The final cause of procrastination is dependence. This is dominated by the word *when*: "I'll do it *when* I'm on top of my
inbox," "I'll do it *when* I have heard back from Chuck," "I'll do
it *when* I have all the information." Returning to Newton's laws
of motion, his third law is often termed the action-reaction law:
every action creates a reaction. The thing is, people who suffer with dependence place these the wrong way around. They
wait for another action before they can react. It is far better to
simply get into action, because that action will inevitably trigger a reaction. For example, rather than doing nothing as you
wait for Chuck to send his report, ask yourself, "What can I do
despite not having heard from Chuck?" or even better, "What
can I send to Chuck so he is forced to react?"

If your procrastination is because you are waiting for more
information, remind yourself that information can become an
addiction. I'll say more about this in the next section, but just
remember two things: First, the desire you feel right now to search
a little bit more is probably based more upon the fact that it
feels good to do this, rather than because that extra information

is necessary. Second, more information almost always makes the final piece of work more intellectually demanding to do (you'll have to react more). By searching more, not only are you using up time now, you're adding complexity and time later too! Most importantly, if you hear yourself explaining your delays by using the word "when," recognize this as a story to justify your procrastination, and do something about it.

Busy Is Defensive

When we are trying to achieve something, we have to exercise a degree of self-control. In psychological terms, this is called self-regulation: the conscious control over our activities in order to achieve our goals. The ability to self-regulate has been shown to significantly affect all kinds of things, including job performance and life satisfaction.

In 1997, Edward Tory Higgins, a psychology professor at Columbia University, developed a concept he called *regulatory focus theory* to describe two fundamentally different forms of self-regulation.[12] Our motivation and the way we control our behavior varies according to which fundamental needs are being served. The first set of needs are those of safety and minimizing risk; the second set involves growth and development. Higgins suggested that each set was driven by different forms of regulation, which he called a *prevention focus* and *promotion focus*, respectively.

A prevention focus is all about avoiding negative outcomes, and promotion focus is all about positive outcomes: striving to achieve goals that are important to us. In 2012, researchers at Michigan State University carried out a thorough review of all the studies into self-regulation.[13] Using a clever statistical technique called meta-analysis, they analyzed studies involving over 25,000 people. Their interest lay in the relationship between regulatory focus and performance. What they found was that

a promotion focus was strongly related to task and job performance. It was also positively related to other good things like
openness, innovation, helpfulness, job satisfaction and organizational commitment. Prevention, on the other hand, was
not related to job performance: in other words, trying to stop
bad things from happening does not improve performance. In
addition, prevention-focused people tended to be less open,
less innovative, less helpful, less satisfied with their job and
less committed to the organization. This is possibly because
the greater fear of bad outcomes means prevention-focused
people play it safe. A primarily preventative strategy seems to
be a great way to make sure you don't thrive.

In this section, I have suggested that busyness is a strategy
many people adopt to try to achieve success (ineffectively).
However, for these people busyness often isn't a success strategy, it's a strategy to avoid failure; in other words, busyness is
a prevention strategy. Here's how to deal with the anxiety to
allow you to move to a more positive, promoting approach.

Anxiety and Prevention

Steve Peters is a psychiatrist with a history of working with
the worst offenders in maximum-security prisons. In 2001, he
began working with elite cyclists on the British cycling team
including Sir Chris Hoy, Victoria Pendleton and Bradley Wiggins to help them to manage their emotions better. In the years
following, British cycling moved from a marginal sport to the
dominant country in Olympic cycling, winning nine medals at
the 2012 Olympic Games. Sir Chris Hoy claimed it was Steve
Peters that helped him win the Olympics; Pendleton—winner
of two Olympics and nine world championships—said, "Steve
Peters is the most important person in my career."

Peters has learned a lot about how anxiety, fear and anger
can reduce performance. In what he accepts is a massive

oversimplification, he has developed a working model of emotion.[14] I love it, because, with simplicity and a bit of humor, it describes very complex science. Peters describes two brains: the frontal and the limbic. The frontal brain he calls the Human; the limbic brain he calls the Chimp.

The Human is rational and logical. When we think about ourselves, it is the Human we are thinking of. Theoretically, since it is the Human that plans and makes the ultimate decisions, it is the Human that is in charge. In reality, this is often not the case. The Chimp thinks emotionally and catastrophically, worrying about the worst possible consequences; it is also paranoid, continually scanning for threats to safety or status. In the same way that a real chimp would be five times stronger than a person, the Chimp can easily overpower the Human. This is one of the biggest reasons that so much of our behavior isn't in line with what we know is the right thing to do, or with our good intentions: if something is bothering the Chimp, the Human can lose any semblance of control.

Part of what fuels our wild bouts of busyness, or stops us from pursuing the areas we know will make a difference, is the anxiety resulting from the Chimp's catastrophic and paranoid thinking: the terrible consequences of not submitting that summary or the earth-shatteringly important email we'll miss if we don't get to the bottom of our inbox. We fear that others will judge us harshly if we don't get it all done. We worry that if we don't stretch ourselves to the limit, we may fall behind in the perpetual race for recognition and promotion. The Chimp won't be settled unless we work harder and churn out more and more stuff. To the Chimp, each one of those activities is our badge of commitment to the cause, our guarantee of safe passage through troubled times. It's all a form of defensive, protective busyness—a prevention mind-set.

The Human recognizes it should prioritize important things over the electronic white noise, that thinking and creating aren't done best at one hundred miles per hour, and that a lack of attention is damaging its most life-affirming relationships. However, the Human can do little until the Chimp is settled. These days, with all the pressure and competition, the Chimp hardly ever relaxes. So we wait "until things settle down," and year after year, they don't. We soldier on, expending all our energy on maintaining our force field of certifiable busyness, and have little left for what's important to us. As we flop onto the sofa and dull our pain with wine and TV, the Chimp is satisfied but the Human in us knows it's all wrong.

Calming the Chimp

If you want the Human in you to make good choices, you have to calm the Chimp. The Chimp will never change: its drives and instincts are what they are. The Human needs to work out how to operate despite these drives so that it is in the position to make rational choices.

Don't Bottle It Up

The first thing to realize is that it's a pretty bad idea to bottle up your emotions. James Gross, professor of psychology at Stanford University, showed that when we suppress our emotions, they actually become more potent.[15] He found that when people try not to show their emotions, they feel distracted, because they are trying to do two things at once; their blood pressure rises; and, bizarrely, it makes other people uncomfortable. It seems that, not only does suppression not work very well, but it also bothers those around us. Clearly a better tactic is needed to satisfy the Chimp.

Reappraisal

That better tactic would be *reappraisal*. It involves changing our interpretation of an event, thought or experience—like the prisoners in the concentration camp who were able to find some happiness despite the most horrific situation. We don't feel fear or anxiety because of events in and of themselves, but because of the meaning we give to them. Change our meanings, and we change our emotions.

Gross measured the brain activity of those watching scary movies. He noticed a large increase in limbic activity in those trying to suppress emotion; those who were reappraising had a reduced amount of limbic activity. When we reappraise, the brain no longer sees a threat, and so the Chimp calms down. Going further, Gross collected data on hundreds of people and grouped them according to whether they tended to use suppression or reappraisal to manage their emotions. He then tested them for optimism, life satisfaction, environmental mastery and the quality of their relationships. Reappraisers were significantly better on all these measures: they thrived more.

Reappraisal takes cognitive effort, but it is absolutely critical. Unless we can calm the Chimp through reappraisal, we will suffer from persistent anxiety and stress. More importantly, we will be unable to think clearly about our priorities and will revert to the "safe" option of busyness. As Kevin Ochsner, director of Social Cognitive Neuroscience at Columbia University, said, "If our emotional responses fundamentally flow out of interpretations, or appraisals, of the world, and we can change those appraisals, then we have to try to do so. And to not do so, at some level, is rather irresponsible."[16]

When I started public speaking, I found myself getting scared. My stomach would tie up in knots, my mouth would go dry, and my heart would start pounding so strongly I could feel it in my neck. More importantly, when I was in the grip of these emotions, I'd mumble and rush my words, and fail to connect with the audience. But I was keen to develop the capability to present and facilitate, so I needed to find a solution. At that time in my life I was also a wannabe adrenaline junkie: I had taken up surfing, was listening to grunge music and had been paragliding. My goatee beard and long hair did little to disguise the fact that it was all image, but it was an important image to me at the time. It was also an image that helped me totally change my relationship with presenting. I'm not sure how it occurred to me, but one day I told myself, as I started to feel the pre-presentation tension rising, "Wow! I'd pay a lot of money to jump out of a plane and get a rush like this!" My reappraisal worked like magic. I had reinterpreted nerves as the very thing I craved: adrenaline and experience.

In charting a new path through too much, you will need to find ways of reinterpreting a lot of experiences and emotions to allow you to think clearly. As well as learning to reinterpret your silent panic at the sight of 171 unread emails, you may also have to help others to reinterpret your behavior. I found a while ago that when I didn't respond immediately to email, it caused irritation to a particular client until I explained I only checked email once a day to allow me to think, create and focus on the important things. Once he knew that, rather than being annoyed, he was a little inspired.

These are the four reappraisal strategies I find most useful:

- Make it less scary or more fun. The adrenaline junkie reinterpretation was an example of that. Imagining the interviewer in underwear is the famous one.
- Zoom out. We often get highly anxious about situations that, when put in a broader context, seem ridiculous. For example, dealing with your anxiety about 171 unread emails by reminding yourself that the risk of not reading these is a lot less than the risk of not working toward your strategy. Another form of zooming out is to look at the situation from a point in the distant future: "In ten years' time, what would I tell myself about this situation?"

- Learning. Perhaps my favorite reappraisal technique is to look on difficult situations as learning opportunities. I might look inside myself, at how I feel, and say "That's interesting!" My fears help me to understand better. Before a big radio interview once I told myself "I might not be perfect, but I'll learn a lot through the experience." This also helped afterward when I was churning about a terrible answer I gave: "Well, it's all great learning!"
- Acceptance. The final form of reappraisal is simply to accept your emotions and recognize they are fleeting.

Regaining Perspective

Have you ever had a moment you wanted to shout, to cry, to punch the wall and to crawl into a corner and hide...all at the same time? A few months ago I was in exactly that state. Work was piling up, deadlines loomed, an unexpected and urgent issue had arisen, and I had a big event the next day that I was worried about. I needed more time. I didn't have more time. Help!

In a mad fluster of activity I tried to work through it all, but I made next to no progress. Fortunately, I had a flight to catch and had to drag myself from my desk for the sixty-five-minute drive to the airport. There is no way on earth, at that point, that I would have voluntarily taken a break. I was in it up to my armpits, Chimp jumping all over the place, unable to think properly, unable to work, but also unable to realize how useless I was being. My forced break turned out to be miraculous. Somehow, the drive allowed me to step back, to allow my attention to broaden again, to allow me to gain perspective. The low-level distraction of driving made the anxieties and fears feel less overwhelming—the raging of the Chimp was no longer so deafening. It allowed me to see the priorities more clearly. I could think again. By the time I had arrived at the airport, I had not only calmed the Chimp, I had formulated a plan. I was ready to engage in purposeful, focused activity.

When those moments hit us, we feel entirely compelled to put our heads down and do stuff. Two things are almost certain: In the grip of those emotions, your decision-making and priorities will be hopeless, and the last thing you will want to do is take a break—but it is what you need.

Confidence

Learning to manage our emotions is a critical first step in the progression from prevention to promotion. However, to move from a defensive to a positive strategy, we need to do more than just control our negative emotions; we need to feel confident. Specifically, we need to believe more strongly in our capability, our ability to deliver value in ways other than busyness. When we feel confident in our ability, we are more likely to make our own choices and take risks, to walk our own path.

The Power of Self-Efficacy

One hundred and fifty-five undergraduate smokers were given four short academic papers. Each one contained a convincing argument backed up with evidence and research citations. These four papers were on the following topics:

1. Just how bad is it if you develop lung cancer? (Severity)
2. What are the risks of developing lung cancer if you're a smoker? (Probability)
3. Does stopping smoking reduce your risk? (Effectiveness)
4. How successful are most students at giving up smoking? (Self-efficacy)

Each person was given one of two possible versions of each paper. So, for example, in the case of paper number one, a person could receive a version giving a fairly unpleasant and graphic account of the disease, or one (based on fabricated evidence) that explained that lung cancer wasn't so bad really.

Though each of those factors influenced the intention to act, none had so strong an effect as the one on self-efficacy. The students' confidence that they could quit had a greater impact on their intentions than the severity of the disease, the risk, or the effectiveness of quitting. Even when the papers painted a much less threatening picture, or described the benefits of giving up smoking as marginal, if the person believed they'd be *capable* of making a change, their intention was influenced. It's as if they thought, "It might not be that important, but what the heck, I can do it, so why don't I?"[17]

Self-efficacy increases your belief that you will succeed, lets you persist longer in the face of challenges, and makes you more likely to experience flow. It increases our likelihood of doing new things—difficult things. Since nearly everything we need to do to move beyond busy will be new and difficult, self-efficacy is critical. Think of your typical day. I'm sure you're working terribly hard. I'm sure you're under a lot of pressure. I'm also sure a bunch of the stuff you fill your day with is probably pretty mundane and unimportant (even though it may be terribly urgent). If, by contrast, you were to start thinking of something you would do if you were to truly focus on what was important to you, it would almost certainly be more challenging.

To walk your own path takes a leap of faith. It takes a belief that, even though you don't yet know what challenges you'll face, you hold one thing to be true: you will be able to cope with whatever you encounter. That step takes courage, that step requires belief, and the name of that belief is "self-efficacy."

It's Your Performance That Matters, Not the Outcome

If you follow English soccer, you will know of the great history of Liverpool Football Club, and that, in more recent years, their success has faded. Desperate to achieve again, Liverpool reached out to our old friend Steve Peters to help them regain their former glory. He recognized the burden of history the players and coaching staff were carrying and the weight of expectation from fans. He realized that the whole organization was struggling with fear: that it would never live up to its glorious past, and that this generation would always be seen as a failure. Specifically, Peters realized that the perennial goal of the team, to win the league, was the wrong goal. No matter how hard they tried, how much they developed, the league might still remain out of the team's reach because they had no control over what their rivals did.[18]

Peters's work with other elite athletes had shown that confidence-building goals have to be within the control of the team. Self-efficacy builds via the experience of goal achievement, so goals must be achievable. Peters differentiates dreams from goals. It is okay to work toward, and dream about, winning the league, but Liverpool shouldn't make it their concrete goal. Instead, they should build their goals around their own performance levels, their own fitness levels. They should simply identify goals that push them, plan how they will deliver them and build confidence in their achievement.

We should build our goals and our confidence on our performance, not our outcomes. In what aspects of your life are your goals too outcome-focused? Where are you basing your confidence on things beyond your control? How could you refocus on aiming to do a brilliant job yourself, rather than getting a great result?

Confidence to Cope with Failure

If we are trying to innovate, and do things differently, it stands to reason that we will fail sometimes. How do we stop our confidence from taking a nosedive after failure? The answer is simple, but profound: build your confidence around your ability to cope with whatever happens.

A recent study by Joachim Stoeber and Dirk Janssen at the University of Kent found that the most effective strategies for coping with failure are reappraisal (see earlier), acceptance and humor.[19] Interestingly, these worked better than social support and venting. So fail and don't moan about it, reappraise ("What have I learned?"), accept it ("I can't expect to be perfect all the time") or laugh about it ("What on earth was I thinking!!!"). Trust in your capacity to deal with whatever happens; you will be okay. If you walk into a situation confident that you are prepared, confident that you will do your best and confident that, no matter what response you get, you will be able to cope, you have developed strong self-efficacy.

Practice Makes Perfect

The most reliable and powerful way to build self-efficacy is through mastery experiences: through doing things, and through succeeding. When we achieve things and overcome obstacles, we build an enhanced sense of capability, which increases our self-efficacy. It has been shown that self-efficacy on specific tasks tends to spread out and boost confidence in other areas of your life too, especially those that have some similarity to the task you nailed.

Start small: experiment with an activity that is meaningful to you. It may be something that you have been putting off (because you're terribly busy), or it may be a change in habit, such as only checking email periodically, which you feel is a risk. Whatever it is, start small with little experiments. As you start to achieve success, you'll start to feel your self-efficacy grow.

What small step could you take to start building self-efficacy?

THE BIG MESSAGES IN "WALK YOUR OWN PATH"

We all know what we should do, yet day after day we **fail to bring real focus** to the big, impactful stuff we know we should do. Why?

Busy Is Avoidance
The biggest temptation of all isn't goofing off, it's **the lure of the small** over the complex task. Through being busy, **we can feel productive while avoiding the hard work**.

Avoiding the Temptation of Busy
- Don't try to resist the temptation. Those people with the strongest willpower aren't any better at resisting, they just develop very good habits.
- Prisoners get fat because they don't wear belts. We are more able to control our behavior when we actively monitor it.

Stop Procrastinating!
- Procrastination is all about momentum. It is hard to start a big task, but once you are in motion, continuing is much easier and more rewarding.
- If we understand the effects of dopamine and norepinephrine, we can more easily get ourselves in the right mood for heavy thinking.

Busy Is Defensive

There are two main strategies to regulate our behavior and emotions: **prevention** (of bad things happening) and **promotion** (positively pursuing our goals). Promotion is the more successful strategy, and is also better for your motivation and well-being. **Busyness is a prevention strategy.**

Anxiety and Prevention

- Learning to manage our emotions is a critical first step in moving to a **promotion strategy**.
- Our emotions are like an **unruly chimp**. You **can't change the Chimp**, but you are **responsible for managing it**.
- **Reappraisal** is a powerful way to manage your emotions. Change your interpretation of an experience and you'll change your emotions.

Confidence

- To move to a less defensive, more positive approach requires confidence.
- High self-efficacy makes you more able to walk your own path—it increases your belief, lets you persist longer in the face of challenges and allows you to experience more flow.
- Build your confidence based on personal performance, not on outcomes.
- When you're confident you will be able to cope no matter what, you will have self-efficacy.
- We build self-efficacy through "mastery" experiences, so practice trying things and succeeding.

Go-Do

The Right Goal

Set yourself important goals, but make sure they are concrete goals that are within your control and more focused on your performance than the uncontrollable outcome.

Eat That Frog

Start each day with a period of email-free activity, where you focus on your biggest and most important task.

Experiment

Reappraise

Practice dealing with negative emotions by reinterpreting their meaning, and deal with failure through humor and acceptance that you aren't perfect (and that's okay).

Thin-Slicing

Get started on that big piece of work by just doing a short burst of activity on it (say thirty minutes or less). You'll create momentum this way.

Section Three

ENGAGEMENT

This section goes a little deeper. It looks at the third face of busy: an approach to happiness. Building on the last section, it argues that the "More" game will also not deliver happiness. More specifically, our attempts to improve our lives through acquiring more money, more status and more friends are flawed; and filling our lives with more empty stimulation and mindless activity does little for our well-being. It explains how we can achieve more happiness through putting our values first and focusing more attention on what really matters to us. It explains how we will gain more happiness from a deeper engagement with fewer friends. It provides ideas on building more moments of joy into our lives, rather than relying on the superficial charms of electronic stimulation. Finally, it provides guidance on moving beyond busy by making our good intentions stick. Overall, it provides a practical guide to being happier in a world of too much.

Chapter 9

Stop Striving for "More"!
(Put Your Values First)

Imperial Chemical Industries (ICI) had a glorious history. It was founded in 1926 through the merger of four companies, including that of Alfred Nobel's dynamite business, an organization whose explosives allowed major engineering projects like the Suez Canal to become possible. For most of the twentieth century, it rightfully earned a reputation as one of the most innovative companies on the planet, gaining 150,000 patents on many life-changing inventions and discoveries. Commercially, it was also one of the most successful companies emerging from the UK, dominating the manufacturing and chemical industries. At its zenith, it was the largest manufacturing company in the British Empire. The ICI tradition was based on science and innovation. In 1990, its mission statement was to be the "world's leading chemical company; serving customers internationally through the innovative and responsible application of chemistry."

Through the '90s, the historical focus on chemistry first, profit and sales second, was overturned. Concerned about increasingly fierce global competition and driven by ambitious CEOs, the company became more focused on maximizing profitability and shareholder return. In 1997, ICI changed its strategy: the new strategy was summarized by the mission to "be the industry leader in creating value for customers and shareholders through market leadership, technological edge and a world-competitive cost base." No mention of chemistry was made. This new, profit-centered approach didn't work for ICI. After eighty years of scientific progress, innovative break-throughs and sustainable commercial success, it experienced a rapid fall from grace. In 2008, ICI ceased to exist.

There was a reason ICI was so outstandingly successful for so long, and it wasn't its ability to manage the bottom line and the cost base. It was successful because of its values: it valued deep expertise and a passion for science. Chemistry was the heart and soul of the business, delivering innovation that, in turn, brought profits. In moving to a more directly profit-centric model, the business lost its vitality. The chemists weren't fired up by spreadsheets, saving money and inventory management. The last ten years for ICI were spent scrambling for efficien-cies and productivities as it increasingly relinquished its unique place in the market.

This story should stand as a salutary reminder of the perils of trading the heart and soul of a business for a balance sheet. It should also set off warning bells for you and me. In this chapter, I'll clarify the corrosive effect of a perpetual focus on the balance sheet in our lives: the insatiable quest for more money, more status and more stuff. Importantly, it will explain how happiness and well-being don't come from a constant striving for more, but from our lives, our moments and our loved ones. It will show how we can start to reengage in what matters again.

Disengagement

How many meals have been ruined by one person or the other picking up emails or receiving calls? How many evenings have you wasted watching TV? How many days did you come home from work, bored but exhausted? How many days in the last month did you go to bed feeling you had really been the person you wanted to be that day?

I see a lot of disengagement around me: people switching off—a little or a lot—from their careers, from their loved ones and from themselves. I see people start on career paths for all the right reasons, and day by day, email by email, drift away from what was important to them. It never happens suddenly, or even consciously. It's just that a lack of attention on these things, over time, takes its toll. As we disconnect, we always have a very good story for why this is the case; most of the time, we may even believe this story. But there is a sadness that creeps into our quiet moments—a kind of existential angst whose one refuge is activity. Busyness quiets (and dulls) the mind.

The problem isn't technology. We don't disconnect from our values because we can easily look at Facebook or email, or because we have so much great stimulation available to us via one of our many screens. The problem also isn't work. We don't disconnect because we have jobs that are simply too demanding. The problem is our values.

"More" and Disconnection

I talked a lot about the "More" game in the last section: the endless (and futile) quest for success through productivity. "More" plays a big role in disconnection too. The busyness provoked by our desire for "More" causes us to neglect things that really matter, and an unhealthy triangle results. The three components of the triangle are busyness, "More" (externals like money or status) and disconnection.

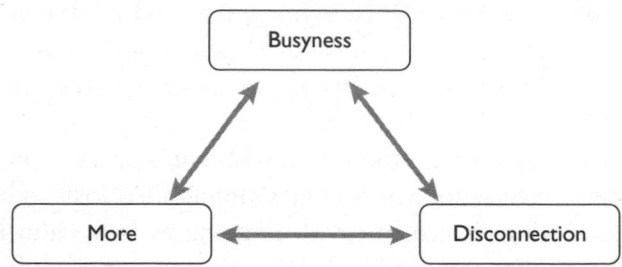

This is how it goes. We are driven to achieve success in the form of earnings, status and/or reputation. This leads to busyness as we strive for our external goals. By being busy we disconnect from our core values and the people and activities that nourish us. This causes us to feel detached and hollow, so we fill the emptiness with more busyness, which gives us a buzz and more stimulation, but little real joy. And so we disconnect further, acquiring more connections on social media, but genuinely connecting with fewer people. We justify the busyness and disconnection because of our external "More" goals; we salve our emptiness with materialism and consumption: "I deserve this." The external "More" doesn't satisfy us, ever. We've replaced the protein of life with chocolate. It doesn't strengthen us or help us to grow; it doesn't satisfy, but it does whet our appetite for more.

In this section, I'm making a stand on behalf of depth over distraction, engagement over stimulation, genuine relationships over Facebook friends. It will help you to cut through the distractions of the world of too much by reorienting yourself back to the fundamentals in your life: the sources of real happiness and well-being.

Rethinking Success

I used the word "thrive" in the book's subtitle because I wanted to emphasize a broader view of success. By "success" I mean financial rewards and positions of greater status. I also mean a lot more: an increased excitement in your work, deeper intimacy with your loved ones, and more joy in your life. It is the increased density of cherished moments, experiences that slice their way through the humdrum, that sear an expression, a sunset conversation, or a child's unintended joke into your longest of long-term memory. It is going to bed, calm in the knowledge that the world, your work and your family have seen the best of you that day, and feeling gently eager for the new possibilities of tomorrow.

I told the story of ICI because I also want to crush an overly narrow, external definition of success. ICI shifted from "better chemistry means success" to "more profits mean success." It killed them. I see a similar mentality in the people I work with today, and it's killing them too. Their actions shout a rapacious focus on the extrinsic "More": more money, more status, more fame, more cool stuff or simply more than the neighbor! They push to improve their balance sheets and neglect their heart and soul, trading what could truly nourish them for "More." The problem is, when the goal is "More," we can never be satisfied. "More" is limitless and, as we get "More," we have to make greater trade-offs to maintain what we have achieved. It's not working.

"More" Is Not Enough

Let me be clear: I'm no hippy—I'm a psychologist and a businessman. I just think you have to pay attention to the hard evidence that "More" doesn't mean happier. For example, in a review of some of the evidence in the United States, David

Myers and Ed Diener comment that wealth has a remarkable lack of connection to well-being.[1] Even though Americans are twice as rich as they were in 1957, the amount of people telling researchers from the National Opinion Research Center (NORC) that they are very happy has declined from 35 percent to 29 percent. Those on the *Forbes* list of the one hundred wealthiest Americans were only slightly happier than average. When people were tracked for a decade, those whose income increased significantly over that time were no happier than those people whose income had remained stagnant. In fact, in cross-cultural studies, it is only in the very poorest countries like Bangladesh that wealth has a good correlation with happiness.

The Wrong Values

Tim Kasser is possibly the world's leading researcher into the effects of materialism on well-being. We often talk about people having different values, assuming that all values are equally valid. Kasser would ask, from a psychological point of view, are some sets of values more beneficial than others? First, he analyzed different people's values and found they tended to cluster into external and internal values. The external values were the aspiration for wealth, image, status, popularity and fame. The internal values were *personal growth*, *affiliation* (close relationships with family and friends) and *community feeling* (the desire to make the world a better place). Most of us value all of the above, to a greater or lesser extent. What he analyzed was relative importance: if pushed to choose, what was more important to that person.

His many studies with thousands of American adults and students showed a remarkably consistent pattern. Those who had stronger external than internal values—who aspire to be wealthy, have a great image and be popular—are less fulfilled, less secure, less vital, more depressed and more anxious. In addition, they complain of more headaches, rate the quality of their day-to-day experience more negatively, have less fun, are less satisfied in their life and with their families, are more narcissistic, and are more likely to engage in substance abuse. Furthermore, these findings apply across the globe.[2]

On one level, Kasser's findings are unremarkable. They simply confirm the old adage "money can't buy you happiness." Yet, on another level, they are shattering. Our whole society is driven by external values, our motivational systems at work are external, and our explanations to ourselves and our families for why we are so busy are external. What's also worth noting from Kasser's research is that it isn't how much money people have that matters, it's how much they *aspire* to be wealthy.

To answer the question posed at the start of this section, some values *are* more valuable than others. And of all the values, the worst of all, from a psychological point of view, are the external ones: wealth, image, status, popularity and fame. So, if you want to ensure you lead a *less* happy and healthy life, strive for these!

Conspicuous Consumption

Before he started Silicon Graphics, Jim Clark said a fortune of $10 million would satisfy him. Before founding Netscape, he thought $100 million would make him happy. Before initiating myCFO and Healtheon, he believed $1 billion would be needed. More recently he said, "Once I have more money than Larry Ellison, I'll be satisfied."[3] Ellison, the founder of the software giant Oracle, is worth $13 billion. How much is enough for you? Don't worry about answering that question, because as soon as you get close to reaching that amount, your definition of enough will have changed.

In 1899, the sociologist and economist Thorstein Veblen coined the term "conspicuous consumption" to describe a certain group of people who, during the Industrial Revolution, had become extremely rich. These people, the nouveau riche, were using money to visibly demonstrate their status and power.

More than one hundred years later, we're all at it. Our desire for wealth isn't about a number on a bank statement; it's about how we appear to others. That's why other external values like status, image and popularity are all linked, and each has the same effect on our well-being. That's why our desires for the externals are infinite—because we don't think of them in absolute terms, but in relation to other people, and there are always wealthier people than us.

"More" Doesn't Satisfy

Goal-setting has proved to be one of the most simple and robust motivational mechanisms we have. From that perspective, even if a drive to succeed in terms of external rewards, such as wealth or popularity, is associated with lower levels of well-being, there must be some satisfaction in working toward these goals, in making progress. In fact, surely one of the appeals of external goals is that progress is so noticeable. It's hard to track a change in your wisdom or your relationships, but you can easily notice a change in your bank balance. So does progress against external goals make us feel better, even if the end goal keeps moving further away?

In further research, Tim Kasser found that progress against external, materialistic goals made no difference to well-being, neither in the short term nor the long term. On the other hand, making progress against more personal goals—such as relationships and growth—made significant differences to all measures of well-being, including drug use and self-esteem.[4]

We all have a cocktail of values and goals that mobilize and drive us. I want to challenge the often taken-for-granted belief that aspiring to "More" is a natural and good thing. In today's world, it seems self-evident that we should sacrifice and make certain choices to get that promotion, or increase our earning power. I want to place a question mark over these aspirations, and the sacrifices they ask us to make. The achievement of external goals such as wealth, status, power, popularity or fame is a hollow victory. It takes a lot from us to achieve them, we don't benefit from the progress we make, and the finish line persistently recedes into the distance.

Unless we can realign our belief system about how we will achieve happy, satisfying lives, we are in grave danger of defaulting to the obvious, external definitions of success. Which brings us right back to busy: the more we focus on external values and goals, the more we will be driven to sacrifice our time and attention for an empty goal, and the more we will throw our lives away in a flurry of self-defeating activity. Through the fog of our frenzy, we will barely notice the increasing disconnection from things that truly matter to us and that could nourish and complete us. In striving for "More," we make ourselves busier and we become less happy and less healthy.

So what should we strive for instead?

A Different Success

In 1973, psychologists Mark R. Lepper and David Greene from Stanford and Richard Nisbitt from the University of Michigan ran an experiment with children who loved drawing. They asked the children to draw for six minutes. Here's the catch: some were told they would be rewarded for drawing, others were not. The children drew. Some were rewarded and some were not. What is important though, is what happened over the coming weeks. The researchers observed how often the children chose to draw of their own free will, when no reward was involved. Those who hadn't been rewarded spent around twice as much time drawing as those who had been rewarded.[5]

This is the classic study that launched a focus on intrinsic motivation: motivation that comes from the activity itself, not from rewards. Remember, the children loved drawing, but after being rewarded, they were less interested *unless* there was a reward. They had a *reason* for drawing, and it wasn't for the fun of it. The reward turned play into work, and it stayed work. Studies like this have been shown to apply to adults as well as children. If the reason people do things is for the reward, they will find interesting activities less engaging.

We thrive when we love our work, our lives and those close to us. That is success. We are succeeding when the *reason* we put effort in at work, when the *reason* we try to improve, is that we love what we do. Work *is* intrinsically interesting, especially these days when there are so many opportunities for us to shape what we do. The problem is, if the primary reason and driving force in all our decisions is money, or status, or fame, we turn what we do from play to work. It becomes less interesting, less engaging. When this happens, we are in danger of turning a big percentage of our waking time into drudgery, which can't be success.

To counter this, we should shift to what I call values-first careers. That means that, while you may want more money and that promotion, your primary focus, your primary decision criteria are your core values. We focus on what's important and interesting to us, on using our greatest skills and on doing what we love. We work to improve in these areas. When we change our priorities to values-first, we change our reasons for working. Work becomes lighter and more fun. Our interesting work stays interesting. We bring more play into our work and our lives.

Values-First Careers

John Stuart Mill was a utilitarian, possibly the greatest of them all. Utilitarians believed the right course of action was the one that directly maximized happiness and minimized suffering.

Having spent his life believing in a direct and simple approach to achieving good outcomes, Mill realized late in life that the best way to achieve something is often indirectly. In his book *Obliquity*, John Kay argues that the same is true for successful companies and people.[6] ICI was successful as long as it focused on chemistry and innovation rather than business success; Bill Gates and David Beckham succeeded, not by trying to make money, but by trying to be great at what they loved. When ICI switched its focus to business success and the bottom line, the company lost its vitality and embarked on a rapid path to oblivion.

Too much focus on success in external terms, or money-first careers, will make you unhappy and unhealthy. When we lead money-first, balance-sheet careers, we seek to achieve by accomplishing what is asked of us and keeping those around us happy. These very activities can drive us toward busyness. In any choice between actions, we take the more immediate, people-satisfying, problem-avoiding approach—behaviors that drive busyness and actually undermine success.

Further research into intrinsic motivation shows that, when people are focused on the rewards, they not only become less motivated, they also become less creative and worse at solving problems. They are less engaged. On the other hand, when we focus primarily on our core values, such as learning, making a difference or, in my case, creativity, our focus naturally shifts to the longer term. We want to invest our time and energy in improving our capability; we are more motivated to explore our passions. The result of this is that our interests naturally drive exactly the kind of focus we discussed in the last chapter: We focus on the important, big stuff; we develop and grow and so differentiate ourselves. This may seem an indirect way to success, but consciously focusing on our values first, and seeking to grow our capability in these areas, like ICI found, is the true path to sustainable success.

The Nobel Prize–winning Indian economist Amartya Sen suggested that we should think of wealth not in terms of what we have, but in terms of what we can do. I would argue a similar shift is possible for success. We should not think of our success as the rewards we get; but in terms of what we can contribute. Or indeed, success is the degree to which your life is lived in-line with your values.

What would be different if you led a values-first career? How would it change your priorities? How could you redefine your success in terms of what you can contribute?

It Will Make You Less Happy Than You Think

Imagine you were told that one of two things would happen tomorrow: either you would become permanently paralyzed from the neck down, or you would win $27 million in the lottery. You were then asked to predict how happy you would be in a year's time as either a paraplegic, or as a multimillionaire. How much of a difference between your levels of happiness do you think there would be?

Dan Gilbert, psychology professor at Harvard, uses this example to demonstrate how bad we are at predicting happiness. In fact, after a year, there would be hardly any difference in happiness levels![7] Hard to believe, but true. This is an example of what Gilbert calls the "impact bias." We massively overestimate the impact things will have on us, and the duration of that impact.

What does this mean for busyness? Those potential achievements, those balls you are terrified you might drop and that job you might gain or lose, will have much, much less impact on your well-being than you think. Blind to our impact bias, we sacrifice too much for successes that will provide too little in return; we struggle too hard to avoid failures that won't really matter.

We all have great reasons to give up on the present in favor of a compelling-sounding future success (or to avoid a horrific failure), but success and happiness aren't found in the outcome; they're to be found in the journey.

So commit to what you value the most, focus on what you love and where you are strong. If our justification to ourselves for crazy busyness is future success, we are giving up our effectiveness, relationships and well-being for a flawed belief. Future successes or failures will take care of themselves; they should not be your focus. Focus on what you value.

What Do You Value?

I have argued that a major driver of busyness is the aspiration for more: the materialistic, external desire for acquisition. It's easy to attribute the cause of this desire to global capitalism: in the modern world, the markets, the advertising and the norms suggest that we are better people if we have more stuff. However, I think there is another significant cause; it's just a little more subtle.

To understand what I mean, think about the setting of objectives at work. If you look at most people's objectives, these are a list of things that are easy to measure. Does this suggest that the only things that matter to job performance are things that are easy to measure? Not at all. It's just that things like improving communication are simply too hard to meaningfully measure, so we set nice, neat (relatively meaningless) SMART (specific, measurable, attainable, relevant, time-bound) objectives, such as to "halve complaints by the end of the year."

In the same way, materialism is easier to latch on to as a personal goal, partly because everyone else seems to be operating that way, but also because it's more readily measurable: $1,000 is better than $500, an iPhone 6 is better than an iPhone 3G, and being a senior manager is better than manager. Material, external values are obvious, self-evident and easy to work toward—ready to use straight out of the box! As a result, materialism steps into the breach when we haven't worked out what our values are.

Personal values on the other hand—clarity regarding what really matters to you—need more work. Many of us have vague notions of things that matter, nebulous clouds of concepts, ideas and goals. However, like light beams, unless they are really focused, they have no power to illuminate decisions and to cut through confusion. When our personal values and priorities are unsorted and unfocused, we default to the clarity of materialism.

What Are Your Core Values, and Why?

Most of the lists of values people create, whether at a personal or a corporate level, are a waste of time. They are simply a list of nice adjectives that feel important to you. Here's my golden rule: when it comes to values, limit your list to two or three. Why? Values should direct attention, decisions and action. You can't possibly hold half a dozen or more values in your head at the same time. In corporate terms, values are one of the most central strategic decisions a business makes. They should be for you too. Take the time to identify your core values, those that energize you the most, and you will be able to draw on a lifetime of inspiration when you align your activity with them.

Three Core Values

This activity will help you to lead a values-first career. It will help to hone your list of values, to move from a nebulous sense that stuff is important to you, to concrete, focused values that become your guide and compass in how you live your life. Here's how it works.

- From the list of "values" circle all those that really resonate for you.

- Add any values you feel are missing from the list in the blank boxes below.

Delivering results	Progression	Learning	Safety	Energy
Variety	Fun	Contributing to society	Peace	Change
Quality	Relationships	Integrity	Fulfillment	Recognition
Competition	Time	Belonging	Creativity	Pride
Interest	Status	Making a difference	Friendship	Wealth
Stretching yourself	Wisdom	Reputation	Speed	Autonomy

- Now reduce that list to three (if it's not already that low) by prioritizing the ones you feel are most important to you.
- Now wear these for a while. If you've done the job right, they should feel vibrant, powerful. You might change the wording a bit so it's in your language.

When you have established your values, use them. Put them first. Remind yourself of them regularly. Reflect on the degree to which you live those values each day.

Why?

> *He who has a strong enough why can bear almost any how.*
>
> —Friedrich Nietzsche

Five and a half years ago I was approaching the big 4-0. Turn-ing thirty hadn't been an issue for me at all, and I wasn't really expecting trouble over my fortieth either. Then I started notic-ing a curious feeling. It wasn't anything strong like depression or frustration, but it was something. After a while, I began to recognize this sensation as some kind of yearning, some kind of need that I was obviously failing to satisfy. On paper, every-thing was going well in my life, so what was this feeling? At around this time I sat down with a colleague and coach. She started asking me questions. Previous conversations I'd had on the topic with other people had focused on what I felt. Instead, she asked me "why?" Why did I feel this way? I can't pretend that I came to a crashing revelation in that conversation, but it did get me thinking; it got me asking, why? In time I came to realize the yearning was for something I'd never considered to be one of my values before: creativity. I might never have recognized it because I was terrible at art, and more of a sci-entist. It's also possible it wasn't important to me earlier in life. In truth, I don't know. All I know is that around my fortieth birthday I became aware that I wanted to create; in fact, I needed to create. Over the years since that realization, I have taken up photography and writing; I've even tried (joyfully but rather unsuccessfully) to paint. More significantly, the desire to create has fed into my work, informing my approach and inspiring my activity. I find it hard to imagine a life without the clarity that creativity is at the core of what I do—and that clarity came from "why?"

I think we have a terrible habit of wasting our crises, our sadness and our frustrations. We proudly boast that we had no problems turning forty. We see it as a sign of strength that we sail through our major turning points unscathed. It is pos-sible, that rather than a sign of strength, it is simply a lack of awareness! Either way, when you feel an unexplained sadness, a yearning or dissatisfaction, it could be your subconscious trying to grapple with something truly important; don't waste it! Stop and pay attention.

Sakichi Toyoda, the son of a poor carpenter, ultimately became one of the most famous industrialists in the country, founding Toyota. He recognized that getting to the root cause of problems was a powerful way to improve quality and fast track innovation. He developed a process which he called the *Five Whys*, which is now used in manufacturing processes all over the world.

The Five Whys is an incredibly simple process that gets under the surface of issues very quickly. You approach a topic and ask "Why?" On receiving the answer, you again ask "Why?" You do this five times. If you are feeling unsettled, don't ignore it; it's great data! Ask why, repeatedly (it may not need to be five times), until you understand your feeling, understand the root cause. Understanding your whys can help you get to the core of your values. After all, our values *are* our big whys.

What's Your Purpose in Life?

Sir Galahad was quite the man. Born as a result of sorcery, when Sir Lancelot was tricked into believing that Elaine of Corbenic was his beloved Queen Guinevere, he was raised by a great-aunt. On reaching adulthood he was reunited with his father, who brought him to King Arthur's court. On entering court, he was led to an infamous seat, the "Siege Perilous," which had been bewitched by Merlin and instantly killed all who sat in it. Sir Galahad survived. Impressed, King Arthur took him out to a sword in a stone (a favored pastime of his, it appears) inscribed with the words, "Never shall man take me hence but only he by whose side I ought to hang, and he shall be the best knight of the world." Galahad pulled the sword free with ease, to be proclaimed by Arthur to be the greatest knight ever.

What made the Sir Galahad legend so potent and popular through the Middle Ages wasn't his battles, conquests or sword-pulling; it was his quest. He, more than any other knight of the Round Table, is associated with the quest for the Holy Grail. Patiently Sir Galahad faces danger, he rescues maidens and saves Sir Percival, until, ultimately, he finds the Holy Grail. Sir Galahad had a quest that was important and worthwhile. It energized, sustained and directed him. Sir Galahad is a legend because he had a purpose and, no matter what tribulations he encountered, that gave him strength.

Joseph Campbell, the great mythologist, suggests that the Holy Grail represents our purpose in life—our own quest.[8] It is a mythical symbol representing the journey that each of us needs to go on to achieve what we are truly capable of. Whatever you might feel about this, I think it's a great thing to ponder. Fundamentally, it's a question that we all have to grapple with at some point. If our values are what are important to us, our purpose clarifies what we want to achieve with those values. Once we are clear about our purpose, it helps steer our course toward what we're most uniquely able to achieve, toward true success.

It's a pretty big question, but a great one...What's *your* purpose in life?

THE BIG MESSAGES IN "STOP STRIVING FOR 'MORE'!"

Our life has **meaning and a purpose** when it is built on our core values. These are the ultimate source of our energy, creativity and resilience. A **life disconnected from core values soon loses its potency** and vitality. **We thrive when we are deeply**

engaged in what is most important to us. **Success is a life of engagement** and meaningful connection, not wealth and fame.

Rethinking Success

- **Not all values are equally valuable.** When people focus on external "More" values, such as the desire for **wealth, status and popularity**, they are **less happy** and less healthy. Internally rewarding values, such as **growth, close relationships** and **community feeling**, are strongly linked to thriving.
- Switch your focus from **external** to **internal values** that make a big impact on your satisfaction and health.

A Different Success

- When we focus primarily on the rewards, we turn play into work; we are less intrinsically motivated.
- We are better off leading **values-first careers**, focusing first on what really matters to us, engaging deeply in our careers and what we contribute, and allowing success to follow.
- Whatever external gain or achievement you are striving for, it won't make you as happy as you think. So **commit to what you value most; don't sacrifice it** in the belief that the end goal will be worth it.

What Do You Value?

- To lead a life in line with your core values, consider what these values are and whether they are **reflected in the way you spend your time**.
- Transform your values from an academic exercise to a **lifelong source of direction and energy** by identifying **two or three core values** to focus on, instead of a long list.

Go-Do

What Does the Evidence Say?

Draw a pie chart that shows how you spend your time. To what extent is that in line with your core values? Make one change in the way you are spending time to bring it more in line with your values.

Identify Your Values

It's hard to motivate any kind of shift in lifestyle unless it's powered by strong personal values. Identify your core two or three values by doing the "Three Core Values" (pages 172–173) exercise.

A Different Goal

If "More" is not a great thing to work for, what should you strive for instead? Set yourself a clear goal to describe a completely different form of success.

Experiment

Ask "Why?"

Next time you feel blue, confused or frustrated and don't know why, take some time to ponder. Go for a walk and allow yourself to wonder "why?" Keep asking "why?" until you understand what your unconscious is trying to say.

Chapter 10

Reconnect
(Why We're Better Off with Fewer Friends)

In 1990, British schoolteacher turned aid worker Monica McDaid walked into a drab gray building at the heart of the medieval town of Siret, Romania. What she saw in that building was, in her words, "beyond belief." She found children listlessly lying three or four to a bed, starved of attention, filthy and ill due to a lack of medicines or washing facilities. In that year, aid workers such as Ms. McDaid discovered similar scenes repeatedly across Romania. Cighid Orphanage, a nineteenth-century manor house housing three hundred children, was one such place in which children were isolated from human and physical warmth. Ill-trained and overwhelmed staff numbed themselves to the horror, distancing themselves from the orphans: children got minimal treatment, and next to no care. They even gave drugs to the children so they would sleep and allow the staff some respite. These places were worse than kennels for babies: harsh, cold and loveless. Between 1987 and 1989, in Cighid Orphanage alone, 137 of the 300 children died.

Following the Second World War, thousands of children

across the world were growing up as orphans while countries struggled to recover from the ravages of that terrible conflict. Orphanages around Britain were designed to offer the very best in physical care. These children grew up in safe, clean, warm environments where they were well fed and watered. Yet pediatricians started becoming alarmed at the high death rates in these places, and began to wonder whether priorities were in the right place. One pediatrician even went so far as to replace a sign that read WASH YOUR HANDS TWICE BEFORE ENTERING THIS WARD with one that read DO NOT ENTER THIS NURSERY WITHOUT PICKING UP A BABY.

Many years later, studies of the survivors of the Romanian orphanages show that the biggest long-term damage to these children was caused by the lack of attention, stimulation or affection. As we now know, touch, attention and time—love—are not just helpful in a child's development; they are critical. Without it, even many of the well-fed, warm children in the UK couldn't prosper, couldn't develop, and died. Doctors gave a name to the condition arising in babies, starved of attention and love. They called it *failure to thrive*.

What these examples demonstrate is the centrality of relationships, the necessity of touch and the lasting consequences of loneliness. My contention is that it isn't just infants that *fail to thrive* if their relationships are impoverished; lives of isolation diminish all of us. No one can thrive unless nourished by the love and attention of those they cherish.

Everyone Needs Relationships

Lisa Berkman is an internationally respected expert on the effects of social and public policy on health. Over her years of experiments and careful statistical analysis of populations, she has become clear on what drives health and well-being: quality relationships, or, in her terms, "social connectedness."[1] In one study of seven thousand adults, those with fewer social ties at the beginning of the study were two to three times more likely to die during the nine years of her study than those who had plentiful relationships.[2] On a cultural level, she suggests that this is the reason that the United States, despite spending more than any other OECD country on health (about twice its nearest competitor per head of population), ranks in the bottom third of those countries in longevity: other countries have stronger social connectedness. Jonathan Haidt, the brilliant professor of psychology and author of *The Happiness Hypothesis*, summarizes the research by saying that good relationships strengthen the immune system, speed up recovery from surgery, sustain mental functioning in old age, and minimize the risk of anxiety and depression.[3] Relationships even boost the mood and well-being of introverts who don't feel they want more relationships.[4] In fact, loneliness and isolation have been shown to be bigger health risk factors than either smoking or obesity![5] This isn't simply because of the support we receive: research suggests that giving support is even more beneficial than receiving it.[6]

We're not just healthier as a result of better relationships; we're also happier. Ed Diener, a senior scientist for Gallup, and Martin Seligman studied very happy people to see what we can learn from them. They found that the common factor linking the happiest people was "their strong ties to friends and family and commitment to spending time with them."[7] Other research shows that the single best way to have more in-the-moment *experiences of happiness* is to spend more quality time with loved ones, and that people are most happy when spending time with friends, followed by family, and are least happy on their own.

Relationships and Busyness

If we have a high level of engagement with those who are important to us, our lives are good. If we don't, our lives are bad. It's pretty much as simple as that. We cannot thrive without great relationships, and relationships cannot thrive without time and attention.

Despite their importance, our most cherished relationships are on the front line of the war with busyness. Our nearest and dearest are the first to suffer and are injured most by our physical or psychological absence. We pillage and plunder those relationships for the time, attention and energy to devote to email, Facebook and that report that has to be done for Monday. We steal attention from those relationships because we can. We feel confident they *understand* that we *have to* do this work, that we *need* to answer that call. We trust them to deal with the scraps of us: serving them only what's left of us after we've spent all our energy, creativity and focus in dopamine-fueled activity binges.

Unbridled busyness destroys our relationships from the inside out—slowly, imperceptibly, but surely. In doing so it erodes our foundation, the only thing that really matters in life. In siphoning attention away from those who are closest to us, we don't end those relationships, but we do suck the richness and color out of them. We impoverish them and consequently they nourish us and fulfill us less, which means we thrive less (and so do our loved ones). This is where we tip back into the busyness cycle: as our relationships nourish us less, we feel more isolated and alone, so we fill our isolation with activity.

Busyness is a gentle poison whose effects will be seen, not in a year, but over a decade as the telltale cancers take hold. Unfortunately for many people, by the time the symptoms have become visible, it is already too late.

Focus on Fewer People: Less Is More

In earlier chapters I discussed how one of the underlying causes of busyness is the constant striving for "More": we attempt to succeed through doing *more*, and we fuel our desire for busyness through striving for *more* stuff. "More" spills over into our relationships too. We want *more* relationships, *more* connectivity and to be *more* popular. There appears to be an insecurity that propels many of us to seek affirmation of our value in the size of our social networks, in the number of "likes" we achieve, or in our Klout (a website calculating online social influence) rating. There is an acquisitiveness in gaining Facebook friends and Twitter followers: whatever the number, we want more.

Undeniably, email, Facebook, Twitter, LinkedIn, WhatsApp, text and IM help us to connect to more people, more easily. Who hasn't thrilled at the rekindling of friendships with very old school friends or acquaintances, glad that, in a very small way, they have reentered your life? Technological tools of communication make mass broadcasting or brief messaging easy, so old connections no longer need prohibitively time-consuming phone calls to bring them back into the realms of active contacts (and what would I say anyway?)—just a couple of words on their Facebook wall and you're back up and running. Social media and electronic communication has extended our reach across the planet, and back in time; we are potent and omnipotent.

But ease and scale of connectivity come with a catch. When you send messages out and connect, people are likely to respond—lots of them, and often. Very soon, keeping up with all the messages, maintaining all those relationships, becomes exhausting. In fear our popularity score may drop, we set about managing the electronic stream of updates, pictures and messages. We talk of getting rid of emails, cleaning our text inbox.

Even outside of work, these social "relationships" can soon
become tasks to be executed. It can all become something of
a burden. Where is the nourishing, life-enriching joy of connecting in this mass of electronic jabber? Our friends, family
and acquaintances can become just one more job to add to the
list, one more thing to increase your busyness.

When Sherry Turkle, author of *Alone Together*, interviewed
sixteen-year-old Sanjay, he explained how much pressure he
felt in trying to keep up with all the texts he received. As he
finished the interview he commented, "I can't imagine doing
this when I'm older," and then more quietly, "How long do I
have to continue doing this?"[8]

Affinity vs. Popularity

One of the things that I find most interesting about Tim Kasser's
research is the distinction he finds between affinity and popularity. Affinity means "being together" and deepening key relationships. This stands in contrast to the attempt to be popular
across the larger population. When I came across this research
it got me thinking. I guess I had always lumped all kinds of
socializing together, regarding intimacy with close friends and
family as the same thing, albeit on a different scale, to banter
and friendliness at a party. His research made me question this.

Kasser's research relates to people's priorities. Are they aspiring to have deeper relationships with close friends and family,
or to become more popular and have more friends? His findings indicate that those with a powerful focus on "affinity" tend
to enjoy happiness, health and mental well-being. On the other
hand, the reverse was found with those who strove for popularity: they were less happy, more depressed and more anxious. It seems that striving to deepen and strengthen important
relationships is nourishing, fulfilling and life-enhancing. Going

for "More" is a great way to increase your likelihood of having a miserable life.

Despite all the TV images, joy is not to be found in *more*, but in *less*. If we want to be happier, we should shift our attention to those special people, many of whom are probably not anywhere in your social network, but who are central to your existence. I personally believe this has always been the case, but I think the argument for a greater focus on our central relationships has never been stronger. We have limited time and attention, so we have to decide where to place it. We should shift more of our energy away from the many and onto the few. We should focus, unremittingly, on deepening, strengthening and nurturing important relationships, and cease trying to become important through our relationships. As in so many aspects of busyness, if we focus more and scatter our attention less, we will start to thrive again.

Who Are Your 15?

Primates have complex social groups. The maintenance of these groups takes effort, often termed "social grooming." As a group gets larger, the grooming required increases, as does the effort to know everyone and understand how they relate to everyone else. British anthropologist Robin Dunbar proved this theory when he found a strong correlation between primate brain size and average group size.[9] It appears that when groupings of apes and monkeys get too big, they start to fall apart: they are just too difficult to maintain. On the basis of his work with other primates, Dunbar calculated the size of social groupings that humans could manage based on their cognitive capacity. His answer was 150. This has become known as "Dunbar's number." He then went a step further and started analyzing historical records to see if social groupings, across cultures, tended to conform to his theory. He found that Neolithic villages tended to average around 150 people. Evidence suggested Hutterite settlements split up when they reached 150, and 150 was often the basic unit size of armies, and remains the size of a company in the modern military.

Dunbar's analysis went a little deeper: through careful study of social groupings, he found remarkable consistency in the shape of social structures. He identified that our level of relationships can be thought of as concentric circles. We tend to have five people who are closest to us, who will often be immediate family and our partner. The next circle contains 15 people, the next 50, then 150. If you combine Dunbar's findings with those of Tim Kasser, the implication for me is that well-being, satisfaction and joy come from the 15. It is these magic 15 people, your closest friends and family, who will trigger more flow experiences, who will make you assess your life as better and who will reduce your depression. The juice of life isn't in the 500 Facebook friends; it's in the 15. I'm not suggesting there isn't fun to be found in larger, more disparate, weak ties through social media or at parties; it's just that this activity can in no way replace the deeper meaning that comes from the 15.

If you remember nothing else from this chapter, remember this: overinvest your time and attention in your 15; revel in being together with them, support them and understand them. Any increase in the quality of these relationships will be a direct increase in your overall life satisfaction. You can be disastrous on social media, you can fail to develop a large network of acquaintances, and it will have little impact on the quality of your life. But unless you get the 15 right, you will not be happy; you will not thrive.

So, who are your 15?

Your Support Network

When we get busy, we can close off from our friends, from our 15, because we are too drained to devote the time to them. As our sense of busyness increases, so our active support network can diminish as we cancel nights out with friends, as we exit quietly from the baseball team. We can end up, at our busiest times, with an active support system of only one or two people just at the time when our need for support is greatest. These needs are unlikely to be met by the superficiality of social media relationships. They need something more meaningful, more present.

One way to help motivate you to put the time into your full 15 is to think about which aspects of you are supported by each person. The experience most people have when doing this is twofold: First, it makes them realize how overly reliant they are on their partner to support them in areas they are not equipped or inclined to do. Second, they realize that painted across the 15 is their full personality. Collectively, their 15 support the vast majority of all their needs, aspirations and passions.

Take Mary, for example, a hardworking lawyer married to another lawyer. She loves Joe dearly, and he understands her well, but there are times she wants to howl with laughter and gossip. Joe doesn't do that for Mary, but Helen and Eva do. There are times Mary wants to create. She loves art and poetry, Joe doesn't, but Bill and Asiya do. At times she wants the unquestioning maternal love of her mum, or to be with Lucy, her running and weight-loss partner. Engagement across the full 15, in Mary's case, makes her more complete and fulfilled. Your 15 should not be trimmed back as you get busy; cut back the 50, the 150 and the 500, but don't cut back the 15. Your 15 can support you, in all those deep and meaningful ways, through your darkest periods of workload and demand.

Giving More

There's an old adage that it's better to give than receive. It turns out that this is supported by evidence. Research into altruism has persistently shown benefits to health, happiness and psychological well-being. One study into sufferers of multiple sclerosis, for example, found that patients who offered support to other MS patients actually experienced more benefits than those they helped—in terms of confidence, self-esteem, depression and daily functioning.[10] Another study showed that giving also builds our resilience, helping to protect us from the stress of modern life.

How could you give more to feel better? Specifically, how could you give more to your 15?

Being Together

When Sherry Turkle started working on her book *Alone Together,* she found children and teens driven to exasperation by call-interrupted dinners, by email-perforated conversations, and by parents too distracted to notice the important "unimportants" of growing up: the proudly shown handmade paper airplane, the new skateboard trick, the disappearance of the first "moustache." She chronicled mothers who used breastfeeding time to catch up on their texts, missing the subtle flickers of emotion across their baby's face. And fathers who are barely present with their children at the park, playing with their iPhones rather than playing ball. She met Audrey, a teen who fantasized about the day when her mother would greet her from school, expectant and focused. Instead, her reality involved arriving at the car to find her mum head down over her phone, too busy to acknowledge Audrey. She simply wanted the opportunity to share the ups and downs of her day, but she had to accept that her mum was focused on more "important" things; she had to accept that her ups and downs were trivial. She was learning to accept that she too was trivial.

Of course we know that those we love are more important than the inbox. Of course we realize that we care less about keeping up to date with texts or WhatsApp than we do about our family and friends. It's just we have a lot on, and we are sure, if they love us, they'll understand this. Next year should be a little quieter...

If we do allow busyness to steal the micro-moments, we disembowel relationships. All relationships comprise two elements: being together and doing things together. If we remove the "being together," we are left with relationships that are focused around activity, tasks or even chores. It is in the "being together" that most of the happiness comes and from where most of the emotional connectedness comes. If we strip the "being together" component into simple physical presence in the same location, our attention consumed in other orbits, we downgrade relationships into activity or transactions. Relationships become less rewarding, so they attract less of our attention and buffer us less and less against the tides of busyness.

In a world of too much, we need to practice and relearn how to be together, unaided and uninterrupted by devices, because that is where trust is built, and that is where joy comes from. Here are some suggestions on how to practice becoming more fully present with that other person, whether they are a child, a partner, a sibling, a parent or a friend.

Connected but Isolated

It was all a little awkward. A large man, in height and in width, sat down opposite me on the train and started talking at me, very animatedly. He was clearly cross about something. What he was saying didn't make a lot of sense; I felt as though I was missing a big chunk of the full picture, like there were gaps in his story. Suddenly, with no apparent warning, his whole body relaxed; he sat back, smiled, then started laughing—great shoulder-shaking guffaws. Finally, in a tender voice, looking at me, but not directly in the eye, he said, "Okay. I'll speak to you later. Love you. Bye," and he hung up his phone. After a moment's pause and reflection, his picked up his phone and made another call.

This odd behavior made me reflect on the weirdness of our private bubbles these days. While technology has, superficially at least, helped us to connect, it has also isolated us. Our technology allows us to connect to many people far and wide, but in so doing, it sucks our presence away from those who are near. We wander around on our streets, in our trains and in our homes wrapped up in a private bubble, physically present, but mentally elsewhere—and that's not good for our relationships with those who are near.

Here's the challenge. Over the next week, double the amount of time you, and those you live with, are simultaneously out of your bubbles, together physically and mentally, connected and sharing attention.

- Switch the phones off.
- Put the phones out of sight (research shows people like you less when you put a phone on the table during a conversation).
- Have technology- and TV-free time, together, built into the daily routine.

The Good Samaritan

If you saw a man collapse in front of you, in a clearly distressed state, would you stop and help? The answer is that it depends. In a famous experiment, social psychologists John Darley and Daniel Batson ran an experiment with people who might be expected to help: trainee priests. Just before leaving for the lecture, some trainee priests were told they were late, others that they had plenty of time. The effects were dramatic. Only 10 percent of the trainee priests who were late stopped to help the collapsed man (who they had no way of knowing was an actor). Of those with more time, 63 percent stopped![11]

When we are in a rush, we are less likely to stop for other people. Our busyness makes us more selfish and self-centered. We are more likely to ignore or put other people on pause in our haste to do whatever our inbox or to-do list is telling us. For example, if you're a parent to young children, let me ask you this: How many times a week do you say, "Wait a minute," in response to a request for attention from a child? Every single time we say that, we signal our priorities and our child's lack of importance. My wife and I caught ourselves (and still catch ourselves) doing this regularly as we rushed around the house in our oh-so-important daily busyness. We wondered what would happen if we didn't say, "Wait a minute." What would happen if we paused our busyness instead of pausing our child? What happened shocked me. I found I started entering a lot more of these random little moments. One minute I'd be tidying the kitchen, the next I'd be helping to attach a propeller to a LEGO biplane, watching a lizard or dressing a doll. I'd be plunged into special moments of togetherness that were light and trivial, and in that triviality I found myself smiling more, connecting more. These were sublime distractions. I was shocked by how quickly the children could drag me into joy if I didn't pause them. I was even more shocked by how brief these moments were.

Recently, my five-year-old daughter asked me to dance with her. I, of course, was involved in something terribly important, though I'm struggling to remember what it was. I put my thing on pause, and got up to dance. We danced and laughed for about twenty seconds. After that, my daughter was done; satisfied, she moved on to the next thing. I don't say this to suggest those twenty seconds weren't important to her, or great moments for me, it's just her attention, as a five-year-old, had scuttled on to something new. I had been assuming that the requests my children made for my attention were adult-sized requests. In most cases, it turns out, they weren't. They were tiny fragments of joy, brief beautiful butterflies, asking for little effort—just a moment to pause and enjoy and, in this joy, to deepen our relationship.

I am now practicing the pause. I don't pretend I always pause my busyness, but at least I now pause it more often than I pause my children.

Creating Rituals

When I was at university I had a theory. This theory sprang from the responses I would get from people when I asked them "What are you doing for the holiday season?" I was struck by the vast differences in the answers. Some would light up as they recounted, in great depth, the family traditions they had. Others would talk vaguely about turkey and knitted sweaters. My theory went like this: you could use the depth and quantity of family traditions as a proxy for how happy that person's childhood was. I appreciate this is a fairly flaky theory, but I have been left with a belief that there is something potent, symbolic and binding in rituals within relationships. More than that, recent research shows that rituals can increase our enjoyment of experiences because they are predictable, and so help build our anticipation.[12]

I can't remember where I first heard the term, but I'm a big fan of "date nights." This is the practice of putting a regular night aside, often once a week, for a nice, one-on-one meal with your partner. I'm told even Barack and Michelle have a date night. If your schedules are crammed with activity, it can become easy to pass like ships in the night for weeks. Scheduling time for each other can be a way of managing this. Dulcie and I have our own spin on this. We like our food, so every now and then (certainly not weekly) we have our own date night. We have rules for this. These meals are four courses. She cooks two and I cook the other two. Neither of us knows what the other is cooking (apart from the main ingredients), and every course has to be something we have never cooked before. The anticipation, the planning and the cooking are every bit as much part of the experience as the meal itself.

However, date nights are nowhere near as important as another of our rituals that developed by chance: our "three-cup-of-tea mornings." At least once a week, more if we can make it, we sit down for a tea-drinking marathon. We cover more ground in those three teas, conversationally, than we might do in days otherwise. We plan our finances, we discuss the children and we dream. We are seldom more together than over those cups of tea. So we stretch out the moment. We stay for three cups.

Rituals work on two principles: the activities are extremely specific, repeatable and predictable and therefore build anticipation; there is a rhythm with which they happen, which is normally daily, weekly or monthly and so they are more likely to happen.

Think about your 15: What rituals could you start to deepen those relationships?

The Power of Positive Emotions

What's the point of positive emotions? From an evolutionary perspective, how could joy help? Positive emotions were considered an evolutionary anomaly, albeit a pleasurable one, until Barbara Fredrickson, professor of psychology at the University of North Carolina, started her work. Through her work,

Fredrickson developed the *broaden and build* theory for positive emotions.[13] She found that people in the grip of positive emotions such as amusement or contentment were more creative and had more of a "big picture" focus. Further work showed that these emotions undo the cardiovascular effects of negative emotions, helping us to relax quicker and, over time, dissipating the effects of stress. Positive emotions, it seems, help us to grow and learn. Through positive emotions we lay down the resources and psychological capital that will be used for the rest of our lives. Negative emotions are about short-term survival; positive emotions are about long-term growth and capability.

The same applies to our emotions in relationships. When we're in the grip of anger or anxiety, we focus on ourselves, on winning or getting out of the situation; all attention is focused on the short term with no regard for long-term damage. Positive emotions, on the other hand, broaden and build our relationships in a couple of ways. First, they broaden your attention, making you more likely to notice subtle signals from the other person, which helps you to navigate the dance better. When our attention is broadened we are more likely to "get out of our heads" and more readily appreciate and empathize with the other person's viewpoint and feelings. By increasing our powers of observation and understanding, we also learn more about that person and ourselves. We grow, and in so doing, help the relationship to grow.

In addition, positive emotions are typically shared. When we're enjoying positive times with a friend, family member or partner, our *mutual* attention broadens. I often think that a simple gauge of the strength of a relationship is the range and depth of things you are able to discuss together. As relationships develop we go through a process called *social penetration*[14] (a horrible term, I know) where we increasingly know, understand and can talk about more things. In less positive moments, our mutual attention is focused on the bare minimum required to complete the interaction; we are transacting in the narrowest sense. As our joint mood improves, conversations open up, the things we discuss together increase and our relationship unfolds. Positive emotions enlarge our moments together, they expand our interactions and deepen the relationship.

Positive to Negative Ratios

The broaden and build theory was reinforced in private relationships and in business through work by Marcial Losada, a colleague of Fredrickson. Losada went into sixty companies and started transcribing every word that was said in their business meetings. A third of those companies were flourishing economically, a third were doing okay, and a third were failing. Losada looked at the ratio of positive to negative comments and found a clear link to performance. Companies where the ratio was higher than 2.9 positive comments for every one negative remark were doing well. Any companies with a worse than 2.9:1 ratio were doing badly. This has become known as the *Losada ratio*.[15] John Gottman used the same principle to calculate optimum ratios with married couples. He found the benchmark was higher in couples: a 2.9:1 ratio predicted divorce; you need a ratio of 5:1 to predict strong, healthy marriages.[16]

The principle of the ratio has been applied to numerous aspects of positive emotions. Now, a recent article has challenged the accuracy of Losada's ratio,[17] questioning the differential equations and the nonlinear dynamics used. All very clever stuff, but I say blah, blah. In the end, what matters is not the exact ratio, but the principle that the proportion of positive to negative emotions has a lasting impact on the health and strength of those relationships.

Think of a key relationship—one of your 15 (or even one of your 5). What's your ratio? ·

Celebrate Better

What do you think is a better predictor of a strong relationship: the way you argue or the way you celebrate? I would have thought the answer was obvious: it is how we act in the heat of battle when the unspeakables are spoken, when we put aside our respect for the other person in favor of a victory. I was wrong. Shelly Gable, professor of psychology at the University of California, has demonstrated that how we celebrate is a better predictor of relationship strength.[18] It appears that how we behave in those moments of triumph and joy makes a huge difference; it can either build or undermine the relationship.

So what is the secret of a great celebration? Martin Seligman suggests that there are four basic types of response when you hear some great news.

News: "I've been asked to be on the regional gymnastics team. The team is going to compete in Paris, France, next month in an international competition."
Response:

	Passive	*Active*
Constructive	"That's great news. You deserve it. They should have selected you ages ago."	"That's amazing. How do you feel? How did they tell you? How did you react? Tell me more about the trip."
Destructive	"Oh. Can you pass the salt?"	"Ahh. Paris is a long way away. Will the trip be expensive? Will you still have enough time for your homework?"

It isn't hard to see the strongest approach. Yet after I came across this distinction, I became painfully aware how often I reverted to passive constructive celebrations with my children. I realized how I was missing so many micro-celebrations: the news of a rare and long-awaited soccer victory, the unexpected school "diploma," and the proud display of a sculpture that Granny had said was fabulous were all greeted with well-meaning comments like, "Brilliant. I'm so proud of you." My responses were heartfelt and true, and they were well received, but they were unsubstantial. They weren't just driven from ignorance, but also from being in a rush, always—too busy to stop and drop into a celebration.

I now celebrate better. Real celebration, for the small and big stuff, isn't about verbal pats on the back and drive-by congratulations; it's not even about my thoughts and feelings, thrown at them like so many flowers to the victor. It's about taking the time to help the other person—partner, child or friend—celebrate. It's about urging them to relive the experience, and joining them in their emotions.

I can't pretend I always celebrate brilliantly. However, at least I stop a little more often to ask questions about exactly what happened and how they felt. I help my 15, whether adult or child, to revel a bit more. This is my favorite kind of psychology: simple, blinking obvious (once explained) and life-enhancing.

Go celebrate!

Better Than Prozac

If I told you I could prescribe something for you that would make you happier than Prozac, would cost you nothing, was very simple and would have no negative side effects, would you be interested? The following is an exercise developed by

Martin Seligman and his team.[19] It has been tested using random controls. It works, and what is more, it is a practice that many find to be sticky: a new behavior that can rapidly become a habit. In fact, it works so well that those people tested with deep, dark, can-hardly-get-out-of-bed depression, in just a few weeks had improved to a state of mild depression (the typical state of people while watching TV).

Here's how it goes. Every night, write down three things about the day that went well, or that you are happy about. Write a little bit of detail, but you don't need to go overboard. That's it!

Why does it work? We tend to overfocus on the negative; we ruminate, worry about and remember the mistakes, the problems and the fears. A simple activity like this can help to rebalance our focus. I don't mean you fake it or try to fool yourself into thinking what was bad is good. I simply mean trying to balance your memory to be more accurate, and in so doing, you start to be more satisfied with your overall life.

You might be thinking, "Why isn't this technique listed in the chapter on happiness?" I have included it here because I've adapted it with my children. For years I would ask, on the drive home from school or at bedtime, "How was your day?" It was a boring question, and I got perfunctory answers like "Good" (full stop). One day I asked instead, "What were the best three things today?" The conversation was infinitely richer; the children started thinking and vying with each other to come up with the best answers. It has become a regular and brilliant conversation for the children and me, and has helped to strengthen our relationship. I also like to think that it might make a small impact on developing their happiness, though of course that's only conjecture.

THE BIG MESSAGES IN "RECONNECT"

Relationships are not "nice to haves": they are central to our lives and well-being. Strong relationships help us to **live longer and to be happier and healthier**, physically and mentally. **We cannot thrive unless we have strong relationships.**

The **first victims of busyness are often those who are closest to us**. We siphon our attention away from these relationships, trusting our loved ones will "understand," and in doing this we are diminished.

Focus on Fewer People

- Research shows we are better off **focusing on fewer close, deep relationships** than lots of (shallower) relationships.
- Using Robin Dunbar's research, perhaps the people to **focus on are your closest 15** relationships.
- Think about how your 15 support you. **Could you spread the support role** more evenly across your 15 to improve your well-being?
- **Giving is good for you**: it makes you healthier, happier and more resilient to stress, so think about how you can give more to your 15.

Being Together

- Technology has enabled us to connect to more people, but due to the demand all those relationships place on us, we have more shallow interactions; we are **more connected but more isolated**.
- Relationships have two parts: being together and doing things together. It is in being together and sharing attention that the joy and connectedness come.

The Power of Positive Emotions

- **Positive emotions** help to broaden and build your relationships, so make an effort to generate these emotions. Consider the **ratio of positive to negative comments** in your relationships and how you can **improve this balance**.

- Relationships deepen not just as a result of getting through tough times, but also in how good times are **celebrated**. Make an effort to celebrate positive moments in an **active and constructive** manner.

- Engage with the positive moments in the lives of your loved ones by asking: **What three things went well today?** It will build your relationship and might also improve their personal narrative.

GO-DO

Your 15

In one respect, happiness is very simple. Identify the 15 people in the world whom you cherish the most, and spend as much quality time as you can with them.

Rituals

Rituals can be powerful and easy to maintain. Start a new one this week with one or more of your 15. Make it really specific, and create a regular rhythm for its occurrence (daily, weekly, monthly).

EXPERIMENT

Phone-Free Moments

Forget the phone when you're with important people. Practice prioritizing them over your calls or emails. At the very least, don't put your phone on the table when you're talking or eating!

Celebrate Better

When someone important has good news, stop and ask them how it feels and what happened; don't default to a drive-by pat of congratulation.

Chapter 11

From Buzz to Joy
(An Ode to Depth)

He loved the sea and so, in 1930, he joined the navy. But he wasn't satisfied with just skimming the surface; he wanted to understand the sea, to go deep. He started diving using a pair of underwater goggles, but enthralled, he wanted more. Together with Emile Gagnan, an engineer, he built the aqua-lung, the first self-contained underwater breathing appara-tus. In so doing, he invented scuba diving. Leaving the navy, he set off on a lifetime's expedition into the sea, exploring and discovering. He was the first to recognize that porpoises could use echolocation, and he made films such as the Oscar-winning *The Silent World*, introducing millions to the realm beneath the sea's surface. He went deep, and lived a life of adventure and joy. He inspired a generation, started the scuba industry, and pioneered marine conservation. His name was Jacques Cousteau.

Cousteau recognized that the true joy in life wasn't to be found on the surface, but down below, and so he immersed himself, deeply. Whether we are discussing work or life, we only achieve real happiness and full satisfaction when we are able and willing to dive deep into our activity, our moments and ourselves.

Yet we live in a world that's scattered and diffuse. Messages, information and stimulation hit us from every angle, at every second. Our attention is pulled in every direction, never really sticking. When we get hooked on busy, we constantly scan for the next thing, skipping onward, only half-present. We seek information in sound bites, relationships in snatches, and activity in bite sizes. We want life in thin slices; we want the buzz of busyness.

Ultimately, however, the buzz of busy is hollow. In fact, you could argue that buzz is the opposite of happiness. Pretty much everything good happens when we go deep: our experiences are richer, our relationships are better and our thinking is more insightful. We are more immersed, more connected and more satisfied. Happiness results from real engagement rather than distraction. It comes from depth rather than diffusion.

This chapter is an ode to depth. It will fire a shot over the bows of the superficial, the shallow and the fractured. We're racing across the surface of the sea, eager to get to our destination, mistaking the fizz of stimulation for the true joy of immersion, oblivious to what we're missing. We need to cut the engine and dive into the wonder and color of the depths below if we want to achieve real and lasting happiness.

Buzz and Happiness

In Chapter 9 I explained the unhealthy triangle of busyness: how an endless striving for "More" leads us to become busier, which leads us to disconnect from what matters and then filling the resulting feelings of emptiness with more busyness. In that chapter I also addressed the first part of the unhealthy triangle by outlining how placing our core values first is a far more reliable approach to happiness than striving for "More." In the last chapter, I explored how to avoid disconnection in our most important relationships. In this chapter I want to address the third part of the triangle: the filling of emptiness. I'll start by suggesting a better way to fill our time (and attention) than the vacuous buzz of busy if we want to achieve happiness. Then I'll address the topic of emptiness.

The Buzz of Busy

Busy is a buzz. It can feel good slashing through your to-do list, skipping from screen to screen, and racing from meeting to meeting. We're alert and ready, like some supercharged task-ninja. The heart is pumping and all kinds of buzz-inducing chemicals are flowing: adrenaline, cocaine-like dopamine and even the internal opiate system,[1] which induces a kind of blissful stupor as we search for ever more information on the web. As our busyness triggers all these chemicals, the brain can get into a wanting cycle: it wants the reward, gets the reward, and as soon as it is rewarded, it starts wanting again. Our dopamine and opiate systems are never satisfied. As neuroscience professor Kent C. Berridge says, "As long as you sit there, the consumption renews the appetite."[2] We want information, so we do a Google search; as soon as we are rewarded we feel compelled, irrationally, to seek that reward again, so one search follows the other.

Many mental health researchers, such as Dr. Kimberly Young, have campaigned for years for medical recognition of *technology addiction disorder*. Countries around the world are taking information addiction seriously.[3] In fact, early in 2014, India opened its first "technology de-addiction clinic" in Bangalore (China already has three hundred!). While calling busyness an addiction may be stretching it, recognize one thing is sure: rampant activity sucks us into more activity. Busy is a buzz, and while it can be fun in small doses, it can take over our lives, our attention and our relationships, and so damage our happiness and well-being.

Going Deep

Busy is a buzz, but it also messes with the brain. While novelty attracts our attention and rewards, the brain doesn't like disorder and chaos. The brain likes it best when everything lines up: our goals, our thoughts and our attention. When novel information arrives, by definition it's inconsistent with our current thinking, our present goals. When we face a lot of novelty, we get knocked off course, distracted from our goals and preferences; energy is diverted from our priorities and we are set on different, less satisfying tracks. Our thoughts become chaotic, hurried and splintered. This mental state is called *psychic entropy*;[4] it is more unpleasant than happy. Busyness may be a buzz, but it induces psychic entropy.

So what's the alternative? Retire to a mountainous hermitage, away from the twenty-first century and its temptations? The answer started with a beeper in Chicago. Professor Mihaly Csikszentmihalyi wanted to understand happiness. Like Cousteau, he wanted to go deeper; he wasn't satisfied that questionnaires asking about life satisfaction were really capturing the essence of happiness. So he got an awful lot of people to carry beepers that sounded at random times. Each time the beep sounded, subjects were tasked with capturing their actions, feelings and thoughts at that exact moment. Through capturing hundreds of thousands of these, his team built up a clear picture of the day-to-day experience of happiness, when it happens and why it happens.

One of the first things he found was a challenge to the stereotype: happiness is not lying on a beach sipping cocktails! He found that people's biggest highs, their peak moments, weren't relaxing or passive at all, but highly active. He described these times as *flow* experiences.[5] When we're in flow, we are deeply immersed in our chosen activity. We lose all sense of time; we lose our sense of self (or the internal dialogue stops anyway). Flow experiences are the very opposite of psychic entropy: our intentions, thoughts and actions are perfectly aligned; our consciousness is coherent and organized. This might be the semi-meditative state you get into on a long bike ride, the quiet focus you find as you rebuild the car engine, or the laughter and giggles of a night out with your friends.

Busyness gets in the way of flow experiences in three ways: We jump from task to task without giving ourselves enough time to become deeply engaged (it can often take fifteen to twenty minutes to get into flow); our attention is scattered as we constantly scan the environment for new inputs, preventing full immersion; and we tend toward the superficial and expedient approach, rather than a more engrossing, thoughtful and skillful one. Our opportunity to experience flow is reduced through frenetic, divergent activity.

Flow is the antidote to psychic entropy and the addiction to buzz. We achieve happiness through deep engagement in what we are doing, whatever it is. We don't need to wait for life to get less frantic or more interesting; we can start by deciding to focus, 100 percent, on the job at hand—to engross ourselves fully by stretching every fiber of our being to improve or excel in that task or activity. The children's bath time, the monthly sales report or the washing up all offer opportunities for great happiness, but only if we sink our attention into them with reckless abandon.

Enjoyment: The Performance Enhancer

Throughout this book I haven't simply been interested in happiness, I am also interested in success. It turns out there is a significant performance enhancement that happens when we are enjoying our work, immersed and in flow. Paul O'Keefe, assistant professor at Yale–NUS College in Singapore and Lisa Linnenbrink-Garcia of Michigan State University showed that when students were enjoying an assignment three things happened: their performance improved, they stayed focused for longer and the work tired them less.[6] When we are loving what we are doing, it's easier and we do it better. As mentioned earlier, immersion reduces our sense of overwhelm. In fact, though research into flow was focused on happiness, and studies of athletes being "in the zone" were about performance, it has become recognized that the two states are pretty much the same thing. Getting into flow means more than just experiencing happiness; it means getting into your optimal performance state as well. So how do you do it?

How to Achieve Flow

If you stop and think about your own moments of flow, you will soon realize that peak moments are never guaranteed. You may passionately love cooking and frequently experience flow as you whip up a soufflé or a sweet and sour. There may also be times when you're just not feeling it, when, no matter how much garlic you crush or fruit you flambé, you are just going through the motions.

Flow is never guaranteed, but there are some conditions under which it is most likely to happen, which we'll look at now.

Challenge

The first component of flow experiences is that of challenge. When we stretch ourselves and our skills, we are more likely to engage deeply. This might come from competitive sports, a fierce debate or an artistic activity. Or it may come from something more mundane in which you have found a way to challenge yourself. I am reminded of my aunty Dymphna. As an early teen, I was tasked with drying the dishes along with her after a big family meal. (Big family = lots of dishes!) I was horrified when I saw the sheer quantity of crockery and cutlery awaiting us, while I knew my siblings and cousins were off playing. I hadn't realized that I would learn a valuable lesson. Dymphna attacked the drying up with an efficacy I had never experienced before. Her trick was, instead of drying a single plate at a time, she'd dry three simultaneously. She would do the same with knives and forks. I started aping her and soon found that by challenging myself to do three at once, not only did I get through the dishes a lot quicker, the time flew. I had discovered how to get into flow while drying dishes!

Goals

Goal-setting is really just another way of increasing challenge. Instead of increasing the task's difficulty, we can set parameters around the task that make us stretch to achieve it. By doing so, we can even transform the process of answering emails from a cause of busyness to a flow-inducing activity. Here's how it works. Set aside a specific time in the day to deal with email. Then, once you have seen how many emails you have, set yourself a goal. For example, "I'll respond to or delete all new emails within thirty-two minutes." Then get a big clock to time yourself, cut off distractions, and go crazy. What happens is that, as you are trying to achieve a tough goal, you also start thinking about new strategies for improving your efficiency, which engrosses you further and pulls you into flow.

Concentration

When an activity requires all your attention, it brings organization to your consciousness, triggering flow. Rock-climbing, playing chess or writing poetry all involve focused attention and so make flow more likely.

I used to row for my university. Often we'd be rowing on cold, wet, windy mornings. You'd get into the boat, knowing you had a hard session ahead of you, wanting to be in bed, or back at home, or pretty much anywhere other than where you were. As you started to row, you could feel the aches from the previous day's training; you felt exhausted before you even began. Then, at some point in the first fifteen minutes, flow would kick in and you would forget all that. Consumed by the rhythm, focused on the micro-movements of the rower in front, trying to get the timing of the catch (the point at which the blade enters the water) in perfect sync...Rowing is an endless quest for the perfect stroke, an intense concentration on your actions, the movement of your crew members and the feel of the boat. Rowing is hard work, but it is also deep concentration. As one stroke merged into the next, so I would glide into a flow state. It was difficult to think of anything else when sunk so deeply into the moment as this; all my consciousness was wrapped in the activity, and the resulting psychic organization, those flow moments, live with me to this day.

Feedback

Optimal experience happens when we're involved in a feedback-rich activity, and when we pay attention to that feedback. When you play tennis, you get feedback from each shot, knowing instantly how well you swung your racket. If you are playing with the intention of improving, this feedback makes you strive to hit better, which absorbs your attention and elicits flow. As the musician plays her violin, she hears how well her fingers and bow combine to create the concerto. The gardener relishes the daily signs of growth—a tribute to his ministrations. When we observe progress, we are rewarded with joy.

The Joy of Commitment

The world of too much can lead us to keep our options open: to try a bit of this and a bit of that, to wait for something better. Overwhelmed by choice and opportunity, we can hedge our bets. We don't simply bounce from task to task at work; we bounce from hobby to hobby outside of work. We start sailing, and are feeling quite good about that until we hear about a friend who is kitesurfing, or waterskiing.

Dan Gilbert wondered if keeping our options open would increase or decrease happiness.[7] He had students in a photography course take pictures of things that were important to them using a film camera. At the end of the course, they were asked to go into the darkroom and print up their two favorite pictures. Gilbert would then ask, "Which one would you like to give up?" One group of students were told that if they changed their minds, they could swap their choice with the other picture. The other group of students were told that they had to make a decision, and that there would be no option of changing their minds, since the photo would be sent away immediately for assessment, never to be seen again. Gilbert followed up with the students to determine how much they ended up liking the picture they chose. Those who were stuck with the picture, who had no option to change it, ended up liking it an awful lot. Those who had the option to change it didn't like the picture much at all.

We enjoy things more when we commit and stop keeping our options open. Yet we are entirely oblivious to this fact. When Gilbert asked these students which photography course they would prefer to enroll in—the course in which they could change their minds, or the one in which they had to commit—two-thirds of all students chose the course that would make them less happy with their ultimate photograph.

In his wonderful book *Mastery*, George Leonard, an aikido

expert, bemoans the fact that so many of us fail to commit to pursuits, activities or areas of expertise in the longer term.[8] We get enticed by new sports and hobbies, thrilled with the initial steep learning curve. When our progress slows, as it always does, when we plateau, we lose interest and seek new activities. We miss the point. True joy, deep engagement and real mastery come from the journey, from the practice, from the persistent immersion in a pursuit; it comes from commitment.

This applies to hobbies and it also applies to careers and areas of expertise. My world changed when I decided to really commit to my subject, when I stopped trying to have a successful career and started trying to be a better psychologist. The change was subtle enough at first, but as I built my knowledge, my interest grew; I started falling back in love with psychology. Then, projects became transformed with the insights I was gaining; the conversations I was having changed and amazing opportunities began appearing. My career and life satisfaction were transformed. None of this came through working harder; it came through commitment. The deep engagement brought joy, but it also brought opportunity.

The Importance of Boredom

We don't just fill time for ourselves; we fill it for our children too. We sign them up for endless after-school activities to stretch their minds and bodies. We race them from class to class, sure that the resulting pressure the endless shuttling of children is making on you and them is worth it for their future wealth and health. Are we right in that assumption? Yuko Munakata, a professor in the psychology and neuroscience department at the University of Colorado, was interested in the effect of unstructured time on children. She found that children who had more unstructured time, less time in formal after-school activities, had stronger executive functioning:[9] that means they thought and focused better.

I now have a saying with my children when they turn to me and say, "I'm bored." I reply, "Your boredom is the greatest gift I could give you." It's wonderful to give our children opportunities to learn and develop, but they also need time without adults structuring their time or activity. They need time when they have to use their imagination to turn a stick into a lightsaber, or a milk carton into a mold for mud bricks. Boredom is valuable; don't deprive your children of it!

Deep Into Your Three Seconds

When René Descartes provided the inspiration for the Keanu Reeves blockbuster *The Matrix*, back in 1637, he was clear about one thing: the only thing we can be absolutely certain of is our mental experience. (*"Cogito ergo sum"*—"I think, therefore I am.") The world we experience could be real, a dream or the "Matrix," but our thoughts regarding it are certainly real. Whether or not you're a fan of René (or Keanu), Descartes captures something important: our experience, our attention, is all we have.

If our moment-to-moment experience, our attention, is all we can be certain of, how long does it last? How long is the "present" tense? From a psychological perspective, the present lasts about three seconds. Outside of those three seconds, we think of experiences as the past or the future; we are not directly experiencing them as now. You could argue that the whole of your life is one long three-second bubble; it's all we really have. All of our attention is found in those three seconds, so it is important we maximize them. Flow isn't the only way of enhancing your present tense. This section will look at other ways to dive more deeply into the moment, to live and experience your three seconds more deeply.

The Joy of Full Attention

Real joy requires full, undiluted attention, and that's something we're not in the habit of doing: we don't practice being totally present. When we "have a moment," we fill it with the help of our smartphone. We top up experiences with more stimulation; we multitask for pleasure as well as for productivity. We surf the Internet or look at Facebook while speaking on the phone. We tweet while watching TV. We email while playing with the kids. In losing our ability to go deep into the moment, our moments are no longer enough for us in themselves without artificial additives. Unless we regain the ability to notice, to savor, we will be sucked ever more into unrewarding and unsustainable busyness.

Stop for a moment and recall your best moments over the last few weeks. Without exception these will be times when you shone the flashlight of your attention fully onto something, when you dived into the moment and were fully present. Improving your happiness and well-being doesn't have to be complicated, but it does require us to recognize that attention-splicing undermines our focus, weakens our ability to fully experience joy, and squanders our three seconds.

Savor the Moment

How good are you at savoring the moment? How good are you at lingering appreciatively in an experience, at plunging your full attention into the moment, the sensation or the thought? A life of high-octane busyness can diminish our ability to stop and notice, to *feel* rather than *do*. Through busyness we vacate our three seconds, leaving behind only the husks of split, stretched and partial attention.

Fred B. Bryant and Joseph Veroff from Loyola University are the founders of the savoring movement.[10] Through their testing of thousands of undergraduates, they have found techniques that promote savoring. Since our frantic lives diminish our ability to be present and savor, consider these three exercises in bringing you back into the present.

1. **Happy Attacks**

Barry Horner, my father-in-law, is an artist and an inspirational figure. He has developed a fantastic little habit that I, and many around him, have copied. At seemingly random moments—during dinner, a conversation, or an activity—he will call out, "I'm having a happy attack!" He does this when he notices he is really enjoying that moment. This works on three levels: It helps him to amplify and savor great moments as they happen (how often do we realize times were great only after the moment has passed?); it is generous, inviting others to relish the moment; and it is sticky—such a simple behavior easily becomes a habit. Speaking personally, my wife and I have taken this habit on board so fully that when we bought a little dinghy, we called it *Happy Tac!* (Apologies for the bad pun, but the name still makes us smile.)

Inadvertently, Barry hit upon his own version of what Bryant and Veroff would call "sharing with others." (I prefer "happy attack.") The single biggest predictor of pleasure is the ability to tell others about your joy in the moment.

Start noticing and calling out your happy attacks!

2. **Sharpening Perceptions**

This is the deliberate attempt to focus on certain elements of your present experience and the blocking out of others. This may involve paying particular attention to the drumming in a favorite rock track, noticing all the different colors and hues of green in a forest view or trying to discern the song of a specific bird.

On a personal level, this happened for me by accident. My work involves a lot of travel around the world—often to amazing cities. I was struck by how unmoved I was by some of the sights I saw in incredible cities like Istanbul, Hyderabad or Lima. I would often, out of boredom and tiredness, drift back to my hotel room and work. I realized why this was: without Dulcie, my wife and best friend, I wasn't able to savor the moment to the same degree. I had no one with whom to share the experience, no one to call out my happy attacks to. By chance, Barry had started a photography club at the same time. I had no history of artistic ability or even visual fluency; all my photos up to that point were the worst kind of holiday snaps. However, for the fun of it, Dulcie and I decided to join. What I hadn't expected was that this simple act transformed my travel. I now had a mission when I was out and about in strange and exotic cities. I wasn't simply seeing the sights; I was looking for great photographs. As my camera lens focused and zoomed, so did my attention. I drank in the sights, hungry for more. I initiated conversations with locals (whose photo I wanted to take) whom I would otherwise have passed by, oblivious. I learned to truly savor the travel and the cities; I was excited and energized by what I experienced. I stopped drifting back to the hotel room.

Consider a potentially pleasurable activity that you have lined up today, at work or outside. How could you direct your attention onto a specific aspect of that experience to help you savor it more deeply?

3. **Absorption**
   "Shut up!" This technique for savoring is the deliberate quieting of the internal dialogue in your head. We

now appreciate that not thinking is a deliberate act: the natural state of the brain is to bounce and jump between thoughts, images and memories. Collectively, these inner distractions take you elsewhere intellectually. Absorption is the attempt to stop thinking and immerse ourselves totally in the senses. An example might be the experience of sinking into a deep bath, taking the time to notice the touch of the hot water on your skin, feeling the bubbles and the ripples and sinking into the gentle embrace as the warmth seeps through to your core. Or it might be intensely focusing on the taste of a fine meal, straining every aspect of your attention to wallow in the unfolding flavors. Both of these experiences stand in stark contrast to jumping into a bath and reaching reflexively for a celebrity magazine, or simply chewing and swallowing your meal, barely noticing the flavor and the texture.

What sensory experience could you wallow in and, by sinking all your attention into your feelings, use to quiet your overactive brain (at least for a few minutes)?

Less Is More

I went on a couple of stag weekends a few years ago. On one of them we flew to a foreign city for a fun-packed, activity-filled two days. We saw the sights, did the clubs and even went on a trip to another famous resort an hour away. It was beautifully planned and executed. A few months later I went on another stag weekend in which the same number of people went into the mountains to stay in a hut, with an ample supply of food and beer. We simply hung out together and did a little walking. The question is, which one was better? Unreservedly, the second weekend was better: we had more time to simply be together. All the activity of the first weekend got in the way of our enjoying time together.

We were acquiring stories to tell on our return, rather than focusing on the present. The fact is, nearly every (positive) thing we do is better if we give it a bit more time, a bit more attention.

On the first stag weekend, we were so busy planning the next activity, or getting there, there wasn't much time left to have a good time. We scattered and stretched our attention between too many things rather than allowing it to sink deeply into the conversations and the location. We were so busy *doing*, we didn't give ourselves the chance to just *be*.

Sometimes deeper enjoyment starts with something as simple as deliberately doing less.

- How could you do less to enjoy the experience more?
- How could having fewer interests or hobbies improve your life by allowing you to focus on fewer, better?

Deep Inside

So far I have positioned the fragmented, distracted and shallow attention of busy at one end of the spectrum, and placed deep engagement and focused attention at the other. I have suggested that while busy is a buzz, it is not the route to happiness. To find joy we need to sink deep into our experiences and our moments. However, this is not a full picture. In actual fact, there is another place that is equally important for our happiness, one that is under threat every bit as much in today's world as deep attention. That place is inside ourselves, alone with our thoughts, with nothing to do.

Alone with Your Thoughts

How much do you like being alone with yourself? If you are like most of us, the answer is "not very much." In fact, in an amazing series of experiments led by the influential professor of psychology Timothy D. Wilson, it was shown that many people prefer to give themselves electric shocks rather than be left alone and unstimulated![11] These people, earlier in the day, had received this same electric shock and been willing to pay in order to never receive it again. Yet, when faced with a period of between six and fifteen minutes without external stimulation, the electric shock was preferable to their own thoughts.

You may be thinking that the above study is crazy (despite the fact it was published in *Science*), but Wilson's findings are in line with other studies. For example, Christopher K. Hsee of the Booth School of Business found that, given the slightest excuse, people would jump at the chance to do meaningless activity rather than spend time inactive.[12] He also found, as did Wilson, that people are happier when they are meaninglessly busy than when they are idle.

The Default Network

One of the most significant findings from neuroscience in recent years is the discovery of the default network.[13] This is the network of neural activity that fires up when we are not externally stimulated with information or activity. It is what happens when we are in the doctor's waiting room with no magazines, when we are in the shower or walking to the train station, when we sink into ourselves, when we are alone with our thoughts, dreams and ruminations. We had expected a lot to be going on in the brain when we are busy, or when we are focused. We hadn't expected a lot to be happening when we were neither of these; we were wrong. When we are not on task, the brain becomes extremely active. The question we have to ask is, "Why?"

What is happening here is that the default network is *creating you*! If you look inside yourself and ask, "Who am I?"

your sense of "I" comes from a collection of experiences, roles, beliefs, ideas, cultural associations and feelings. Somehow, from that tapestry of disconnected thoughts and memories comes a sense of identity. When we are on task, we generate input and stimulation for the brain. This information is raw and external. It is only when we play with this input, associating it with our own experiences, that it begins to have meaning. It is only when we integrate it into our understanding of the world that we learn and develop. It is that process that turns raw, external data into something more personal; into *your* opinion, *your* insight and your *wisdom*.

The Importance of Idleness

This brings us right back to busyness: How much time do you have to quietly process, reflect and integrate? We have talked about the impact of all the demands we experience in the world of too much: our racing, multitasking and cramming drive out focused attention and engagement. However, our world of too much stimulation may be having an equally big impact. We now have stimulation devices with us all the time, ready for any moment when we are not on task. At home, we have multiple additional devices to ensure our brains are never left on their own.

Focused attention and engagement are the foods we need to provide the energy and the nourishment to survive and thrive. Stimulation and consumption of media is like bubble gum; it keeps us occupied, but offers little. The default network is like the digestive system: absolutely essential to allow that food to be integrated, to allow you to grow. I don't think we're doing enough digesting these days.

Resolving Our Emptiness

I explained in the busyness triangle that a consequence of too much busyness is an increasing sense of emptiness in our lives;

which we fill with activity. I have suggested that focusing on
values rather than "More" drives less frenetic busyness. I have
also suggested deep engagement and flow generate more happiness than the buzz of busy. Both of these strategies will help
to reduce the inner sense of emptiness. Now I want to talk
about another strategy for happiness: getting comfortable with
your emptiness.

What do I mean by emptiness? The notion of an emptiness
in people has been explored by many in recent history, including Friedrich Nietzsche, Jean-Paul Sartre and Mark Rothko. In
my view, we all contain a space inside us of utter emptiness;
and it's not a happy place. It originates from our unmet needs,
unsolved problems and thwarted desires. This emptiness
affects all of us in some way: it's the source of our doubt, fear
or yearning and it's the darkness from which our ruminations
emanate.

Back in the 1950s, Martin Heidegger predicted that we might
become so dazzled and bewitched by technology that our only
way of thinking might be calculative thinking; this would come
at a loss of meditative thinking, the essence of our humanity.[14]
When we meditate, we reflect on our being, our truths, and
the meaning of our lives. We make sense of everything about
ourselves, good and bad, and develop authenticity. A lack of
meditative thinking leaves our emptiness untended, raw and
dark. If many of us, as Hsee suggests, have developed an aversion to idleness, our stimulation devices are helping us avoid
doing the critical psychological work we need to do to become
whole. If we fail to spend time inside ourselves, facing our
demons as well as our dreams, we can't resolve our problems,
find meaning from our troubles, and make sense of the future
we want. If we fail to spend time with our thoughts and worries, we can't learn from them and grow stronger. If we fail to
spend time inside ourselves, we can't become ourselves, in all
our possibilities and potential.

The Happiness Paradox

My wife sprained her ankle badly. Her foot swelled painfully, making her want to rest it all the time. Her doctor, on the other hand, had different ideas. He told her to walk with a normal step, rotating through the full movement, each stride. It was excruciating. At any given point, she would have been much happier resting that foot. Yet, the only way to improve was to walk through the pain, and so step by painful step, she walked and she healed.

It is true, as Wilson and Hsee found, that we are happier when active (even if the activity is meaningless). However, this misses the point. It is only by walking through our thoughts—and all the worries, problems and emptiness—that we build up our internal resources to face future troubles. If we don't do this, we cannot stem the creeping cloud of hollowness. In many, that might mean we yearn for more external validation through money, image or popularity, which drives us to more busyness. In others it may simply mean that we try to drown out the wails of our existential angst through mindless, frenetic activity. Either way, unresolved emptiness drives us, unsatisfyingly, into the skeletal arms of busyness.

Earning Happiness

Happiness is something earned. It is only through focused effort and stretching ourselves, for example, that we experience flow. The same applies when we are not active. Happiness in your thoughts—alone and unstimulated—takes time and the willingness to do the work. We have to earn it through periods of idleness and meditation. In my view, both active and passive happiness are critical. We will not lead completely happy lives unless we can be completely engaged in our activity; and quietly content in our idleness.

Getting Practical

Going inside and working through what's there is a little messy. It takes time, and there is no universal solution. Having said that, in the practical spirit of the book, here are a few pointers.

Dead Time

A recent American Time Use Survey, by the Bureau of Labor Statistics, found that that 83 percent of people in the US spend no time at all "relaxing or thinking."[15] Caught between production and consumption, we manage to keep ourselves almost totally occupied. In doing this, we are the first generation who are living without downtime; no previous generation has had so little time alone with their thoughts. Our fabulous devices are allowing us to hyperstimulate ourselves away from happiness and fulfillment.

What are the best times in your day to create "dead time"? For me it is travel time: I fly a lot. I used to be intent on making that time useful, or at least interesting. Between podcasts of recorded lectures, my Kindle, and the odd book, I would make sure every second of my travel time, including driving to the airport and going through security, were learning filled. What I became aware of, is in learning and learning and learning, I had no time and space to stand back, to integrate and to make the research and ideas I was reading and hearing into my own. I have started creating dead time on these trips: time without input or stimulation, time for intellectual ambling. All the best ideas for this book came from those times.

Notice the Chimp

One of the things I like most about Steve Peters's concept of the Chimp (mentioned in Chapter 8), is that it somehow externalizes emotions. It helps people see emotions and thought separately, to see irrational worries and fears as belonging to the Chimp, and as being normal. This allows the Human to observe them, reflect and learn. One of the core concepts of mindfulness is the ability to be alert and notice what's passing through your mind, but to stay detached from it, at a distance, not judging or getting wrapped up in it. It seems to me that noticing the grip of fear or anxiety, it is easier to say to yourself, "There goes the Chimp again," and in so doing retain a separateness from those emotions. In Latin-based languages for example, people would say, "I *have* fear," (*tengo miedo* in Spanish), which seems a much more helpful description than "I *am* scared."

Personal Pronoun Proofing

How do you talk to yourself? Ethan Kross, assistant professor of psychology at the University of Michigan, was curious when he ran a red light and caught himself saying, "Ethan, you idiot!" He wondered what effect speaking to himself (in his head) in the third person would have versus using "I." He asked people to give a presentation with only five minutes to prepare. Some of those people he asked to talk to themselves using "I." Others he asked to use their own names. He found that those who talked to themselves using "I" had an internal monologue full of emotion: "I can't do this. I'll look stupid. I'll forget my words. I wish I'd worn my other pants!" On the other hand, those that talked to themselves in the third person tended to be more rational and supportive: "Tony, you'll be okay. You've done loads of presentations before." Using this subtle change in inner language helped people to get more emotional distance.[16]

When your time alone with your thoughts turns sour, catch yourself using "I" statements. Don't force yourself to make ridiculously overpositive affirmations, just start talking in the third person. Your voices will naturally step away from the emotion and start supporting you through your challenge.

The Big Messages in "From Buzz to Joy"

This chapter explains how the path to joy is not in the buzz of activity and stimulation, but in diving deep into experiences and moments, or deeply into ourselves.

Buzz and Happiness

- **Busyness is a buzz**, getting all the chemicals flowing: adrenaline, dopamine and opiates. It can be fun in small doses, but it can also, too easily, take over our lives.

Going Deep

- **Flow moments are states of optimal experience** in which we are deeply engaged with what we're doing, losing all sense of ourselves and of time.
- Flow experiences motivate us to follow **the path of engagement**; we naturally go deeper into activities that are uniquely aligned to our strengths and values, and we **naturally become more differentiated**.
- **Flow is the antidote** to a life of distraction, to the addiction of buzz.
- **Create flow** by challenging yourself, setting goals, concentrating on experiences and getting feedback.

Deep into Your Three Seconds

- From a psychological perspective, **the present moment lasts three seconds**. All we ever experience is held in those three-second bubbles. To replace buzz with depth, we need to be more engaged within our three seconds.
- **Time management** tends to drive us toward slicing time and splitting attention, and away from engagement. **Focus on managing attention instead**.

- **Savor moments** more fully by noticing **"happy attacks,"
  sharpening your perceptions** and increasing your capability
  to **get absorbed** in the moment.

Deep Inside

- We have a dread of idleness, because it forces us to come
  face-to-face with our emptiness. In fact, many of us would
  rather electrocute ourselves than be alone with our thoughts!
- When we are idle, the amount of blood to our brain increases,
  because the default network is doing important work.
- The default network integrates what we've experienced; it is
  essential for learning, growth and resolving the problems and
  pain of our emptiness.
- The happiness paradox: we are happier when we are active, but
  we won't be truly happy and fulfilled unless we are idle.

Go-Do

Increase Your Joy

Identify when you experience flow in your typical week and increase the amount of time you spend doing the most flow-inducing activities.

Trigger Flow

Identify one important activity or piece of work you are currently spending a lot of time on. Increase the intellectual or physical challenge by making the task harder (drying three plates at once) or by setting yourself a tough goal. By doing this you are likely to concentrate harder and experience more flow.

Dead Time

Make sure you waste some time—every day. In that time, be alone; just you and your thoughts.

Experiment

Do Less

Try, for the next week, to do fewer things, both at work and in your personal life. This doesn't mean you work or play less hard, it's just the overall number of things you are doing is lower, so you spend longer on each activity.

Happy Attacks

When you are in a moment of true joy, don't let it pass unnoticed. Give it your full attention by calling out that you're having a happy attack.

Personal Pronoun Proofing

Catch the voices in your head using "I." You'll find your time alone with your thoughts is more constructive and less emotive if you create distance by changing your inner monologue to "you."

Chapter 12

Beyond Busy
(Making Good Intentions Stick)

On a bitterly cold morning in 1916, Floyd and Glenn Cunningham arrived at their schoolhouse in rural Kansas. There was no one at school yet so, like most days, the two boys went to the stove, soaked the wood in kerosene (so it caught more easily) and lit the fire. Unfortunately, by mistake, someone had put gasoline in the can rather than kerosene. The resulting explosion and fire killed thirteen-year-old Floyd. His younger brother, Glenn, woke up in the hospital a few days later, screaming in pain; his lower body had been ravaged by flames. At first the doctors believed he would die. He survived, but needed to have his legs amputated: his skin had been burned away, he had lost all his toes on his left foot and his right leg was so deformed by the fire it had become two inches shorter. Glenn, however, had other ideas. He screamed so loud and so persistently, they decided to let him try to cope with his tattered legs.[1]

Bringing life back into his legs would not be easy. He needed horrific stretching exercises and massages, which, in his words, "hurt like hell." Most young children would have given up, but he was determined to walk again. When his father grew tired from administering the painful stretches and massages, he asked his mother to take over, then when she tired, he continued himself.

In 1919, his mother wheeled him outside only to return and find him on his knees. She rushed to help, assuming a problem, but was brushed aside as he crawled to the picket fence. Stake by stake he clambered along the wall, willing his legs to move. Over the coming months, he worked so hard along that fence that he wore a path in the grass.

After many months of this self-inflicted ordeal, to the astonishment of everyone, Glenn took his first unaided steps in years. He recalls how painful it was. Bizarrely, he found it hurt less if he did a kind of hopping, running step than if he walked. So that's what he did. For the next six years pretty much every step he took was running.

Six years after the accident, not only was he running, he was outrunning everyone in the town (even though it was still uncomfortable to walk). True to form though, Glenn didn't stop there; he continued pushing himself. Over the following years he became one of the greatest middle-distance American runners of all time, setting the world record for the mile, 800-meter, and the indoor mile.

Glenn Cunningham achieved amazing things because he persisted. He knew what he wanted and he kept pushing for it. It was hard; his injuries bothered him for a decade, but he willed his body back onto its feet. He willed himself to become the best. I like this story because teaching himself to walk again wasn't a one-off challenge he faced. It was a long-term struggle. I can only imagine how many days he woke up not in the mood for the difficulties facing him that day. At so many points in his journey he could have settled for something less than he dreamed of. At many points those around him believed he should accept his lot. Yet he pushed on.

The challenge with busy is not a one off-change either; it's a long-term struggle. It takes work, persistence and, at times, defying those around you. To walk, or run your own path, to move beyond busy is most certainly not the easy route. You could settle for less, you could accept busy; I just encourage you not to.

Most Change Attempts Fail

The truth is that, each and every day, we mess our lives up a little bit by not making the changes we know will make a difference to us, our businesses and our loved ones. We have good intentions, but, somehow, we fail to follow through on them. Think about your own life for a second: How many times have you "decided" to do something different? How many New Year's Resolutions have you broken? Kerry Patterson claims that 98 percent of us fail to break bad habits despite wanting to, and 95 percent of our attempts to diet are unsuccessful.[2] What I find curious is not that we don't follow through on our intentions, it's that we don't *learn*. We still seem to believe that if we know something, and decide something, and are sufficiently motivated, we will change.

We are wrong.

It is certainly possible to modify behavior; it just takes more than good intentions. Fortunately, we now know a lot about how people respond to change. This chapter is devoted to one thing and one thing only: helping you to be happier by doing what you want to do. You may have enjoyed this book; it may even have inspired you to make changes and move beyond busy. All that means little, unless you actually change something as a result.

So the question is…

What Are You Going to Change?

I suggest you focus on changing only one thing. This isn't just because of the challenges of making changes and because you are so busy. It's because of the value of *keystone habits*. In researching his book *The Power of Habit*, journalist Charles Duhigg came across Lisa Allen, a women who had gone from obese to fit and toned, had stopped smoking and drinking, escaped from chronic debts and transformed her career. It all started when she gave up smoking. She changed that one behavior, and in doing so, understood how to change other habits in her life. All the examples of significant change he came across had all started with a single habit; this habit became the keystone to transforming their lives.[3]

If you want to transform your busyness, focus totally on one habit you want to change. Once you succeed in establishing a single habit you will find it much easier to change others.

So, **STOP!** Pause your reading.

Get out of the role of the person being stimulated with ideas—and into a more active state, of someone who will make things happen. Get a pen and paper and spend a few minutes reflecting on what you really want to change. Is your priority to regain a sense of mastery over your life again? Do you want to differentiate yourself at work? Or do you want to engage in your work, your relationships and your life?

Whatever you want to focus on, you will find this chapter infinitely more useful if you read it with a clear idea of the specific habit you want to change.

Seven Strategies

Making personal change is a subject that I'm passionate about. However, I won't even try to do it full justice here. What I will

do is suggest seven specific strategies that have been shown
to help people make personal change, and that I have found
useful. The central point behind all these strategies is that our
intentions need some help if we want them to deliver a lasting change in our behavior or habits. All of these strategies
are simple, and none of them replace the need for motivation.
They act like Glenn Cunningham's picket fence. They will support your efforts; they will help you convert your intentions
into action.

Make Your Goals Clear

One way to avoid the inertia that follows good intentions is to
make your goals for change as clear as possible. The benefits
of doing this were demonstrated by Steve Booth-Butterfield
and Bill Reger, professors at West Virginia University, when
they were thinking of an effective way to persuade people to
eat more healthily. They looked at how they might simplify the
message. They identified that if the average American switched
from whole milk to 1 percent milk, their diet would immediately attain the USDA recommended levels for saturated fats.
So they focused on creating a single, specific behavioral shift
in a specific context: they told people that when they were in
the grocery store, they should buy 1 percent milk rather than
whole milk. The clarity of this message worked like magic:
market share for 1 percent milk doubled and, as a result, people dramatically changed their saturated fat consumption.[4]

The principle of clarity works on ourselves too. Saying we
want to have more impact at work is like saying we want to
eat more healthily. It's a broad and relatively ill-defined goal. To
move forward you have to get to the clarity of 1 percent milk.
What is the specific behavior that you feel, if adopted regularly, will drive this change? What is the context in which that
behavior will happen? Is it switching off your email notifier all

morning at work, is it persistently practicing Plan B thinking on all projects, or is it "thin-slicing" the big stuff at work first thing each day? Getting clear about the specific behavior, and the context required, to achieve your goal makes it a lot more likely you'll be successful.

Keep It Really Small

Sometimes it can help, to start with at least, to not set your sights too high. Robert Cialdini, the leading expert in the psychology of influence, had his researchers go door to door to collect money for the American Cancer Society. One group of researchers asked, "Would you be willing to help by making a donation?" The other researchers asked the same question, but followed their request with "Even a penny will help." Of those asked by the first group of researchers, 29 percent donated money. Of the latter group, 50 percent donated. The extra "Even a penny..." almost doubled the likelihood of donating, but made no change to the average size of the donation as compared to those who donated without the "Even a penny..." addition. It simply increased the likelihood of triggering action.[5]

To build momentum, start very small.

Plan Your Next Step

In a classic example of the importance of clarifying the next step is Howard Leventhal's seminal study into the power of fear to mobilize action. Leventhal and his colleagues wanted to persuade more students to get vaccinated for tetanus. They showed graphic pictures and lectured students on the consequences of tetanus and how easily it could be contracted. Their efforts had a powerful effect on the beliefs of the students: most were totally sold on the danger of tetanus and the value of getting a vaccination, but only 3 percent actually got that vaccination.

In a follow-up, Leventhal added something to the persuasion tactics: he included a simple map of the campus, with the health clinic and its opening hours highlighted, and the recommendation that they make an appointment.[6] The lectures and pictures were the same. However, the addition of this simple map, explaining the next step, increased the number of students getting vaccinated by more than nine times, to 28 percent. This was despite the fact that all the students knew very well where the clinic was!

The fact is that, especially when we're busy, if we have to do more than one thing at a time, we can get distracted away from our intention. In this case, those without the map had to decide if they wanted to go, and what to do next. Those with the map had only to decide if they wanted the vaccination; the next step was super clear. David Allen suggests that a goal isn't enough for any project, or, in this case, change intention: what we need to do is identify the very next step. Mostly these next steps will be incredibly small and easy, but cumulatively they can add up to a huge change.

Use Social Influence

At Newcastle University, employees were expected to pay for their drinks, and so an honesty box was left with recommended prices listed. For ten weeks, researchers placed images above the prices, giving no explanation. Every week the image changed. The images were either of eyes, which appeared to be looking at the person making their drink, or of flowers. No one commented on the images; no one asked about their significance. When the money in the honesty box was counted at the end of each week, the difference was dramatic. In the weeks when flowers were shown, the average contribution made per liter of milk was 15 pence. In the weeks that the eyes were displayed, that figure more than quadrupled to 70 pence.[7]

Many studies have shown that we are more likely to act in a desirable manner when we are being watched, and we can harness this fact to help us make changes. I unwittingly walked into this type of support myself. My sister-in-law Shiv and I had both been talking about writing, and "working" on our books for ages. At a certain point I started challenging Shiv's excuses for a lack of progress. I thought she was letting herself off too lightly for not progressing with something that was important. Anyway, she finished soon afterward, and made a reciprocal offer to me: to hold me to account for my own writing progress. She asked me to draw up a timetable for chapter completion and if I slipped from my schedule, which I did often, she came down on me like a ton of bricks. I can't pretend I wasn't irked by some of her chasing, even though I knew it was what we agreed and that she was going out of her way to help me. However, there is no doubt I made a lot more progress as a direct result of trying not to let Shiv down, trying to deliver on my commitments. Shiv, thanks for nagging; it made all of the difference. (And I look forward to getting my own back when you start your next book!)

Slipstream Habits

If you've ever cycled long distances with a group of people, you'll realize the massive benefit of tucking into the slipstream of the cyclist in front. We can apply the same principle to establishing new habits. It's much, much easier to build a healthy new habit on the back of an old one. In doing this, the new behavior seems to get swept along more easily by the automatic motion of the established habit.

This is one of the reasons I think Brian Tracy's simple idea of "Eat that frog"—which I discussed in Chapter 8—works so

powerfully. In eating frogs, we build on the established rituals that we perform at the start of our day—often some of the
strongest in a working day. The early morning rituals have
more than strength; they are pure, unbattered by the flak of
daily office life. It is much easier to retain choice before for-
mally opening up the inbox. So, if you make it part of your
morning ritual that—along with unpacking your laptop, grab-
bing a coffee and chatting with Maria—you will spend thirty
minutes on big stuff, you can benefit from the morning routine's slipstream.

The slipstream effect works for most new behaviors. If you
want to have better conversations with your son, why not
build a post–football match routine, or a pre-bedtime chat? If
you want to create more time for your default network to be
active, don't just think, "I'll create more task-free, stimulation-
free time"; rather decide, for example, to do your commute
device-free.

Think of the behavior you want to change; which of your current habits or routines could you slipstream?

Reward Good Behavior

Another way to help you move beyond busy is to use simple
behaviorism: our choices are significantly influenced by the
rewards we get immediately. When it comes to busyness, even
though our long-term rewards are a life of focus and engagement, the immediate rewards of this goal may seem less compelling than the relief of an empty inbox. One client dealt with
this head-on. He wanted to bring real focus to a project he was
passionate about—one he thought could make a big impact on
the business—but which no one was shouting for. Persistently
he would get lured into reactivity. He decided to fight fire with
fire. Around the corner from his office was his favorite coffee

shop, which had a lovely vibe and served a vanilla latte he loved. Instead of going straight to the office, he "treated" himself to forty-five minutes every morning in this coffee shop on the condition that he was working on his project. He also never signed up for their Wi-Fi, so he was "dark" during his time in the coffee shop. After a while he didn't stick to doing this first thing every day; he went there at other points in the day, but he always saw it as his project place—a place which rewarded him into change.

"What the Hell!"

Participants in a study were asked to turn up to a laboratory hungry. On arrival, some people were given nothing; others were given two very large milkshakes, enough to make a person feel very full. They were then taken to the experiment, which they were told was a taste test. They were put in private rooms in front of big plates of cookies and crackers, and asked to rate the flavors. Those who were still hungry ate quite a lot; those who had been filled with the milkshakes nibbled a bit, assessed the taste and left. This is what everyone did— apart from those on diets. They did the opposite! Those who had drunk the giant milkshakes actually ate *more* cookies and crackers than those who hadn't eaten for many hours![8]

Why? This pattern showed up in repeated experiments, and Peter Herman and his colleagues eventually called it "counter-regulatory eating." I, however, prefer Roy Baumeister's term— the "what the hell" effect. The dieters, once they'd already blown their diet for the day with the massive milkshakes, lost any willpower. They thought, "What the hell; I've ruined the diet today, so I may as well have fun and start again tomorrow." The risk is that, tomorrow, the "what the hell" feeling may be extended a little longer, and a little longer...and then the diet is over.

"What the hell" is a dangerous moment for any change effort. Any change involves resisting some form of temptation. We will almost always slip at times, or be "forced" to act counter to our change plans, like the dieters who were asked to drink the milkshakes. There will always be that urgent call that derails your best intentions, or the project crisis that has you jabbing away at your keyboard through the night. The issue that will determine your long-term success is not whether or not you were 100 percent true to your change plan, but how quickly and persistently you got back onto the horse after you fell off.

So, don't just choose the change you want to make; come up with a plan for how you will get back on the horse immediately after you fall off.

Imagine you are committed to switching your smartphone off at night, so you can be more present with your family. Accept, right from the start, that you may not be able to follow through on this every night, and prevent the odd slip from killing your momentum by any, or all of the following:

- Every time you do use your phone, send yourself an email, which reminds you to recommit to your goal, to read in the cold light of the morning.
- Ask your partner to challenge you when they see you using your phone at night. In particular, their job is to ask you this question: "Okay, so you are letting your goal slip tonight. Will you restart your commitment to phone-free nights tomorrow?"
- Give yourself phone "jokers." The idea is to acknowledge in advance that, a few evenings a month, you will want to use the phone. For each of those nights you can play the "joker" as your permit for a phone night. This tactic builds exceptions into your change effort: the odd night doesn't break momentum—it's part of the pattern.

Deep Change

There are times when, despite our best efforts, certain aspects of our behavior stubbornly resist change. I think a lot of us, when it comes to the way we live our lives, might be there right now: we've tried loads of tips and techniques, but remain hopelessly distracted, stretched and disconnected. If you recognize this situation, if the techniques and the reminders aren't working but you remain keen to change, you will have to go deeper. To succeed, it will not be enough to *make* a change; *you* will have to change.

Technical and Adaptive Problems

There are two fundamentally different kinds of problems we might face. Some of those problems require information, practice and skill development. Ronald Heifetz, a leadership expert, calls these types of changes *technical problems.*[9] These are not necessarily simple, or unimportant, but there are recognized ways to address them. Examples of technical problems might range from completing the Rubik's Cube in under a minute to landing a fighter jet on an aircraft carrier. They might be tough, but with enough learning and practice, you could succeed.

Adaptive problems are a different matter. A problem is considered adaptive if there isn't a correct way to solve it or a proven solution; there isn't an instruction manual. A problem is adaptive if the only way to resolve it is through changing the person with the problem: their mind-set, beliefs and assumptions. Time and again, I see people endlessly seeking "the solution" to problems they have had for years. They misdiagnose their problem as being a technical one, seek technical solutions, come up with a plan, and fail—repeatedly. They don't need to solve the *problem*; they need to change *themselves* in order to progress. A classic example of this is losing weight.

On one level it appears to be a straightforward technical problem: just eat less food and exercise more. However, anyone who has persistently grappled with this problem knows the repeated cycle of excitement and despair as they go from diet to diet. The technical solutions seldom work sustainably. What is normally needed is a more adaptive response: a fundamental change to their relationships with food and exercise.

If you think your change is an adaptive challenge (and there is a very good chance it will be) the following section is for you.

Competing Commitments

There are often very good reasons why we do things as we do today—very compelling reasons for us not to make the change. These reasons don't disappear when we decide we want to make a change. Robert Kegan would call these our *competing commitments*. So when we try to make a change, those commitments actively fight against the thing we want to do.[10] Even though the change we want to make will meet certain desires or needs we have, our competing commitments are also servicing needs—often quite deep needs; they will not give up the fight easily. Unless we unearth these competing commitments, we will be fighting blind and, more often than not, our attempts to change will stall.

To bring this to life, I'll share something of my own experience. Ever since I left university, I talked about writing a book. At various points I have played with getting started, but never made much progress. All this time, I would happily tell people, "I'm going to write a book." Finally I started researching in earnest about six years ago, but failed to put pen to paper for about four years. During this time I promoted my story to "I'm working on a book."

Naturally, when people met up with me they would often ask how my "book" was coming on. It started to get a little embarrassing! However, I had a story. I explained how I was very "busy" (yes, I did use *that* word) and I was traveling a lot. So it was simple: if I was to start writing a book, the time to work on the book would come directly out of precious family time. People accepted this; I believed it too. Until one day I decided to take my own medicine: I decided to really think about why I wasn't making any progress on something I'd been talking about for years. I started working through the competing commitments exercise I'll describe shortly, and quickly realized that my "story" was an excuse, not a reason. The real reason was fear. I had a big fear, an unspoken fear, which was fighting against any moves I might make to write. I was scared I might have nothing to say. I was fearful that I might not be able to write. I was petrified I might fail, and as a result, lose my identity as a "bright bloke who is going to write a book."

As you might imagine, any of the *technical* solutions I might have tried to help me manage my time better or prioritize would have had little effect. Until I named my fear and grappled with it directly, I would make little progress. The solutions that put me onto the path to writing this book were not technical. I did nothing to clear my calendar, or free up space to write. In fact, the year in which I wrote this book has been one with the highest workload that I have ever experienced (independent of the book). The big solution for me was to start writing—publicly—and actively seek feedback. I started blogging. By blogging I was practicing and experimenting: I was practicing writing and getting feedback to see what worked and what didn't; I was experimenting with the possibility that I might be a terrible writer and have little to say, and that might be okay.

My point in sharing this story is not to pat myself on the back, or make some trite motivational. My point is far more humble. I'm a psychologist; I do this stuff for a living, and I fooled myself for over a decade over why I wasn't writing. I was convincing myself with half-truths and excuses. Yet, once I had finally accepted that I wanted to understand why I wasn't changing, once I was determined to get under the surface, the truth wasn't that hard to unearth—and the truth changed everything.

Unearthing Competing Commitments

The heart of Kegan's process for unearthing commitments is very simple. First you identify, at length, the specific things you are doing, or *not* doing, instead of your stated change commitment. So, for example, if your commitment is to focus more on work that you value, you might identify things like "I say 'yes' to everything," "I have my email on all the time," "I prioritize on the basis of urgency, not importance," etc. Or, in my case, the list would have started, "I am not writing anything." Make a list of these. You don't have to interpret anything at this stage, just identify what else you are doing and not doing.

It's the next stage that gets interesting. Go through each of the negative items and imagine what it would feel like if you did the exact opposite—the thing that you are supposed to be doing. Some of the items will elicit little reaction; others will trigger a pronounced feeling—a "Yuck" effect. When you trigger that worry or discomfort, you're often onto something. Ask yourself, "What is the worry or fear that's causing me to feel this way?" and put a name to it. Then ask, "Therefore, what is the competing commitment I am holding on to that prevents me from making the change I am striving for?"

This process can be powerful. A friend of mine went through this exercise. His commitment was to get "race fit" again so he could start competing in marathons like he used to. For years he had been frustrated by his lack of progress. Sure, he exercised at times, but it was fairly light and patchy, and he was putting on weight. The items he went through on the list, when he thought about doing the opposite, caused no emotional reaction until he reached "Go out for gentle runs, not pushing myself." When he thought about doing the opposite—pushing himself really hard—he felt uncomfortable. Even a day later, when he told me the story, his eyes filled with tears. His deep fear, the fear that was stopping him from training, was a fear of getting old. The realization that had hit him like a sledgehammer was that he was committed to feeling young and vital. Whenever he pushed himself, his body ached and felt old; these times highlighted his physical decline. The very act of doing the thing that would make him feel younger in the long term, made him feel old—and feeling old disgusted him. I am happy to say that he is now running and is also slimmer; he is also competing again.

From my own experience, and from watching others go through this, it is the brutal clarity that this process gives that makes the difference. Once the underlying causes of the lack of progress are laid clear, the path toward your goals can be fairly obvious. It typically involves a process of learning and experimentation, where you play with alternative behaviors. Effectively, you are testing and reframing your catastrophic fears. You are creating different and healthier interpretations of the world. To change you are not simply doing stuff; you are growing and becoming more self-aware.

We all need to do a lot more of this to thrive.

THE BIG MESSAGES IN "BEYOND BUSY"

Change Is Hard. All the research shows that **good intentions are not enough**—nor is being motivated to change.

Seven Strategies

- It's easy to get overwhelmed and lapse into inertia. So start building momentum by getting **really clear** about the behavior you want to change, and the **context** you'll make that change in.

- **Start really small**. Build on the fact that we like to be consistent, and make the next step for yourself obvious.
- Always make sure you are clear about your next step.
- Use social influence. Tell someone who you respect about the change you will make; have them hold you accountable for doing it—no excuses!
- Build new, healthy habits by slipstreaming current, established habits.
- Simple behaviorism says that if we get an immediate reward, we are more likely to continue doing something. How could you reward your good behavior, immediately?
- We will all let our good intentions slip at times. It's easy, at those points, to say, "What the hell!" and let your change effort die. Get back on the horse quickly!

Deep Change
- Problems can be **technical or adaptive**. Technical problems have known solutions that require knowledge, skill and practice. **Adaptive problems** don't have known solutions; they involve **personal change**, learning and growth.
- When people are **struggling to change**, after persistent efforts, it is often because the **problem is adaptive** and they are using technical methods to change.
- To solve an adaptive problem and move forward, we have to unearth our **competing commitments**, the behaviors we currently exhibit that are blocking our change.

What I Have Learned

If learning to thrive is an adaptive challenge, what have I learned? First, I don't pretend to have "busy" cracked. It is a work in progress for me, but I have made big progress through the process of writing this book. I have learned some stuff about myself, and I have learned some stuff about how to respond to a world of too much. Some of those lessons have been hard-won, but they have all been valuable. I don't pretend all these will work for you; it is after all an individual journey we must all make, but I share them in the spirit that a fellow traveler will recommend a restaurant here, or a venue there. It is just my experience; you decide if it's useful to you.

Tough Choices

I have taken on too much this year. I have worked too hard. I am exhausted. I didn't need to organize myself better; I just should have made tougher choices. I have become crystal clear that the next frontier for me to address is my ability to predict how long things will take, and then to decline a lot more opportunities. For a few years, when the global economy was struggling, I had to take on everything I could find. I now

244

realize the legacy of that was more than a little debt; it was a fear that the phone may stop ringing again. This fear has hindered me this year by agreeing to too much. What has been valuable is that this year forced this fear to the surface. I can now name it, and so address it.

Focus

Taking on too much at the same time as writing this book did have one positive effect: it forced me to focus like I have never done before. I've included all the theoretical reasons for this earlier in the book. From a more personal level, I was astonished at how much activity I could either drop altogether, delegate or downscale. I won't pretend it didn't have consequences at times, but the scale of the consequences was dwarfed by what I achieved in their stead.

One example of this is the leadership team sessions I run. These are always bespoke, and so I didn't want to cut back on interviewing folks before the event. However, I used to spend ages designing big proposals, and "preparing" for these sessions (which included designing beautiful slide decks). I have increasingly switched to "big idea" proposals, which are much simpler, much shorter and much quicker to write. Clients seem to prefer them to my old Word documents too! I've killed slide decks too. I go into most of my sessions now without slides. In doing this I have also realized that, by not distracting myself with slideware, by going into events "naked," I force myself to be more present with the group, to add value through what I do in the moment. It has triggered me to become braver in my facilitation.

It's Not About Time

On any scale I could use, this was the worst year of my life to write a book. I had no time. Yet I did it. I paid for it at times, but I did it; and I feel good about that. It has really emphasized to me the order of things. Stephen Covey was right: you choose the big rocks first, the ones you are passionate about, then fit the pebbles in around them. I could never have written this book if I hadn't just made it happen, and then dealt with the consequences. Yes, I should have put fewer pebbles in my jar, but I have no doubt that doing this book was the right thing for me.

Dead Time

In the earlier stages of researching and writing this book, I was hyperstimulating. I wasn't doing trivial stuff a lot of the time, I was learning and writing and working, but I was doing it without pause. I learned to be deliberately unproductive and bored as often as I can, at the times when it is most natural. For example, I no longer take my phone or Kindle to appointments like hairdressers or doctors, I deliberately allow all the wasted time traveling through airports (security, etc.) to stay wasted, and I drive and walk without music (mostly). My wasted time has become precious for me. I don't think I would have written this book without all the dead time.

Big Chunks

The principle that made the most dramatic difference for me in writing this book, and in my other work, was big-chunking my time. I hear many authors talk about needing to write every day for momentum, doing a few hours at a set time. For me, that doesn't work at all. I work and write best in massive, great chunks of time. I learned that a huge percentage of the writing I had done in evenings and on flights, the writing I had done in one-hour lumps, I ended up discarding. I worked best when I could put a whole day aside and entirely engross myself in the full chapter.

While in my other work I don't need such big chunks, I have pushed to increase pretty much all the working chunks I have, and squeeze email, etc., between the gaps. It works brilliantly for me.

Boxing

As a development of the big-chunking idea, I have started doing something I call "boxing," which is working really well for me. It's not rocket science, but I allocate slots of time (and even locations) for only one thing. So this evening, for example, I have allocated my flight to designing an event. In doing this, it has a couple of benefits: I relax, knowing this particular task will be taken care of in that "box," I am primed and ready for the task as I go to the airport so I benefit from the Zeigarnik effect, and I don't have to decide what I'll do when I get there (the decision has been premade in a "cold" state) so I get into it quicker.

Out of Sight, Out of Mind

For me the email and phone thing became very simple; if it was out of sight, it was out of mind. I turned off my Outlook and removed all alerts. I do email in bursts at times when I'm tired through the day. I make sure I can never see the phone at night or the evenings. I still often carry it, and will take calls, but I never charge it, for example, on the kitchen counter…it's just too tempting!

Rituals

I mentioned earlier the "three-cup-of-tea-mornings" ritual my wife and I have. In all the craziness of this year, we have maintained rituals such as that. It has seemed that once it's ritualized, once it has a name, it happens more regularly and more often. Our three cups of tea have been critical for easing us both through this year, together.

Presence Is More Than Time

Given how tight time has been, and how much I have traveled or disappeared into my office, I have worked hard at being present with the children. I realize how much time I am in their vicinity in normal life, but not fully present with them. This year, in contrast, some of the ten-minute moments have been rich and energizing, for both of us, because I have dived wholeheartedly into that experience.

In my guilt, at one point as I was disappearing into the office for yet another weekend, I told my children I would buy them each a big present when the book was finished for being so patient with me. A few days later I realized how wrong that was. What they had missed and what I had missed this year wasn't stuff—it was time, presence and engagement. The following day over breakfast, I announced my new plan. I told the children that, when the book was finished, they would all be having a day off school. Each child will do this on a separate day, so they get undiluted attention. The day was theirs to design, to do whatever they wanted. More importantly, it would be spent with Dulcie and me, totally focused on them. When I announced that they wouldn't be getting a big present, but a "Book Day" instead, they all spontaneously cheered! I couldn't help feeling that my children were more naturally tuned in to the principles of this book than the author! At the time of writing, my daughter wants to go swimming in the morning, for a "fancy" lunch and to the beach for the afternoon. My youngest boy wants to play golf and have a big breakfast in a restaurant; and the eldest is keen to try go-carting and hill walking.

More Me

My last, and biggest, insight builds on the previous. This year has been hard, as I have said, but I have experienced periods of sheer elation, times when I could hardly believe what I was doing and how much joy it gave me. It is the joy of walking my own path. I had the sense, on many occasions, that what I was doing at that moment was absolutely the best thing for me to be doing. At times I was hit with waves of something akin to relief that I was finally writing. More commonly, it just felt *right*.

The consequences of this I have experienced in two ways: I have been buoyed up throughout a torrid year with previously unknown levels of energy and perseverance, because I was tapping into a rich source of motivation for me; I was following my purpose. More than that though, I feel a little more *me* at this point than I did last year. I have grown into myself more; I feel more grounded. More like the person I want to be. I'm a long way from becoming what Carl Jung would call "individuated," but being a bit more like Tony Crabbe feels a good place to start.

With that, I close this book. I'm done with busy. I'm off to join my family for dinner.

Many airlines say "We appreciate you had a choice of airlines." I appreciate you had a choice of where to put your scarce attention. Thank you for sharing it with me and this book. Please get in touch via my website, www.tonycrabbe .com, if you have any questions. But for now, I wish you the very best of success and happiness as you wrestle with the demands and distractions in your life.

Tony

Other Books to Read

I am hugely grateful to the following authors. Their research and thinking has inspired this book. I have used their studies to build my argument, and their examples to tell my story. If you want to explore this topic further, you would be well advised to start with the following books, all of which I highly recommend.

Author	Title	Why you should read it
David Allen	*Getting Things Done*	The best book on personal productivity
Roy Baumeister	*Willpower*	The definitive overview on the topic
Robert Cialdini	*Influence*	World expert on the psychology of influence
Dave Coplin	*The Rise of the Humans*	Turning the threat of digital deluge into an advantage
Mihaly Csikszentmihalyi	*Flow*	The classic on happiness through flow

Author	Title	Why you should read it
Charles Duhigg	*The Power of Habit*	Probably the best explanation of the way habits work and can be changed
Viktor Frankl	*Man's Search for Meaning*	Moving story and powerful insights
Daniel Gilbert	*Stumbling on Happiness*	This made me happy! Great research and humor
Daniel Goleman	*Focus*	Describes the importance and mechanisms of focus
Jonathan Haidt	*The Happiness Hypothesis*	Accessible blend of modern and ancient wisdom
Edward Hallowell	*CrazyBusy*	Description of busy, likening it to ADHD
Tim Harford	*Adapt*	Why we have to fail to succeed—a great read
Chip and Dan Heath	*Decisive*	Great book on how we decide
Chip and Dan Heath	*Switch*	One of the best on how to make changes
Arianna Huffington	*Thrive*	Inspiring read on how to thrive today
Maggie Jackson	*Distracted*	This book really influenced my thinking
Daniel Kahneman	*Thinking, Fast and Slow*	A brilliant overview of System One and Two thinking

Author	Title	Why you should read it
Tim Kasser	*The High Price of Materialism*	Explains the research behind Chapter 9
Robert Kegan and Lisa Laskow Lahey	*Immunity to Change*	A great book: make deep, adaptive change
George Leonard	*Mastery*	Describes the joy of practice
Jim Loehr and Tony Schwartz	*The Power of Full Engagement*	Inspiring book on managing your energy
Steve Peters	*The Chimp Paradox*	A simple concept that helps manage emotions
David Rock	*Your Brain at Work*	Remarkably simple application of neuroscience
Brigid Schulte	*Overwhelmed*	Fantastic, and relevant book on the subject of busy
Barry Schwartz	*The Paradox of Choice*	The subtitle says it all: "Why more is less"
Martin Seligman	*Flourish*	The latest book by the founder of Positive Psychology
Sherry Turkle	*Alone Together*	Insightful: our response to technological immersion
Timothy D. Wilson	*Redirect*	Surprising (and simple to use) findings on change

Notes

Epigraph

1. Oliver Burkeman, *The Antidote: Happiness for People Who Can't Stand Positive Thinking* (Edinburgh: Canongate Books, 2012). Kindle edition.

Preface: *Busting Busy*

1. Oliver Burkeman, *The Antidote: Happiness for People Who Can't Stand Positive Thinking* (Edinburgh: Canongate Books, 2012). Kindle edition.

2. Edward M. Hallowell, M.D. and John J. Ratey, M.D., *Delivered from Distraction: Getting the Most Out of Life with Attention Deficit Disorder* (New York: Ballantine Books, 2006).

3. James Roberts and Stephen Pirog, "150 Times a Day: A Preliminary Investigation of Materialism and Impulsiveness as Predictors of Technological Addictions among Young Adults," *Journal of Behavioral Addictions* 2, no. 1 (2012): 56–62.

4. Ann Burnett, Denise Gorsline, Julie Semlak, and Adam Tyma, "Earning the Badge of Honor: The Social Construction of Time and Pace of Life." Paper presented at the Annual Meeting of the NCA 93rd Annual Convention, TBA, Chicago, IL, November 14, 2007.

5. Tom W. Smith et al., *General Social Surveys, 1972–2010* (machine-readable data file) (Chicago: National Opinion Research Center, 2011), in Brigid Schulte, *Overwhelmed: Work, Love, and Play When No One Has the Time* (New York: Sarah Crichton Books, 2014).

6. B. S. McEwen, "Allostasis and allostatic load: implications for neuropsychopharmacology," *Neuropsychopharmacology* 22 (2000): 108–24.

7. Martin Hilbert and Priscella López, "The World's Technological Capacity to Store, Communicate, and Compute Information," *Science* 332, no. 6025 (April 2011): 60–65.

8. Sarah Radicati, *Email Statistics Report, 2014–2018*. http://www.radicati.com/wp/wp-content/uploads/2014/01/Email-Statistics-Report-2014-2018-Executive-Summary.pdf.

9. Gary P. Hayes, Social media counter, http://www.personalizemedia.com/garys-social-media-count.

10. Simon Quicke, "Nadella sets out mobile and cloud first vision to partners," *MicroScope*, July 17, 2014, http://www.microscope.co.uk/news/2240224715/Nadella-sets-out-mobile-and-cloud-first-vision-to-partners. Satya Nadella, CEO of Microsoft, regularly talked in the media about his view that by 2020, three billion people would have Internet connected devices.

11. Jonathan B. Spira, *Overload! How Too Much Information Is Hazardous to Your Organization* (New Jersey: John Wiley and Sons, 2010).

12. David Foster Wallace, "Deciderization 2007—A Special Report," in *Both Flesh and Not: Essays* (New York: Little, Brown and Company, 2012).

13. Martin Hilbert and Priscella López, "The World's Technological Capacity to Store, Communicate, and Compute Information," *Science* 332, no. 6025 (April 2011): 60–65.

14. Kennon M. Sheldon and Tim Kasser, "Pursuing Personal Goals: Skills Enable Progress, but Not All Progress Is Beneficial," *Personality and Social Psychology Bulletin* 24, 1319–31.

15. Tim Kasser, *The High Price of Materialism* (Cambridge, MA: A Bradford Book, The MIT Press, 2002).

Getting Started: *Too Busy to Read This Book?*

1. E. Langer, A. Blank, and B. Chanowitz, "The Mindlessness of Ostensibly Thoughtful Action: The Role of 'Placebic' Information in Interpersonal Interaction," *Journal of Personality and Social Psychology* 36, no. 6 (1978): 639–42.

2. Glenn Wilson, private study for Hewlett-Packard, carried out at the Institute of Psychiatry, University of London, 2005. This was not published, and involved only eight subjects. It was included here as being interesting and illustrative, rather than robust and solid science.

3. Gloria Mark, Victor Gonzalez, and Justin Harris, "No Task Left Behind? Examining the Nature of Fragmented Work," *Proceedings of the Conference on Human Factors in Computer Systems* (Portland, Oregon, 2005), 321–30.

4. "Multitasking: Switching costs," American Psychological Association, March 20, 2006, http://www.apa.org/research/action/multitask.aspx.

5. Nicholas C. Romano, Jr. and J. F. Nunamaker, Jr., "Meeting Analysis: Findings from Research and Practice," *Proceedings of the 34th Hawaii International Conference on System Sciences* 1 (1), 2001.

6. Roger K. Mosvick and Robert B. Nelson, *We've Got to Start Meeting Like This!: A Guide to Successful Business Meeting Management* (Glenview, IL: Scott, Foresman & Co., 1987).

7. 3M Meeting Management Team and Jeannine Drew, *Mastering Meetings: Discovering the Hidden Potential of Effective Business Meetings* (New York: McGraw-Hill, 1994).

8. Michael Doyle and David Straus, *How to Make Meetings Work!* (Time Warner International, 1996).

9. R. Buehler, D. Griffin, and M. Ross, "Exploring the 'Planning Fallacy': Why People Underestimate Their Task Completion Times," *Journal of Personality and Social Psychology* 67, no. 3 (1994): 366–81.

10. J. R. Kelly and S. J. Karau, "Group Decision Making: The Effects of Initial Preferences and Time Pressure," *Personality and Social Psychology Bulletin* 25 (1999): 1342–54.

11. John Maeda, *The Laws of Simplicity* (Cambridge, MA: MIT Press, 2006).

12. David Allen, *Getting Things Done* (New York: Penguin Books, 2003).

13. Daniel Gilbert, *Stumbling on Happiness* (New York: Knopf, 2006).

14. Ron Gutman, "The Hidden Power of Smiling," (TED talk, March 2011), http://www.ted.com/talks/ron_gutman_the_hidden_power_of_smiling.html.

15. Ernest L. Abel and Michael L. Kruger, "Smile Intensity in Photographs Predicts Longevity," *Psychological Science* 21, no. 4 (2010): 542–44.

Chapter 1: *Stop Managing Your Time! (…and Go Surfing)*

1. Basex Survey, "The Knowledge Worker's Day: Our Findings," 2010, http://www.basexblog.com/2010/11/04/our-findings.

2. W. W. Eaton, J. C. Anthony, W. Mandel, and R. Garrison, "Occupations and the Prevalence of Major Depressive Disorder," *Journal of Occupational and Environmental Medicine* 32 (1990): 1079–87.

3. Martin E. P. Seligman, *Flourish: A Visionary New Understanding of Happiness and Well-being* (London: Nicholas Brealey Publishing, 2011).

4. Michael A. DeDonno and Heath A. Demaree, "Perceived Time Pressure and the Iowa Gambling Task," *Judgment and Decision Making* 3, no. 8 (2008): 636–40.

5. "Laird Hamilton takes on Teahupoo," YouTube video, posted by "b0nedry," May 10, 2008, https://www.youtube.com/watch?v=pYQQtxb8wv0.

6. Brené Brown, *Daring Greatly: How the Courage to Be Vulnerable Transforms the Way We Live, Love, Parent, and Lead* (New York: Gotham Books, 2012).

7. Deborah Spar, *Wonder Women: Sex, Power, and the Quest for Perfection* (New York: Sarah Crichton Books, 2013).

8. S. F. Maier and M.E.P. Seligman, "Learned Helplessness: Theory and Evidence," *Journal of Experimental Psychology: General* 105, no. 1 (1976): 3–46.

9. Amy F. T. Arnsten, "The Biology of Being Frazzled," *Science* 280, no. 5370 (June 12, 1998): 1711–12.

10. Victor E. Frankl, *Man's Search for Meaning* (London: Rider Books for Ebury Publishing, 2004).

11. Michael J. Apter, *Reversal Theory: Motivation, Emotion and Personality* (Florence, KY: Routledge, 1989).

Chapter 2: *Make Choices (Fighting Fish and Terminal Consumption)*

1. B. Wansink and J. Sobal, "Mindless Eating: The 200 Daily Food Decisions We Overlook," *Environment and Behavior* 39, no. 1 (2007): 106–23.
2. Daniel Kahneman, *Thinking, Fast and Slow* (New York: Farrar, Straus and Giroux, 2012).
3. G. P. Cipriani and A. Zago, "Productivity or Discrimination? Beauty and the Exams," *Oxford Bulletin of Economics and Statistics* 73, issue 3 (2011): 428–47.
4. B. C. Madrian and D. F. Shea, "The Power of Suggestion: Inertia in 401(k) Participation and Savings Behavior," *The Quarterly Journal of Economics* 116, issue 4 (2001): 1149–87.
5. N. J. Goldstein, R. B. Cialdini, and V. Griskevicius, "A Room with a Viewpoint: Using Social Norms to Motivate Environmental Conservation in Hotels," *Journal of Consumer Research* 35 (2008): 472–82.
6. Paul C. Nutt, "The Identification of Solution Ideas During Organizational Decision Making," *Management Science* 39: 1071–85.
7. Chip and Dan Heath, *Decisive: How to Make Better Choices in Life and Work* (New York: Crown Business, 2013).
8. Shane Frederick, Nathan Novemsky, Jing Want, Ravi Dhar, and Stephen Nowlis, "Opportunity Cost Neglect," *Journal of Consumer Research* 36 (2009): 553–61.
9. S. Danziger, J. Levav, and L. Avnaim-Pesso, "Extraneous Factors in Judicial Decisions," *PNAS* 108, no. 17 (April 26, 2011): 6889–92.
10. Jiwoong Shin and Dan Ariely, "Keeping Doors Open: The Effect of Unavailability on Incentives to Keep Options Viable," *Management Science* 50, no. 5 (May 2004): 575–86.
11. Brian Wansink, James E. Painter, and Jill North, "Bottomless Bowls: Why Visual Cues of Portion Size May Influence Intake," *Obesity Research* 13, no. 1 (January 2005): 93–100.
12. Nassim Nicholas Taleb, *Antifragile: Things That Gain from Disorder* (New York: Random House, 2014).

Chapter 3: *Manage Attention (How to Use Our Blobby Tissue Better)*

1. Edward M. Hallowell, M.D., *CrazyBusy: Overstretched, Overbooked, and About to Snap!* (New York: Ballantine Books, 2006).
2. Maggie Jackson, *Distracted: The Erosion of Attention and the Coming of the Dark Age* (New York: Prometheus Books, 2008).
3. A. D. DeSantis, E. Webb, and S. Noar, "Illicit Use of Prescription ADHD Medications on a College Campus: A Multi-Methodological Approach," *Journal of American College Health* 57, no. 3 (2008): 315–23.

4. J. C. Welch, "On the Measurement of Mental Activity through Muscular Activity and the Determination of a Constant Attention," *American Journal of Physiology* 1, no. 3 (May 1, 1898): 283–306.

5. H. Pashler, J. C. Johnston, and E. Ruthruff, "Attention and Performance," *Annual Review of Psychology* 52 (February 2001): 629–51.

6. David Rock, *Your Brain at Work: Strategies for Overcoming Distraction, Regaining Focus, and Working Smarter All Day Long* (New York: Harper-Business, 2009).

7. David Allen, *Getting Things Done* (New York: Penguin Books, 2003).

8. D. F. Gucciardi and J. A. Dimmock, "Choking Under Pressure in Sensorimotor Skills: Conscious Processing or Depleted Attentional Resources?" *Psychology of Sport and Exercise* 9, issue 1 (January 2008): 45–59.

9. E. J. Masicampo and R. F. Baumeister, "Consider it Done!: Plan Making Can Eliminate the Cognitive Effects of Unfulfilled Goals," *Journal of Personality and Social Psychology* 101, no. 4 (2011): 667–83.

10. Ad Kerkhof, *Stop Worrying: Get Your Life Back with CBT* (Berkshire, England: Open University Press, 2010).

11. Joe Brownstein, "Planning 'Worry Time' May Help Ease Anxiety," *LiveScience*, July 26, 2011, http://www.livescience.com/15233-planning-worry-time-ease -anxiety.html.

12. D. E. Meyer and D. E. Kieras, "A Computational Theory of Executive Cognitive Processes and Multiple-Task Performance: Part 1. Basic Mechanisms," *Psychological Review* 104, no. 1 (January 1997): 3–65.

     Also D. E. Meyer and D. E. Kieras, "A Computational Theory of Executive Cognitive Processes and Multiple-Task Performance: Part 2. Accounts of Psychological Refractory-Period Phenomena," *Psychological Review* 104, no. 1 (January 1997): 749–91.

13. Teresa Amabile, Constance N. Hadley, and Steven J Kramer, "Creativity Under the Gun," *Harvard Business Review* 80, no. 8 (August 2002): 52–61.

14. Jonathan B. Spira, *Overload! How Too Much Information Is Hazardous to Your Organization* (New Jersey: John Wiley and Sons, 2010).

15. E. Ophir, C. Nass, and A. D. Wagner, "Cognitive Control in Media Multitaskers," *PNAS* 106, no. 37: 15583–587.

16. S. Adam Brasel and James Gips, "Media Multitasking Behavior: Concurrent Television and Computer Usage," *Cyberpsychology, Behavior, and Social Networking* 14, no. 9 (2011): 527–34.

17. Gloria Mark, Victor Gonzalez, and Justin Harris, "No Task Left Behind? Examining the Nature of Fragmented Work," *Proceedings of the Conference on Human Factors in Computer Systems* (Portland, Oregon, 2005), 321–30.

18. Cited in Dave Coplin, *The Rise of the Humans: How to Outsmart the Digital Deluge,* (Great Britain: Harriman House, 2014), Kindle edition, location 225.

19. Gloria Mark and Jennifer Robison, "Too Many Interruptions at Work?: Office Distractions Are Worse Than You Think—and Maybe Better," *Business*

Journal (June 8, 2006), http://www.gallup.com/businessjournal/23146/Too
-Many-Interruptions-Work.aspx.

20. Linda Stone coined the term "Continuous Partial Attention" in 1998, http://
    lindastone.net/qa/continuous-partial-attention.

21. Cited in Derek Thompson, "A Formula for Perfect Productivity: Work for
    52 Minutes, Break for 17," *The Atlantic*, (September 17, 2014), http://www
    .theatlantic.com/business/archive/2014/09/science-tells-you-how-many
    -minutes-should-you-take-a-break-for-work-17/380369.

22. Rachel and Stephen Kaplan, *The Experience of Nature: A Psychological Per-
    spective* (Cambridge, England: Cambridge University Press, 1989).

23. Marc G. Berman, Jon Jonides, and Stephen Kaplan, "The Cognitive Ben-
    efits of Interacting with Nature," *Psychological Science* 19, no. 12 (2008):
    1207–12.

24. Leslie A. Perlow and Jessica L. Porter, "Making Time Off Predictable—and
    Required," *Harvard Business Review* 87, no. 10 (October 2009): 102–9, 142.

25. Linda Stone, "Diagnosis: Email Apnea," *Linda Stone* (blog), November 30,
    2009, http://lindastone.net/2009/11/30/diagnosis-email-apnea.

26. Peter Keating, "Sleeping Giants," *ESPN The Magazine*, April 5, 2012, http://
    espn.go.com/espn/commentary/story/_/id/7765998/for-athletes-sleep-new
    -magic-pill.

27. Ronald Kessler, Patricia Berglund, Catherine Coulouvrat, Goeran Hajak,
    Thomas Roth, Victoria Shahly, Alicia Shillington, et al., "Insomnia and the
    Performance of US Workers: Results from the America Insomnia Survey,"
    Sleep 34, issue 9 (2011): 1161–71.

Chapter 4: *Negotiate for Your Life (To Keep Those Missiles at Bay)*

1. Roger Fisher, William Ury, and Bruce Patton, *Getting to Yes: Negotiating an
   Agreement Without Giving In* (London: Random House Business, 1997).

2. Itamar Simonson, "Get Closer to Your Customers by Understanding How
   They Make Choices," *California Management Review* 35, issue 4 (1993):
   68–84.

3. A. G. Greenwald, C. G. Carnot, R. Beach, and B. Young, "Increasing Vot-
   ing Behavior by Asking People If They Expect to Vote," *Journal of Applied
   Psychology* 72, no. 2 (1987): 315–18.

4. Stanley Milgram, "Behavioral Study of Obedience," *The Journal of Abnormal
   and Social Psychology* 67, no. 4 (1963): 371–8.

5. Amy Cuddy, "Your Body Language Shapes Who You Are," (TED talk, June
   2012), http://www.ted.com/talks/amy_cuddy_your_body_language_shapes
   _who_you_are.

6. William Ury, *The Power of a Positive No* (London: Hodder and Stoughton,
   Ltd., 2007).

Chapter 5: *Stop Being So Productive! (Become More Strategic)*

1. David Garlan, Daniel P. Siewiorek, Asim Smailagic, and Peter Steenkiste, "Toward Distraction-free Pervasive Computing," *Pervasive Computing* 1, issue 2 (April–June 2002): 22–31.

2. Cited in Dave Coplin, *The Rise of the Humans: How to Outsmart the Digital Deluge* (Great Britain: Harriman House, 2014), Kindle edition, location 241.

3. Jonathan B. Spira, *Overload! How Too Much Information Is Hazardous to Your Organization* (New Jersey: John Wiley and Sons, 2010).

4. Michael E. Porter, "What Is Strategy?" *Harvard Business Review* 74, no. 6 (November 1996): 61–78.

5. Kjell Nordström and Jonas Ridderstrale, *Karaoke Capitalism* (New York: Financial Times Prentice Hall, 2004).

6. Cited by Susan Adams, "The Test That Measures a Leader's Strengths," *Forbes.com* (August 28, 2009), http://www.forbes.com/2009/08/28/strengthsfinder -skills-test-leadership-managing-jobs.html.

7. Quoted by Dan Frommer, "Apple COO Tim Cook: 'We Have No Interest In Being In The TV Market,'" *Business Insider* (February 23, 2010), http:// www.businessinsider.com/live-apple-coo-tim-cook-at-the-goldman-tech -conference-2010-2.

8. Robert S. Kaplan and David P. Norton, "The Balanced Scorecard: Measures That Drive Performance," *Harvard Business Review* 83 (July–August 2005): 172–80.

9. M. Baghai, S. Coley, and D. White, *The Alchemy of Growth*, (New York: Basic Books, 2000).

10. D. S. Kirschenbaum, L. L. Humphrey, and S. D. Malett, "Specificity of Planning in Adult Self-Control: An Applied Investigation," *Journal of Personality and Social Psychology* 40, no. 5 (May 1981): 941–50.

11. This story is about Brigadier General Rhonda Cornum in Martin Seligman, *Flourish: A Visionary New Understanding of Happiness and Well-being* (London: Nicholas Brealey Publishing, 2011).

Chapter 6: *Impact Through Innovation (Don't Be the Invisible Man)*

1. Reference to the Nomura Institute in John Kao, *Jamming: The Art and Discipline of Business Creativity* (New York: HarperCollins, 1997).

2. Marc Benioff quote in Daniel Goleman, *Focus: The Hidden Driver of Excellence* (London, Bloomsbury Publishing, 2013), Kindle edition, location 549.

3. "First break all the rules," *The Economist* (April 10, 2010), http://www .economist.com/node/15879359.

4. Aza Raskin, "You Are Solving the Wrong Problem," *UX Magazine*, (May 2, 2011), http://uxmag.com/articles/you-are-solving-the-wrong-problem.

5. Mihaly Csikszentmihalyi, *Creativity: Flow and the Psychology of Discovery and Invention* (New York: Harper Perennial, 1997).

6. Stuart Kauffman, *At Home in the Universe: The Search for the Laws of Self-Organization and Complexity* (New York: Oxford University Press, 1996).
7. Tim Harford, *Adapt: Why Success Always Starts with Failure* (New York: Farrar, Straus and Giroux, 2011).
8. Ibid.
9. Ibid.

Chapter 7: *Busy Is a Terrible Brand (Develop a Better Brand)*

1. Fritz Strack, "Priming and Communication: Social Determinants of Information Use in Judgments of Life Satisfaction," *European Journal of Social Psychology* 18, no. 5 (October 1988): 429–42.
2. Adam L. Alter and Daniel M. Oppenheimer, "Predicting short-term stock fluctuations by using processing fluency," *PNAS* 103, no. 24 (2006): 9369–72.
3. Adam L. Alter and Daniel M. Oppenheimer, "Uniting the Tribes of Fluency to Form a Metacognitive Nation," *Personality and Social Psychology Review* 13, no. 3 (2009): 219–35.
4. Zachary Schiller, Greg Burns, and Karen Lowry Miller, "Make It Simple," *BusinessWeek* (September 9, 1996), http://www.businessweek.com/1996/37/b34921.htm.
5. Ron Ashkenas, *Simply Effective: How to Cut Through Complexity in Your Organization and Get Things Done* (Boston, MA: Harvard Business Review Press, 2009).

Chapter 8: *Walk Your Own Path (Fixing Radios by Thinking)*

1. Richard P. Feynman, *Surely You're Joking, Mr. Feynman (Adventures of a Curious Character)* (New York: W. W. Norton and Company, 1985).
2. E. A. Livingstone, ed., *The Concise Oxford Dictionary of the Christian Church* (Oxford: Oxford University Press, 2006).
3. G. Mark, S. T. Iqbal, M. Czerwinski, and P. Johns, "Bored Mondays and Focused Afternoons: The Rhythm of Attention and Online Activity in the Workplace," Proceedings of the SIGCHI Conference on Human Factors in Computing Systems (Toronto, Canada, 2014), 3025–34.
4. W. Hofmann, R. F. Baumeister, G. Förster, and K. D. Vohs, "Everyday Temptations: An Experience Sampling Study of Desire, Conflict, and Self-Control," *Journal of Personality and Social Psychology* 102, no. 6 (2012): 1318–35.
5. D. T. de Ridder, G. Lensvelt-Mulders, C. Finkenauer, F. M. Stok, and R. F. Baumeister, "Taking Stock of Self-Control: A Meta-Analysis of How Trait Self-Control Relates to a Wide Range of Behaviors," *Personality and Social Psychology Review* 16, no. 1 (2012): 76–99.
6. Brian Tracy, *Eat That Frog!: 21 Great Ways to Stop Procrastinating and Get More Done in Less Time* (San Francisco, CA: Berrett-Koehler Publishers, Inc., 2007).

7. Brian Wansink, *Mindless Eating: Why We Eat More Than We Think* (New York: Bantam, 2006).

8. Teresa Amabile and Steven Kramer, *The Progress Principle: Using Small Wins to Ignite Joy, Engagement, and Creativity at Work* (Boston, MA: Harvard Business Review Press, 2011).

9. Alia J. Crum and Ellen J. Langer, "Mind-set Matters: Exercise and the Placebo Effect," *Association for Psychological Science* 18, no. 2 (2007): 165–71.

10. Example given in Chip Heath and Dan Heath, *Switch: How to Change Things When Change Is Hard* (New York: Broadway Books, 2010).

11. Amy Arnsten cited in David Rock, *Your Brain at Work: Strategies for Overcoming Distraction, Regaining Focus, and Working Smarter All Day Long* (New York: HarperBusiness, 2009).

12. Edward Tory Higgins, "Beyond Pleasure and Pain," *American Psychologist* 52, no. 12 (December 1997): 1280–1300.

13. K. Lanaj, C. H. Chang, and R. E. Johnson, "Regulatory Focus and Work-Related Outcomes: A Review and Meta-Analysis," *Psychological Bulletin* 138, no. 5 (September 2012): 998–1034.

14. Steve Peters, *The Chimp Paradox: The Mind Management Program to Help You Achieve Success, Confidence, and Happiness* (New York: Jeremy P. Tarcher/Penguin, 2011).

15. James Gross, "Emotion Regulation: Affective, Cognitive, and Social Consequences," *Psychophysiology* 39, no. 3 (May 2002): 281–91.

16. David Rock, *Your Brain at Work: Strategies for Overcoming Distraction, Regaining Focus, and Working Smarter All Day Long* (New York: HarperBusiness, 2009).

17. J. E. Maddux and R. W. Rogers, "Protection Motivation and Self-Efficacy: A Revised Theory of Fear Appeals and Attitude Change," *Journal of Experimental Social Psychology* 19, no. 5 (September 1983): 469–79.

18. Ian Herbert, "Dr Steve Peters: The Psychiatrist Charged with Ridding Anfield of the Fear Factor," *The Independent*, March 28, 2013.

19. J. Stoeber and D. P. Janssen, "Perfectionism and Coping with Daily Failures: Positive Reframing Helps Achieve Satisfaction at the End of the Day," *Anxiety, Stress, & Coping* 24, issue 5 (October 2011): 477–97.

Chapter 9: *Stop Striving for "More"! (Put Your Values First)*

1. David G. Myers and Ed Diener, "The Pursuit of Happiness," *Scientific American*, April 16, 1996, 54–56.

2. Tim Kasser, *The High Price of Materialism* (Cambridge, MA: A Bradford Book, The MIT Press, 2002).

3. Ibid.

4. Kennon M. Sheldon and Tim Kasser, "Pursuing Personal Goals: Skills Enable Progress, but Not All Progress Is Beneficial," *Personality and Social Psychology Bulletin* 24, 1319–31.

Also T. Kasser and R. M. Ryan, "Be Careful What You Wish For: Optimal Functioning and the Relative Attainment of Intrinsic and Extrinsic Goals," in Peter Schmuck and Kennon M. Sheldon (eds), *Life Goals and Well-Being* (Göttingen, Germany: Hogrefe & Huber Publishers, 2001), 116–31.

5. Mark R. Lepper, David Greene, and Richard E Nisbett, "Undermining Children's Intrinsic Interest with Extrinsic Reward: A Test of the 'Overjustification' Hypothesis," *Journal of Personality and Social Psychology* 28, no. 1 (1973): 129–37.

6. John Kay, *Obliquity: Why Our Goals Are Best Achieved Indirectly* (London: Profile Books, 2011).

7. Daniel Gilbert, *Stumbling on Happiness* (New York: Knopf, 2006).

8. Joseph Campbell, *The Power of Myth* (New York: Random House, 1988).

Chapter 10: *Reconnect (Why We're Better Off with Fewer Friends)*

1. Lisa F. Berkman, "The Role of Social Relations in Health Promotion," *Psychosomatic Medicine* 57, no. 3 (May–June 1995): 245–54.

2. Lisa F. Berkman and S. Leonard Syme, "Social Networks, Host Resistance, and Mortality: A Nine-year Follow-up Study of Alameda County Residents," *American Journal of Epidemiology* 109, no. 2 (February 1979): 186–204.

3. Jonathan Haidt, *The Happiness Hypothesis: Finding Modern Truth in Ancient Wisdom* (London: Arrow, 2007).

4. W. Fleeson, A. B. Malanos, and N. M. Achille, "An Intraindividual Process Approach to the Relationship between Extraversion and Positive Affect: Is Acting Extraverted as 'Good' as Being Extraverted?" *Journal of Personality and Social Psychology* 83, no. 6 (December 2002): 1409–22.

5. S. Cohen and T. B. Herbert, "Health Psychology: Psychological Factors and Physical Disease from the Perspective of Human Psychoneuroimmunology," *Annual Reviews of Psychology* 47, no. 1 (1996): 113–42.

6. S. L. Brown, R. M. Nesse, A. D. Vinokur, and D. M. Smith, "Providing Social Support May be More Beneficial than Receiving It: Results from a Prospective Study of Mortality," *Psychological Science* 14, no. 4 (July 2003) 320–27.

7. Ed Diener and Martin E. P. Seligman, "Very Happy People," *Psychological Science* 13, no. 1 (2002): 80–3.

8. Sherry Turkle, *Alone Together: Why We Expect More from Technology and Less from Each Other* (New York: Basic Books, 2012).

9. RIM Dunbar, "Neocortex Size as a Constraint on Group Size in Primates," *Journal of Human Evolution* 22, issue 6 (1992): 469–93.

10. Carolyn E. Schwartz, Janice Bell Meisenhelder, Yunsheng Ma, and George W. Reed, "Altruistic Social Interest Behaviors Are Associated with Better Mental Health," *Psychosomatic Medicine* 65, no. 5, 2003: 778–85.

11. John M. Darley and C. Daniel Batson, " 'From Jerusalem to Jericho': A Study of Situational and Dispositional Variables in Helping Behavior," *Journal of Personality and Social Psychology* 27, no. 1 (1973): 100–8.

12. Kathleen D. Vohs, Yajin Wang, Francesca Gino, Michael I. Norton, "Rituals Enhance Consumption," *Psychological Science* 24, no. 9 (July 17, 2013): 1714–21.

13. Barbara L. Fredrickson, "What Good Are Positive Emotions?" *Review of General Psychology* 2, no. 3 (1998): 300–19.

14. Irwin Altman and Dalmas A. Taylor, *Social Penetration: The Development of Interpersonal Relationships* (New York: Holt, 1973).

15. M. Losada and E. Heaphy, "The Role of Positivity and Connectivity in the Performance of Business Teams: A Nonlinear Dynamics Model," *American Behavioral Scientist* 47 (2004): 740–65.

   (*Note:* There has been some questioning of the accuracy of some of the complicated mathematics behind this ratio. It's not worth worrying about the specific number, but the principle of the ratio of positive to negative still holds.)

16. John Gottman, *What Predicts Divorce?* (Hillsdale, NJ; Lawrence Erlbaum Associates, Inc., 1994).

17. Nicholas J. L. Brown, Alan D. Sokal, and Harris L. Friedman, "The Complex Dynamics of Wishful Thinking: The Critical Positivity Ratio," *American Psychologist* 68 (July 15, 2013): 801–13.

18. S. L. Gable, H. T. Reis, E. A. Impett, and E. R. Asher, "What Do You Do When Things Go Right? The Intrapersonal and Interpersonal Benefits of Sharing Positive Events," *Journal of Personality and Social Psychology* 87, no. 2 (2004): 228–45.

19. M.E.P. Seligman, T. A. Steen, N. Park, and C. Peterson, "Positive Psychology Progress: Empirical Validation of Interventions," *American Psychologist* 60, vol. 5 (July–August 2005): 410–21.

Chapter 11: *From Buzz to Joy (An Ode to Depth)*

1. Edward M. Hallowell, M.D. and John J. Ratey, M.D., *Delivered from Distraction: Getting the Most Out of Life with Attention Deficit Disorder* (New York: Ballantine Books, 2006).

2. Kent C. Berridge quote from Emily Yoffe, "Seeking," on www.slate.com, Aug 12, 2009.

3. David McNamee, "'Technology Addiction'—How Should It Be Treated?" *Medical News Today*, June 20, 2014, http://www.medicalnewstoday.com/articles/278530.php.

4. Psychic entropy is a concept used in Mihaly Csikszentmihalyi, *Flow: The Classic Work on How to Achieve Happiness* (London: Rider/Random House, 1992).

5. Mihaly Csikszentmihalyi, *Flow: The Classic Work on How to Achieve Happiness* (London: Rider/Random House, 1992).

6. Paul A. O'Keefe and Lisa Linnenbrink-Garcia, "The Role of Interest in Optimizing Performance and Self-regulation," *Journal of Experimental Social Psychology* 53 (July 2014): 70–8.

7. Daniel Gilbert, "The Surprising Science of Happiness," (TED talk, February 2004), http://www.ted.com/talks/dan_gilbert_asks_why_are_we_happy.

8. George Leonard, *Mastery: The Key to Success and Long-Term Fulfilment* (New York: Plume, 1991).

9. Jane E. Barker, Andrei D. Semenov, Laura Michaelson, Lindsay S. Provan, Hannah R. Snyder, and Yuko Munakata, "Less-Structured Time in Children's Daily Lives Predicts Self-Directed Executive Functioning," *Frontiers in Psychology*, June 17, 2014.

10. Fred B. Bryant and Joseph Veroff, *Savoring: A New Model of Positive Experience* (New Jersey: Psychology Press, 2006).

11. Timothy D. Wilson, David A. Reinhard, Erin C. Westgate, Daniel T. Gilbert, Nicole Ellerbeck, Cheryl Hahn, Casey L. Brown, and Adi Shaked, "Just Think: The Challenges of the Disengaged Mind," *Science* 345, issue 6192 (2014): 75–7.

12. K. Hsee, Adelle X. Yang, and Liangyan Wang, "Idleness Aversion and the Need for Justifiable Busyness," *Psychological Science* 21, no. 7 (July 2010): 926–30.

13. M. E. Raichle, A. M. MacLeod, A. Z. Snyder, W. J. Powers, D. A. Gusnard, and G. L. Shulman, "Inaugural Article: A default mode of brain function," *Proceedings of the National Academy of Sciences* 98, no. 2 (2001): 676–82.

14. Martin Heidegger, *Discourse on Thinking* (New York: Torchbooks, 1969).

15. American Time Use Survey—2012 Microdata File, Bureau of Labor Statistics, U.S. Department of Labor, http://www.bls.gov/tus/datafiles_2012.htm.

16. Ethan Kross et al., "Self-Talk as a Regulatory Mechanism: How You Do It Matters," *Journal of Personality and Social Psychology*, 106 no. 2 (February 2014): 304–24.

Chapter 12: *Beyond Busy (Making Good Intentions Stick)*

1. Leroy Watson Jr., "Forgotten Stories of Courage and Inspiration: Glenn Cunningham," *Bleacher Report*, June 12, 2009.

2. K. Patterson, J. Grenny, D. Maxfield, R. McMillan, and A. Switzler, *Change Anything: The New Science of Personal Success* (New York: Hachette Book Group, 2011).

3. Charles Duhigg, *The Power of Habit: Why We Do What We Do in Life and Business* (London: William Heinemann, 2012).

4. Steve Booth-Butterfield and Bill Reger, "The Message Changes Belief and the Rest Is Theory: The '1% Milk or Less' Campaign and Reasoned Action," *Preventive Medicine* 39, (2004): 581–8.

5. R. B. Cialdini and D. A. Schroeder, "Increasing Compliance by Legitimizing Paltry Contributions: When Even a Penny Helps," *Journal of Personality and Social Psychology*, 34, no. 4 (1976): 599–604.

6. Howard Leventhal, Robert Singer, and Susan Jones, "Effects of Fear and Specificity of Recommendation upon Attitudes and Behavior," *Journal of Personality and Social Psychology* 2, no. 1 (July 1965): 20–9.

7. M. Bateson, D. Nettle, and G. Roberts, "Cues of Being Watched Enhance Cooperation in a Real-World Setting," *Biology Letters* (2006): 412–14.

8. C. P. Herman and D. Mack, "Restrained and Unrestrained Eating," *Journal of Personality* 43, no. 4 (December 1975): 647–60.

9. Ronald Heifetz, *Leadership Without Easy Answers* (Boston, MA: Harvard University Press, 1994).

10. R. Kegan and L. Lahey, *Immunity to Change: How to Overcome It and Unlock the Potential in Yourself and Your Organization* (Boston, MA: Harvard Business School Press, 2009).

Index

Action Learning, 110
*Adapt: Why Success Always Starts
    with Failure* (Harford), 111
Adderall, 44
Ali, Muhammad, 113
Allen, David, xxxiii, 46–47, 233
Allen, Lisa, 230
Allostatic load, xix
Alone Together (Turkle), 184, 188
Amabile, Teresa, 53, 136
American Cancer Society, 232
American Time Use Survey, 222
Angry Birds, 58
Anxiety, 143–145
Apple
    iPhone, 171
    iPod, 91
Apps
    Angry Birds, 58
    DeskTime, 57
    Freedom, 134
    RescueTime, 135
    Thinking Time app, xxx
    Twitter, 104, 183
    WhatsApp, 58, 183, 189
Apter, Michael J., 18
Ariely, Dan, 34
Arnsten, Amy, 15, 140
Attention. *See also* distractions;
        relationships
    big-chunking, 53–54

directed and involuntary, 58
and distraction, 44
"FAME," 60
focus and recovery, 56–57
management of, 44–45, 48–50,
    52–53, 59
maximizing, savoring, full, 212–216
Attention deficit disorder (ADD),
    43–44
Attention restoration theory (ART), 58
Attractiveness halo effect, 26
Automatic stimulus-response cycle, 17

Baghai, Mehrdad, 97
Balanced scorecard
    four important practices and focus
        areas, 96–97, 99–100
Basex, 4, 53
Batson, Daniel, 191
Baumeister, Roy, 50, 236
Bayer, 121
Because, xxix
Beckham, David, 169
Berkman, Lisa, 180–181
Berman, Marc, 58
Berocca, 121–122
Berridge, Kent C., 204
The Big Messages
    "Beyond Busy"
        Deep Change, 243
        Seven Strategies, 242

The Big Messages (*Cont.*)
  "Busy Is a Terrible Brand"
    Build Your Brand, 127
    Identify Your Brand, 127
    The Importance of Brands, 127
  "From Buzz to Joy"
    Buzz and Happiness, 224
    Deep Inside, 225
    Deep into Your Three Seconds,
      224–225
    Going Deep, 224
  "Impact Through Innovation"
    Becoming Creative, 114
    From Idea to Innovation, 114
    The Innovation Imperative, 113
  "Make Choices"
    Beating Mindlessness,
      39–40
    Busy Is the Easy Choice, 40
    When Enough Is Enough, 40
  "Manage Attention"
    Focusing Attention, 61
    Maintaining Attention, 62
    Refreshing Attention, 62
  "Negotiate for Your Life"
    Negotiate Beyond Busy, 76
    Time to Say "No," 76–77
  "Reconnect"
    Being Together, 199
    Focus on Fewer People, 199
    The Power of Positive
      Emotions, 200
  "Stop Being So Productive!"
    Less Is More, 101
    The "More" Game, 100
    Strategic Focus, 100–101
  "Stop Managing Your Time"
    Building a Sense of Mastery, 20
    From Control to Mastery, 20
    Time Management Isn't
      Helping, 20
  "Stop Striving for More!"
    A Different Success, 177
    Rethinking Success, 176–177
    What Do You Value?, 177
  "Walk Your Own Path"
    Anxiety and Prevention, 154
    Avoiding the Temptation of Busy,
      153
    Busy Is Avoidance, 153
    Busy Is Defensive, 154
    Confidence, 154
    Stop Procrastinating!, 153
Booth-Butterfield, Steve, 231
Booth School of Business, 218
Boredom, 211–212
Borkovec, Tom, 52
Boston College, 54
Boston Consulting Group, 59
Boundaries
  "Preemptive Strike," 37–39
  "Rules of Engagement," 38–39
"Brain dump," xxxiii–xxxiv
Branding
  and busyness, 119–121
  importance of, 117
  and personal themes, 121–126
  and simplicity, 117–119,
    120–121
Broaden and build theory
    (Fredrickson), 194, 195
Brown, Brené, 10
Bryant, Fred B., 213–214
Bucket
  idea collection list, 47–48, 50
Budweiser, 116–117
Bureau of Labor Statistics, 222
Burnett, Ann, xviii
The Busy Footprint, 36–37
Busy. *See also* busyness; mindlessness
  As an Approach to Happiness
    acquisition, xxii, 157–243
  As an Experience
    time management, xxi, 1–77
  As a Success Strategy
    productivity, xxii, 79–155

Three Faces of Busy
  busy as an approach to
    happiness, xxi, 157–243
  busy as an experience,
    xx–xxi, 1–77
  busy as a success strategy,
    xxi, 79–155
Busyness
  and abdication of choice, xvii,
    23–24, 30–31
  and addiction, xvii–xviii
  and anxiety, 144–145
  and attention, 45–46
  and avoidance, xvii, 131, 134
  and branding, 119–121
  and concave relationships, 36
  and inaction, 131–132
  and lack of happiness, 162
  and limitless information, 22–23,
    134–135
  and more, 143, 162, 170–171,
    183, 220
  and multitasking, xvi, 23, 219
  negotiating beyond, 64–65
  and procrastination, 136–139
  and productivity, 81–82
  and relationships, 182–184
  and social norms, xvii–xviii, 28–30

Campbell, Joseph, 176
Campbell's soup, 35, 118
Carnegie Mellon University, 82
Case Western Reserve University, 6
Cave, Christopher, xv
Change. See also goals
  and failure, 229, 236–238, 239–242
  and habits, 230–231
  "Seven Strategies," 231–237
Chartier, Emile-Auguste, 108
Chesterton, G. K., 103
Choices and decisions. See also
    persistence
  good choices, 33–34

  loss aversion, 34–36
  whether or not, 30–33
  which, 30–33, 34
Chris Rock, 112
Churning, 50–52. See also worry
Cialdini, Robert, 232
Cighid Orphanage, 179
Cilley, Marla, 139
Clark, Jim, 165
Cogito ergo sum (Descartes), 212
Cognitive behavioral therapy (CBT)
  and worry procrastination, 51–52
Cognitive dissonance
  changing behavior, changing
    belief, 13–14
Cognitive fluency, 120
Columbia University, 142
Comedy Central, 112
Competing commitments (Kegan),
    239–240
Concentration camps
  Auschwitz, 16
  Dachau, 16
Conspicuous consumption (Veblen),
    165–166
Continental Airlines
  Continental Lite, 86
Continuous partial attention
    (Stone), 57
Coors, 116
Cornell University, 24
Counter-regulatory eating
    (Herman), 236
Cousteau, Jacques, 202, 205
Covey, Stephen, 96, 246
Crabbe, Dulcie, 193, 215, 248
Crabbe, Tony
  being present, 248
  creating rituals, 247–248
  focus, 245
  making choices, 244–245, 246
  personal motivation, 249
  time-management, 246–247

CrazyBusy (Hallowell), 43
Crum, Alia, 138
Csikszentmihalyi, Mihaly, 110, 205
Cuddy, Amy, 71
Cunningham, Floyd, 227
Cunningham, Glenn, 227–288, 231
*Cyberpsychology, Behavior, and
        Social Networking* (journal), 54

Danziger, Shai, 33
Darley, John, 191
Decisive (Heath), 31
DeDonno, Michael, 6
Default network, 218–219
Delta, 86
Demaree, Heath, 6
Descartes, René, 212
DeskTime, 57
Diener, Ed, 164, 181
Differentiation
    and creativity, 106–107
    and innovation, 103–105, 130–131
Dimmock, James, 49
Disengagement
    and disconnection, 161–162
Distracted (Jackson), 44
Distractions
    avoidance of, 54–55
    "machine-gunning," 56
Doerner, Darrick, 6–7
Doyle, Michael, xxxi
Duhigg, Charles, 230
Dunbar, Robin, 185–186

Eat That Frog (Tracy), 134, 234
Edison, Thomas, 105–106, 111
Edison Portland Cement
        Company, 106
Eichmann, Adolf, 71
Einstein, Albert, 125
Eisenhower, Dwight D., 32
Ellison, Larry, 165
Email apnea, 59

Emotions, 15–17
    and internal monologue, 223
    normalizing, 222–223
    power of positive emotions,
        193–195
    and reappraisal, 145–149
Encarta (Microsoft), 104
Encyclopaedia Britannica, 104
Eras of economic activity
    Agricultural Age, 104
    Creative Age, 105
    Industrial Age, xv, 82, 104, 166
    Information Age, 83, 104
Experiment
    Ask "Why?", 178
    Big Things First, 102
    Celebrate Better, 201
    Churning, 63
    Do Less, 226
    Fail, 115
    Get Sloppy, 21
    Happy Attacks, 226
    High-Leverage Signals, 128
    Killer Question, 115
    Live Up to Your Brand, 128
    The "No" Toolkit, 77
    Offer a Compromise, 77
    Outcasting, 41
    Phone-Free Moments, 201
    Reappraise, 155
    Reverse Your Mood, 21
    Sleep, 63
    Social Norms, 41
    Thin-Slicing, 155
    Trade-Offs, 102

Facebook, 42, 132, 161, 162, 182, 213
Failure
    and blame, 9
    coping strategies, 152
Feynman, Richard, 129–130
Fisher, Roger, 65–66
Five-Minute Room Rescue (Cilley), 139

Five Whys (Toyoda), 175
Florida State University, 50
Forbes (magazine), 164
Ford, Henry, 108
Frankl, Viktor, 15–16
Frederick, Shane, 32
Fredrickson, Barbara, 193–194, 195
Freedom, 134

Gable, Shelly, 196
Gagnan, Emile, 202
Gallup, 181
Gates, Bill, 169
Getting Things Done (Allen), xxxiii,
    46–47
Getting to Yes (Fisher and Ury), 66
Gilbert, Dan, 170, 210
Gilbert, Daniel, xxxiv
Gloria Mark, 55
Goals
  and achievement, 18, 142, 151
  change and, 140–141
  and clarity, 54, 162–163, 205,
    231–232
  and momentum, 232–233
  setting of, 166–167, 208
  "seven strategies," 231–237
Go-Do
  Act "As If," 21
  Big-Chunk Your Time, 63
  Borrow Ideas, 115
  Choose Your Response, 21
  Clarify Your Brand, 128
  Cold Decision-Making, 41
  Dead Time, 226
  A Different Goal, 178
  Eat That Frog, 155
  Identify Your Values, 178
  Increase Your Joy, 226
  Machine-Gun Emails, 63
  Market Research, 128
  Personal Pronoun Proofing, 226
  Plan C, 115

Renegotiate, 77
The Right Goal, 15
Rituals, 201
Say "No," 77
Strategic Position, 102
Trigger Flow, 226
Unchoose, 41
What Does the Evidence Say?, 178
Your 15, 201
Your Balanced Scorecard, 102
Google, 204
Gottman, John, 195
Greene, David, 167
Greenwald, Anthony, 70
Gross, James, 145–146
Gucciardi, Daniel, 49
Gutman, Ron, xxxiv

Haidt, Jonathan, 181
Hallowell, Edward M., 43–44
Hamilton, Laird, 7–8, 48
Happiness. *See also* success;
    time management
  and commitment, 210–212
  and doing less, 216–220
  and emptiness, 220
  and "flow" experiences, 205–206,
    207–209, 212, 221
  and performance enhancement,
    205–206, 210
The Happiness Hypothesis (Haidt), 181
Harford, Tim, 111
Harvard Business Review (magazine),
    86, 89
Harvard Business School, 53
Harvard Law School, 66
Harvard Negotiation Project, 66
Harvard University, xxix, xxxiv,
    136, 170
Head & Shoulders shampoo, 120
Healtheon, 165
HealthTap, xxxiv
Heath, Chip, 31–32

Index

Heath, Dan, 31–32
Heidegger, Martin, 220
Heifetz, Ronald, 238
Hemingway, Ernest, 113
Henkel, 91
Herman, Peter, 236
Higgins, Edward Tory, 142
High-leverage signals, 126
Hofmann, Wilhelm, 133
The Holocaust, 15
Hormones
    cortisol, 71
    testosterone, 71
Horner, Barry, 214
Horner, Damian, 116
Houdini, Harry, 72
How to Make Meetings Work!
        (Doyle and Strauss), xxxi
Hoy, Chris, Sir, 143
Hsee, Christopher K., 218, 220, 221
Huffington, Arianna, 61
Hughes, Ted, 131
Hunnicutt, Ben, xvii

IKEA, 87–88
Impact bias (Gilbert), 170
Imperial Chemical Industries (ICI),
        159–160, 169
Information
    addiction, 204–205, 218–219
    and attention, 52–54, 203
    as a commodity, 104
    excess consumption of, 4, 9,
        43–44, 57
    and novelty, 205–206
    overload and the Internet, xix–xx,
        204–205
    and procrastination, 141–142
    and US economic toll, xix–xx
Innovation. *See also* differentiation
    and evolution, 111–112
    and failure, 112–113
    solving the right problem, 109–112

Input, 11, 13
International Child Support (ICS), 112
The Invisible Man (Chesterton), 103
IPhone, 171
IPod, 91
IQ (Intelligence Quotient)
    and being "on," xxx

Jackson, Maggie, 44
Janssen, Dirk, 152
Jonides, John, 58
Jung, Carl, 249

Kahneman, Daniel, 25, 117
Kaplan, Robert S., 96
Kaplan, Stephen, 58
Kapos, 16
Karoshi, xix
Kasser, Tim, 164–165, 184, 186
Kauffmann, Stuart, 111
Kay, John, 169
Kegan, Robert, 239, 241
Kennedy, John F., 64
Kerkhof, Ad, 51
Kindle, 222, 246
Klout, 183
Kodak, 98
Kremer, Henry, 109
Kross, Ethan, 223

Langer, Ellen, xxix, 138
Lao Tzu, 8
Learned helplessness (Seligman), 14
LEGO, 191
Leonard, George, 210
Lepper, Mark R., 167
Levav, Jonathan, 33
Leventhal, Howard, 232–233
The Life of Brian (movie), 65
LinkedIn, 183
Linnenbrink-Garcia, Lisa, 206
Liverpool Football Club, 151
Losada, Marcial, 195

Losada ratio (Losada), 195
Loyola University, 213

MacCready, Paul, 109
Madrian, Brigitte, 27
Mah, Cheri, 60
Mark, Gloria, 132, 134
Marquardt, Mike, 110
Mastery
    and changing emotional response,
        15–17, 145–146
    feelings of and brain function, 15,
        143–145
    and relinquishing control, 1
Mastery (Leonard), 210
The Matrix (movie), 212
McDaid, Monica, 179
McKinsey and Co., 97
Meyer, David, xxx
Michigan State University, 142, 206
Microsoft, 18–19, 37
Milgram, Stanley, 71
Mill, John Stuart, 168–169
Miller, 116
Mindlessness
    and consumption, 24, 35–36
    and defaults, 26–28
    justifying choices, 26
Monty Python, 65
Motivational states
    changing state, 19
    serious, playful, 18
Moving Beyond Busy
    differentiation, xxiv
    engagement, xxiv
    mastery, xxiii–xxiv
Multitasking. *See also* attention
    dual-task interference, 46
    negative repercussions of, xxx,
        45–46, 52–53, 54, 219
Munakata, Yuko, 211
MyCFO, 165
Myers, David, 164

National Opinion Research Center
    (NORC), 164
National Science Foundation,
    xviii–xix
Negotiation
    and busyness, 64–65
    cognitive dissonance and, 68
    and compromise, 69–71
    principle-based, agreements and
        needs, 66–69
    and saying "no," 72–76
Netscape, 165
Neurotransmitter
    adrenaline, 204
    dopamine, 53, 140–141, 204
    norepinephrine, 140–141
Newcastle University, 233
Newton, Isaac, Sir, 137
    laws of motion, 137, 138, 141
New York Stock Exchange (NYSE), 119
Nietzsche, Friedrich, 220
Nisbitt, Richard, 167
No. *See also* negotiation
    and the important "yes," 73–74
    and truthfulness, 72–73
Nobel, Alfred, 159
Nobel Prize, 25, 110, 129, 170
Nomura Research Institute, 105
Nordström, Kjell, 91
Northwest Airlines, 86
Norton, David P., 96
Nutt, Paul, 31

Obama, Barack, 192
Obama, Michelle, 192
Objectives
    "SMART," 171
Obliquity (Kay), 169
Ocean's Eleven (movie), 3
The Ohio State University, 31
O'Keefe, Paul, 206
O'Leary, Michael, 94
Oracle, 165

Organisation for Economic
    Cooperation and Development
    (OECD), 181
Outlook, 247
Output, 11
  and mastery, 12
*Oxford Concise Dictionary of the
    Christian Church,* 131

Pashler, Harold, 45–46
Pendleton, Victoria, 143
Penn State University, 52
Perfection
  and self-esteem, 10–11
  and vulnerability, 10–11
Persistence, 227–229. *See also* change
Peters, Steve, 143–144, 151, 222
Porter, Michael, 86, 89
Positive psychology, 14
Principia Mathematica (Newton), 137
Pritt Stick, 91
Problems
  adaptive, 238–239
  technical, 238
Procrastination
  action-reaction, 141
  building momentum, 138–139
  and dependence, 137, 141–142
  and fear, 239–242
  and inertia, 137–139
  and mood, 137, 139–141
Procter & Gamble, 120
Productivity
  and doing more, 83–84, 93–94
Progress principle (Amabile), 136
Prozac, 197

Reeves, Keanu, 212
Reger, Bill, 231
Regulatory focus theory (Higgins), 142
  prevention focus, 142–143
  promotion focus, 142–143
Relationships. *See also* emotions

affinity and popularity, 184–185
and celebration, 196–198
creating rituals, 192–193, 198,
    247–248
failure to thrive, 180
importance of social
    connectedness, 179–181,
    188–190, 248
and negative impacts, 181–184
and social grouping, 185–186
and "social penetration," 194
support network, 187–188
RescueTime, 135
Reversal Theory (Apter), 18, 140
Ridderstråle, Jonas, 91
Riemenschneider, Bobbi, 19
Ritalin, 44
Rothko, Mark, 220
Rubik's Cube, 238
Ryanair, 94–95

Sartre, Jean-Paul, 220
Saturday Night Live (television
    show), 112
Science (magazine), 218
Scientific management, 82
Self-control
  and avoiding temptation, 133–136,
    236–237
  and good habits, 133–135, 235–236
  as self-regulation, 142–143
Self-efficacy, 149–150, 152–153
  and achievable goals, 151,
    166–167, 208
Seligman, Martin, 5, 14, 181, 196, 198
Sen, Amartya, 170
"Seven Strategies," 231–237, 242
Shea, Dennis, 27
Shell, 126
Shetty, Devi, 108–109
The Silent World (movie), 202
Silicon Graphics, 165
Sleep, 60–61

Sloppiness
  and failure or success, 9–11
Small, Gary, xxx
Smiling
  and endorphins, xxxiv–xxxv
Social connectedness (Berkman), 181
Social influence, 233–234
Southwest Airlines, 86, 94
Spar, Deborah, 10
Spira, Jonathan B., 53, 84
Stanford Graduate School of
      Business, 33
Stanford University, 54, 60, 145, 167
Stoeber, Joachim, 152
Stone, Linda, 57, 59
Strategic career positioning
  audience-based, 88, 89–91, 93
  cost-based, 88, 89
  everything, everyone, 88–89, 93
  product-based, 88, 91–93
Strategy. *See also* differentiation
  competitive strategy, 87–88
  corporate and delivering success,
      84–85
  corporate strategy
    Horizon One, short-term, 97
    Horizon Three, long-term, 98
    Horizon Two, middle-term,
      97–99
  and loss of focus, 86
  and trade-offs, 94–96
Straus, David, xxxi
Stress, xviii–xix
Success
  and intrinsic motivation, 167–170
  and "More," 161–164, 171
  and values, 164–165, 168–172
Suez Canal, 159
Sun, 98
Surfer (magazine), 7

Taleb, Nassim Nicholas, 36, 82
Target, 117

Task-switching. *See* multitasking
Taylor, Frederick Winslow, 82
Teahupo'o, Tahiti, 6–8
Technology addiction disorder, 204
TED (Technology, Entertainment,
      Design) Talk, xxxiv, 71
Tel Aviv University, 33
The Power of Habit (Duhigg), 230
The Wedding Planner (movie), 3
Thinking process
  calculative thinking, 220
  deliberate act of, 215–216
  externalize, 48
  immersion and focus of, 48–50,
      217–219
  meditative thinking, 220
  System One, 25
  System Two, 25
Thinking Time app, xxx
3M, xxxi
Time management
  and attention, 44
  and control, 4
  and effectiveness, 5–6
  and fractured attention, 5
  goal setting, xxxii, 166–167
  and happiness, 4–5, 205–206
  planning fallacy, xxxi–xxxii
  procrastination, xxxiii, 132
  and sequence, 96
Time mastery, 7–8
  letting go, 8–9
Toyoda, Sakichi, 175
Toyota, 175
Tracy, Brian, 134, 234
Triple Constant Triangle, 74–75, *75,
      162*
Turkle, Sherry, 184, 188
Tversky, Amos, 117
Twitter, 104, 183

UCLA, xxx
Unilever, 111

University of California, 45, 55, 196
University of Chicago, 110
University of Cologne, 133
University of Colorado, 211
University of Kent, 152
University of London, xxx
University of Michigan, xxx,
    167, 223
University of North Carolina, 193
University of Pennsylvania, 14
University of Western Australia, 49
Ury, William, 65–66

Values
  core values, 157, 161–164, 168–170,
    172–173, *173*
  guiding decisions, 34, 39, 87, 130
  internal and external, 105, 149,
    164–165
Veblen, Thorstein, 165
Veroff, Joseph, 213–214
Volvo, 120
Vrije University, 51

Walmart, 117
Wansink, Brian, 24, 35, 135
Websites
  Facebook, 42, 132, 161, 162,
    182, 213

Google, 204
Klout, 183
LinkedIn, 183
www.tonycrabbe.com, 249
Welch, J. C., 45
West Virginia University, 231
What Is Strategy? (Porter), 86
WhatsApp, 58, 183, 189
What the hell effect (Baumeister), 236
Wiggins, Bradley, 143
Wikipedia, 104
Williams-Sonoma, 69
Wilson, Timothy D., 218, 221
Wonder Women (Spar), 10
Worry
  and churning, 50–52
  and procrastination, 51–52
Wright, Tony, 135

Xerox, 98

Yale-NUS College, 206
Young, Kimberly, 204
YouTube, xix, 132

Zeigarnik, Bluma, xxxii–xxxiii, 46
Zeigarnik effect (Zeigarnik),
    xxxii–xxxiii, 46, 139, 247
Zurich Insurance Company, 120

About the Author

Tony Crabbe is a business psychologist who works with multinational companies around the world, including Microsoft, Disney, Salesforce, News Corp, Cisco, HSBC, American Express and the World Bank. He is also an honorary research fellow in the field of organizational psychology at Birkbeck College, University of London. He lives with his family in Spain, but spends a considerable amount of time consulting in the UK and the US.